The Church

ACCORDING *to the* NEW TESTAMENT

The Church

ACCORDING *to the* NEW TESTAMENT

WHAT the WISDOM and WITNESS of EARLY CHRISTIANITY TEACH US TODAY

DANIEL J. HARRINGTON, S.J.

A SHEED & WARD BOOK

ROWMAN & LITTLEFIELD PUBLISHERS, INC.
Lanham • Boulder • New York • Toronto • Oxford

A SHEED & WARD BOOK

ROWMAN & LITTLEFIELD PUBLISHERS, INC.

Published in the United States of America
by Rowman & Littlefield Publishers, Inc.
A wholly owned subsidary of The Rowman & Littlefield Publishing Group, Inc.
4501 Forbes Boulevard, Suite 200, Lanham, Maryland 20706
www.rowmanlittlefield.com

PO Box 317
Oxford
OX2 9RU, UK

Printed in the United States of America

Cover and interior design: Madonna Gauding
Cover art used with permission from The J. Paul Getty Museum, Los Angeles, CA
Scripture quotations are from the New Revised Standard Version of the Bible, copyright
1946, 1952, 1971 by the Division of Christian Education of the National Council of the
Churches of Christ in the USA. Used by permission. All rights reserved.

Quotations from the Second Vatican Council are from *Vatican Council II, The Conciliar and
Post Conciliar Documents*, General Editor, Austin Flannery, OP (Northport, NY: Costello
Publishing Company), © 1975, 1986, 1992, 1996.

Library of Congress Cataloging-in-Publication Data

Harrington, Daniel J.
    The church according to the New Testament : what the wisdom and witness of
early Christianity teach us today / Daniel J. Harrington.
        p. cm.
    Includes bibliographical references and index.
    ISBN 1-58051-111-2 (pbk.)
        1. Church—Biblical teaching. 2. Bible. N.T.—Criticism, interpretation, etc.
        I. Title.

BS2545.C5 H36 2001
262'.012—dc21

2001045861

In memory of
Anthony J. Saldarini (1941–2001)
Scholar and Friend

CONTENTS

PREFACE   xi

1. THE JESUS MOVEMENT   1
   Rooted in Israel   1
   The Kingdom of God   3
   The Values of the Jesus Movement   5
   Jesus' Disciples   7
   The Death of Jesus   8
   Possibilities and Problems   10
   For Reflection and Discussion   12

2. THE JESUS MOVEMENT CONTINUES   13
   The Resurrection of Jesus   13
   The Holy Spirit   15
   External Factors   17
   Kingdom and Church   19
   Did Jesus Found the Church?   20
   Possibilities and Problems   22
   For Reflection and Discussion   25

3. WHAT EARLY CHRISTIANS BELIEVED ABOUT JESUS   27
   Paul's Letters: The Power of Jesus' Death and Resurrection   28
   Pastoral Epistles: "The Saying Is Sure"   31
   Other Early Traditions about Jesus   34
   Jesus as the Wisdom of God   36
   Hymns in Luke's Infancy Narrative   38
   Possibilities and Problems   40
   For Reflection and Discussion   41

4. HOW EARLY CHRISTIANS WORSHIPED   43
   Baptism as Initiation into Christ   43
   The Lord's Supper and Early Christian Life   45
   The House Church   49
   The Christian Assembly   51
   Possibilities and Problems   54
   For Reflection and Discussion   55

5. PAUL ON THE CHURCH   57
   The Spirit-Led Community   58
   The Charismatic Community   61
   The Body of Christ   64
   Possibilities and Problems   67
   For Reflection and Discussion   68

6. THE CHURCH AND THE PEOPLE OF GOD   69
   Old Testament Perspectives   69
   The People of God in 1 Peter 2:9–10   72
   The People of God in Galatians 3   74
   The Mystery of Israel in Romans 9–11   77
   Possibilities and Problems   79
   For Reflection and Discussion   81

7. PAUL'S LEGACY: THEOLOGY, NARRATIVE, AND PRACTICE   83
   Ecumenical Dimensions in Paul's Ecclesiology   83
   Theology: Ephesians   85
   Narrative: The Acts of the Apostles   89
   Practical Advice: The Pastoral Epistles   93
   Possibilities and Problems   96
   For Reflection and Discussion   98

8. THE CHURCHES BEHIND THE SYNOPTIC GOSPELS   99
   From Jesus to the Synoptic Gospels: Windows onto Church Life   99
   Mark: A Church under Pressure   101
   Matthew: The Church and Judaism   104
   Luke: The Church in History and in the World   109
   Possibilities and Problems   112
   For Reflection and Discussion   114

9. THE JOHANNINE COMMUNITIES   115
   John's Book of Signs: Jesus and "the Jews"   115
   John's Book of Glory: The Community of the Beloved Disciple   119
   The Johannine Letters: The Story Continues   122
   Revelation: Hope for Suffering Christians   124
   Possibilities and Problems   126
   For Reflection and Discussion   128

10. THE CHURCH IN THE WORLD   129
   Church and State   129
   Men and Women   132
   Early Christian Values   135
   Hospitality and Compassion   138
   Possibilities and Problems   141
   For Reflection and Discussion   143

11. MINISTRY   145
    Jesus as the Servant Leader   145
    Other Terms and Patterns   148
    Disciples of Jesus   150
    The Ministry of the Word   153
    Possibilities and Problems   156
    For Reflection and Discussion   158

12. MINISTERS   159
    Church Offices   159
    Ignatius of Antioch   162
    Priesthood   165
    Peter   168
    Possibilities and Problems   170
    For Reflection and Discussion   172

GLOSSARY   173

FOR FURTHER STUDY   181

INDEX   187

PREFACE

The idea for this book came to me in the last days of the twentieth century. Amid all the lists looking at the achievements and disasters of the past century and millennium, along with the apocalyptic warnings about the impending Y2K computer crisis, I began to focus on a question that fascinates me as a New Testament scholar and a preacher: What might the church of the first century have to say to the Church of the twenty-first century?

At the dawn of the twenty-first century, the Christian churches, in some settings at least, find themselves full of energy and life while, at the same time, they are divided into various denominations and sects. But there is one thing on which all Christian churches agree: the New Testament is the privileged witness to Jesus Christ and to the early Christian movement. Although various Christian groups attribute different grades of authority to the New Testament and interpret certain texts differently, they all agree that those writings are foundational for Christian faith. Perhaps then a brief synthesis of what the New Testament says and does not say about the Church can be a help toward even greater vitality within the churches and a stimulus toward greater unity among the churches. That is my hope for this little book.

The present work is a study in biblical theology. Its primary sources are the twenty-seven books of the New Testament. It approaches these books with a concern for their historical settings in the first century A.D. and with sensitivity toward the literary conventions by which they communicate their messages. For further information on these matters, see my book *Who Is Jesus? Why Is He Important? An Invitation to the New Testament* (Sheed & Ward, 1999). The focus of this work is the theological content of these books with particular attention to what they say about the Church.

The format follows the pattern developed in *Why Do We Suffer? A Scriptural Approach to the Human Condition* (Sheed & Ward, 2000). Each of the twelve chapters is divided into three or four sections that treat various aspects of the general topic under consideration. At the end of each chapter there is a final section entitled "Possibilities and Problems" that summarizes the main points while noting the positive contributions raised by the New Testament texts and the problems they may pose for Christians in the twenty-first century. Three questions, "For Reflection and Discussion," complete each chapter. The biblical quotations are from the New Revised Standard Version.

I confess that there are some repetitions in my presentation, but I feel they are necessary from a pedagogical perspective in order to help nonspecialists to understand the full dimensions of the topic under discussion. For example, in treating the early Jesus movement, Mark's Gospel, and ministry, respectively, it seemed necessary in each case to discuss discipleship. I tried to vary the wording and content, but the basic points are the same. A cross-reference would not do the job, I think. Those who wish to move on when they reach such points can easily do so. The general bibliography (For Further Study, pages 000–000) provides resources for more in-depth study of the major topics.

I write here primarily as a New Testament specialist addressing a general audience of Christians or those interested in Christianity. While I am a Roman Catholic priest, I see my task here not as promoting or defending distinctively Catholic positions but rather as helping Christians (and their friends) appreciate better what the New Testament says and does not say about the Church. In the framework of a short book intended for a wide (nonspecialist) audience, I want to help Christian readers to better understand what the writings—that they all regard as privileged and foundational—teach about the Church. I imagine that this book might even work best in classes or Bible study groups in which the participants represent different Christian traditions. In that respect, this is a work of biblical and ecumenical theology.

The New Testament, of course, is a collection of many books, not just one book. The New Testament did not drop down from heaven at the end of the first century A.D. Rather, the canon of the New Testament was the result of a long and complex process of development that reached its final form in the late fourth century A.D. This collection contains many different theological voices and perspectives on Jesus and the Church. Thus the New Testament is paradoxically the source of both Christian unity and Christian diversity. There is something for everybody in it, and yet it is unified by its focus on Jesus of Nazareth and on how the movement begun by him was carried on in the first century A.D.

The New Testament writings do not tell the whole story about Christianity in the first century. Nor do they solve all our problems today. But I am confident that Christians in the twenty-first century have much to learn about the Church from these writings. Study of them has been my life's work, and they never fail to surprise, challenge, and delight me with their fresh and wise teachings.

chapter one

THE JESUS MOVEMENT

It recently has become customary in academic circles to refer to the *Jesus movement*. The term refers to the public ministry of Jesus of Nazareth and the impact that it had on other people. The term captures the dynamism that Jesus and his first followers displayed as they moved about the land of Israel and proclaimed the kingdom of God. Conversely, it avoids the static and institutional connotations that are often attached to the word *church*. And it leaves open whether it is proper to speak of "the Church" prior to Jesus' death and resurrection.

This chapter will consider the roots of the Jesus movement in Israel, the kingdom of God as its central symbol, the teachings of Jesus that flow from this symbol, those who followed Jesus, and the implications for the relationship between Jesus and the Church. In other words, it concerns where the Jesus movement came from, what it stood for, and how it developed into what we call "the Church." The presentation relies on material in the Synoptic Gospels (Matthew, Mark, and Luke) that can be traced with some historical certainty to Jesus himself.

ROOTED IN ISRAEL

Jesus was born, lived, and died in the land of Israel. He read the Jewish Scriptures and participated in the rituals of his people. His public ministry was directed mainly toward his people and sought their spiritual renewal.

The movement that Jesus began had its roots in Israel's consciousness of itself as the People of God. According to Deuteronomy 7:6–8, Israel was "a people holy to the LORD your God" precisely because God had chosen it out of all the peoples of the earth. It was not because of its size or any other merit that God chose Israel. Rather, the initiative came from God: it was "because the LORD loved you." According to the prophet Ezekiel writing in the early sixth century B.C., even though Israel had profaned God's name and suffered defeat and exile, God remained faithful to his part of the promise: "I will sanctify my great name . . . and gather you from all countries. . . . I will sprinkle clean water upon you. . . . A new heart I will give you, and a new spirit I will put within you" (Ezekiel 36:22–26). The prophet Zechariah looks forward to that day when "ten men from nations of every language shall take hold of a Jew, grasping his garment and

saying, 'Let us go with you, for we have heard that God is with you'"
(Zechariah 8:23). These quotations make important points about Israel's
consciousness of itself as the People of God by God's initiative and favor,
about God's fidelity to this relationship despite the people's infidelity, and
about Israel's significance for all the nations of the world.

While Jews in Jesus' time had a lively sense of being God's people,
there was much controversy about who within Israel best represented God's
people. With the return from exile in the late sixth century B.C., and
onward, there was conflict between those who took an inclusive view (see
Isaiah 40–66) and those who fostered a more exclusive definition of God's
people (see Ezra, Nehemiah).

The Book of Daniel represents the perspective of a Jewish apocalyptic
group in Judea that looked to the God of Israel as its defender and vindi-
cator against the threat of Israel being swallowed up by paganism. The
Pharisees arose in the second century B.C. as a Jewish renewal movement
dedicated to living the kind of holiness in everyday life that was appropriate to the priests in the Jerusalem Temple. The Essenes (the group most
likely responsible for writing and preserving the Dead Sea Scrolls), having
been shut out from the administration of the Temple, regarded themselves
as the true Israel, and their communities as the places where the authentic
worship of God was carried on. The Sadducees retreated to controlling
the temple administration and appealing to the Torah (the Pentateuch) as
God's Law, while various revolutionary groups such as the Zealots undertook violent resistance in the hope of overthrowing their Roman rulers
and bringing about the kingdom of God (which they perceived as a theocracy in which God was the real ruler).

These movements within Second Temple Judaism (and there were
many more) provide the context for understanding the Jesus movement.
They all assume and take as their starting point the election of Israel as
God's people. But they all are dissatisfied with the present condition of
God's people. Some were dissatisfied for religious reasons: the Temple
being in the wrong hands, the threat of paganism, or poor observance of
the Torah. Others were dissatisfied for political reasons, especially the subjugation of Israel to a series of foreign powers: Babylonians, Persians, Greeks,
and Romans. And, of course, in Jesus' time, the religious, economic, political, and cultural spheres were closely related and even intertwined.

In this context, the Jesus movement emerged as a renewal or reform
movement within Judaism. It was started by the Jew Jesus of Nazareth, and
gathered followers from the Jewish population of the land of Israel.
It presupposed that God had chosen Israel to be a special people with
significance for the other nations of the world. Its proclamation of God's
kingdom as its theological center was an echo of the Old Testament

pronouncement: "The LORD is king! Let the earth rejoice" (Psalms 97:1). And the goal of all its teachings and activities was to show how God's people should live in expectation of the coming fullness of God's kingdom.

THE KINGDOM OF GOD

Mark 1:15 (see Matthew 4:17) aptly summarizes the teaching of Jesus in the following way: "The time is fulfilled, and the kingdom of God has drawn near; repent, and believe in the good news." This saying presents the ministry of Jesus as a decisive moment in the coming of God's kingdom, and insists on repentance and faith as the proper responses to it.

The kingship of God is an important theme in the Old Testament. When Israel demands that Samuel appoint a human king, God consoles him with the words: "...they have not rejected you, but they have rejected me from being king over them" (1 Samuel 8:7). A large block of Psalms (see 93, 95–97, 99) celebrates the God of Israel as king over all the earth: "The LORD is king; let the peoples tremble" (99:1). Especially after the exile to Babylon in the early sixth century B.C., there is a growing belief that the God of Israel is not simply the national God of the Jewish people, but also the sovereign Lord over all creation.

The claim that the God of Israel rules over all creation flew in the face of Israel's ongoing subjugation to foreign rule in postexilic times. In response, there developed the idea of the future kingdom of God—that time in the future when the sovereignty of Israel's God will be so manifest that all peoples and indeed all creation will have to acknowledge it.

For example, Daniel 12:1–3 looks for divine intervention through "Michael, the great prince, the protector of your people" that will issue in the resurrection of the dead, the last judgment, and rewards for the wise and righteous. The "Apocalypse of Weeks" in *1 Enoch* 91:12–17 foresees the vindication of the righteous in Israel, a righteous judgment revealed to the whole world, and the appearance of a new heaven. And the *Assumption* (or *Testament*) *of Moses* 10:1 envisions the time when "His kingdom shall appear throughout all creation, and then Satan shall be no more." The tension between the theological claim that the God of Israel is sovereign over all creation and the political reality that Israel in postexilic times was subject to one foreign power after another (and to the Maccabees and the Herods who generated many opponents within Israel) was resolved by appeal to a future and transcendent kingdom to be ushered in by God or his agents.

In his teachings about the kingdom of God, Jesus combines the preexilic faith in the present kingship of God and the postexilic hope for a future definitive display of God's kingship. His short parables about the mustard seed and the leaven (see Matthew 13:31–33; Mark 4:30–32; Luke 13:18–21) combine the two dimensions by insisting that something is already present (the mustard seed, the leaven) and that what will appear in the future will be unmistakable (a huge bush, large quantities of bread). Likewise, his short parables about the treasure in the field and the pearl (see Matthew 13:44–46) underscore the surpassing value of God's kingdom and the total commitment that it will elicit.

Several sayings with good claims to represent the mind of Jesus emphasize the presence of God's kingdom. For example, in Luke 11:20 (see Matthew 12:28) Jesus says: "But if it is by the finger of God that I cast out the demons, then the kingdom of God has come upon you." And in Luke 17:21, Jesus warns against seeking signs, and asserts that "the kingdom of God is among you." He also speaks about the kingdom of God having suffered violence (see Matthew 11:12; Luke 16:16) and holds out the possibility of "entering" the kingdom of God now (see Matthew 5:20; 7:21; 18:3; 21:31; etc.).

At the same time, Jesus perceives the fullness of God's kingdom as future, and so he instructs his followers to pray "Your kingdom come" (Matthew 6:10; Luke 11:2). His parables of the wheat and the weeds (see Matthew 13:24–30, 36–43) and the fishnet (see Matthew 13:47–50) look toward a future judgment when the righteous and the wicked will be distinguished and rewarded or punished accordingly. Some sayings (which also have good claims to authenticity) suggest that God's kingdom will come in its fullness very soon: "Truly I tell you, this generation will not pass away until all these things have taken place" (Mark 13:30; see also Mark 9:1; Matthew 10:23). At the same time, Jesus acknowledges that not even he knows the exact time (see Mark 13:32), and admits that God can shorten the time for the sake of his elect ones (see Mark 13:20) or lengthen it to allow sinners to repent (see Luke 13:6–9).

The fullness of God's kingdom, according to Jesus, is future. Yet the kingdom is present not only in the history of God's people but also (and especially) in the person of Jesus and in his teaching and healing activity. Those who follow him in the "Jesus movement" bear witness to the future and the present dimensions of God's kingdom.

While the New Testament never identifies the Church as the kingdom of God, it does indicate that the Church is to be a sign of the presence of God's kingdom and a symbol of hope for its future fullness. To enter God's kingdom is to acknowledge the sovereignty of the God of Israel (who is the Father of Jesus) and to follow the way of Jesus. The Church lives against the background or horizon of the kingdom of God, and tries to be faithful to Jesus' vision of God's kingdom and to put into practice the values and attitudes that are appropriate to it.

THE VALUES OF THE JESUS MOVEMENT

What set Jews apart from other nations in the Roman Empire and what reinforced their own identity as a special people were their observances of circumcision, food and purity laws, and the Sabbath. According to Luke 2:21, Jesus' parents had him circumcised eight days after his birth, and in the Gospels, Jesus never questions the ritual of circumcision. With regard to the food and purity laws, Jesus is depicted in the Gospels as taking a free attitude on various issues without rejecting the biblical commandments associated with these matters (see Mark 1:40–45; 5:21–43; 7:1–23). He insists, however, that "there is nothing outside a person that by going in can defile but the things that come out are what defile" (Mark 7:15).

Likewise, Jesus' teachings about the Sabbath do not abolish the biblical commandment. Rather, they fit within contemporary debates among Jewish teachers about what constitutes "work" on the Sabbath. His principle is that it is lawful to do good and to save life on the Sabbath (see Mark 2:23–3:6; Matthew 12:9–14; Luke 13:10–17)—something that most of his Jewish contemporaries would have affirmed as well. The idea is that if killing in self-defense is permitted on the Sabbath (see 1 Maccabees 2:41), how much more is it allowed to do good and to save life. So on the three issues that set Jews apart as a people in Jesus' time, Jesus stood within the parameters of contemporary Jewish debate while promoting the primacy of moral purity and the principle of doing good on the Sabbath.

What stands out as especially characteristic among the teachings of Jesus are his invitation to approach God as Father, his embrace of the double love commandment, his concern for marginal persons, his radical ethical teachings, and his emphasis on forgiveness. While other Jewish teachers taught these and similar things, the combination of these five teachings gives us a good picture of what was characteristic of Jesus' teachings and what presumably should be carried on by his followers in the Church.

Jesus invites his followers to address God as *Father* in prayer (see Luke 11:2; Matthew 6:9). That simple epithet reflects Jesus' own experience of God as "Abba, Father" (Mark 14:36). This intimate relationship with God is established by the narratives about Jesus' baptism (see Mark 1:9–11) and transfiguration (see Mark 9:2–8). That Jesus urged his followers to approach God as a loving parent is confirmed not only by his address in the Lord's Prayer but also by the use of "Abba" (Aramaic for "Father") in the Greek-speaking churches (see Romans 8:15; Galatians 4:6).

When asked for his summary of the 613 commandments in the Torah, Jesus puts forward two commandments: love of God and love of neighbor (see Mark 12:28–34; Matthew 22:34–40; Luke 10:25–28). These two commandments, of course, are direct quotations from Deuteronomy6:4–5 and Leviticus 19:18. Associated with the double love commandment is Jesus' challenge to love one's enemies (see Matthew 5:43–48; Luke 6:27–36). Those who practice love of enemies imitate the example of "your Father in heaven" who shows loving care for not only the good and righteous but also for the evil and unrighteous (see Matthew 5:45).

In word and deed Jesus provides a good example of concern for marginal persons. Indeed, one of the most controversial features of his ministry is his willingness to minister to "tax collectors and sinners"—persons whose Jewish identity was suspect on the grounds of their occupation, social status, and conduct. Jesus actively attracts people who are on the social and religious margins of society, including the economically poor and the prostitutes. He is criticized as "a glutton and a drunkard, a friend of tax collectors and sinners" (Matthew 11:19). What shocks many of Jesus' contemporaries is his willingness to share meals with such disreputable people (see Mark 2:13–17). For Jesus, however, these meals with marginal persons are signs pointing toward the great banquet in the kingdom of God (see Matthew 8:5–13).

While Jesus freely accepts marginal persons among his first followers, he also challenges them to live out his radical teachings. The word *radical* means going to the "root" (*radix* in Latin) of things. And so in Mark 10, Jesus counsels "no divorce" (10:2–12) and urges that those who wish to follow him should put aside their desire for security based on material possessions (see 10:17–31). In the six antitheses ("You have heard . . . but I say . . .") in Matthew 5:21–48, Jesus shows how to avoid infringing upon the biblical commandments by going to their roots: if you wish to avoid murder (or adultery, divorce procedures, false oaths, etc.), then avoid their root causes (anger, lust, divorce, oaths, etc.). In this sense, Jesus promotes a "radical" ethic and way of life.

Despite the demanding and radical character of his teachings, Jesus also insists on the possibility of forgiveness. The parables of the lost sheep, the lost coin, and the lost son in Luke 15 illustrate how God, through Jesus as his agent, actively seeks out those who seem to be lost. Jesus teaches his followers to beg God for forgiveness and to be willing to show forgiveness to others: "And forgive us our sins, for we ourselves forgive everyone indebted to us" (Luke 11:4). Indeed, there is a close link made between our willingness to forgive others and God's willingness to forgive us (see Matthew 6:14–15; 18:21–35).

These five core values—closeness to God, the primacy of love, concern for marginal persons, radical ethical stances, and forgiveness—emerge from the Synoptic Gospels as characteristic of the Jesus movement.

JESUS' DISCIPLES

Jesus did not write books. Nor did he have access to the various media of communication that are part of life in the twenty-first century. Rather, he (like other religious teachers and philosophers in the Greco-Roman world) spread his message primarily by word of mouth. So in the Gospels, Jesus is portrayed as going from place to place, gathering an audience, and putting forth his wisdom. Having a reputation for being a healer and an exorcist surely helped him to draw a crowd. But if the Jesus movement was to make a lasting impact, its principal figure needed others to help spread the word and expand his influence.

In Judaism of Jesus' time (and especially in later rabbinic times) it was customary for prospective disciples to seek out a distinguished teacher and be received by him. In the Gospels, however, this process is reversed, with Jesus actively seeking out his followers. The call of the first disciples in Mark 1:16–20 serves as a model. While walking by the shore of the Sea of Galilee, Jesus encounters two sets of brothers—Simon (Peter) and Andrew, and James and John—working at their trade as fishermen. There is no indication that these men have ever met Jesus or know anything about him. Nevertheless, when Jesus says "Follow me," they leave behind their family and business, and immediately become his disciples. By way of indirection, the narrative suggests that Jesus' person and call are so persuasive and attractive that the four fishermen leave everything to follow him.

The first four disciples along with eight others constitute the group of Twelve Apostles (see Mark 3:13–19). They are called to be with Jesus and to be sent forth to proclaim his message (see Mark 3:14). The number "twelve" is important because it evokes the motif of the twelve tribes of Israel and suggests that Jesus and his first followers represent Israel as God's people. The call of these men to accompany Jesus and to share in his mission expresses the essence of discipleship in the Jesus movement.

Those who follow Jesus—and not just the Twelve—constitute the true family of Jesus. When family members seek to restrain Jesus because they fear that "he has gone out of his mind" (Mark 3:21), Jesus defines those who make up his real family in this way: "Whoever does the will of God is my brother and sister and mother" (3:35). With this saying, Jesus diminishes the importance of "blood" family relationships and provides the charter for the Jesus movement and for the Church in all ages. What binds the disciples to Jesus and to one another is their commitment to do the will of God as interpreted by Jesus.

In Mark 6:7–13 Jesus sends out the Twelve to do what he does, thus making them active participants in his mission. They are to adopt the simple lifestyle of Jesus as they go from place to place. They are to take no extra food or money; their clothing is to be as simple as is necessary; and they are to rely upon the hospitality that is offered to them. Their main task is to proclaim repentance in the face of the coming kingdom of God and to heal those who are sick and possessed by demons. The Jesus movement was spread first by itinerant missionaries in Galilee.

The Gospels, however, are remarkably frank about the failures of Jesus' first disciples. Since this is not the kind of thing that later admirers might make up, it very likely reflects historical reality. According to Mark 8:14–21, Jesus' public ministry in Galilee ends with his indictment of his followers' inability to grasp who he is and what he is about: "Do you still not perceive or understand? Are your hearts hardened?" (8:17). On the way up to Jerusalem (see 8:22–10:52) the disciples repeatedly turn a deaf ear to Jesus' passion predictions (see 8:31; 9:31; 10:33–34) and exhibit fundamental misunderstandings about the necessity of the cross (see 8:32–33), greatness in the Jesus movement (see 9:33–34), and greatness in the kingdom of God (see 10:35–37).

In the passion narrative, the plot to arrest Jesus is put into action by the willingness of one of the Twelve—Judas—to betray Jesus to the chief priests and scribes (see Mark 14:1–2, 10–11). The arrest of Jesus is made possible by the signal agreed upon between Judas and the captors—the "kiss" that a disciple might give to his teacher as a sign of respect (see Mark 14:44–45). At Jesus' arrest, his closest disciples abandon him: "All of them deserted him and fled" (14:50). Why they too were not arrested remains a mystery to historians.

According to Mark 14:66–72, Peter denies Jesus three times. Again this is not the kind of thing that later admirers might invent, since it presents a great early Christian leader in such poor light. Peter, who had answered Jesus' call with enthusiasm in Mark 1:16–18 and accompanies Jesus throughout his ministry of teaching and healing, now swears: "I do not know this man you are talking about" (14:71).

The first followers of Jesus provide a positive example in their enthusiastic response to Jesus and in their being with him and doing what he did. However, the Gospels do not shrink from portraying their many failures in grasping who Jesus is and in following him on the way to the cross.

THE DEATH OF JESUS

In the short time—one year according to the Synoptic Gospels, three years according to John—that the Jesus movement was active, it did make an impact in the land of Israel. Many people were convinced that Jesus was a prophet: "A great prophet has risen among us" (Luke 7:16). There was speculation that Jesus might be Elijah whose return was prophesied in

Malachi 4:5–6, the prophet like Moses described in Deuteronomy 18:15, or John the Baptist (see Mark 6:14; 8:28). Some went so far as to identify Jesus as the Messiah, the descendant of King David who was to restore the glory of Israel (see Mark 8:29; Acts 1:6). These speculations about the identity of Jesus drew the attention of Herod Antipas in Galilee (see Mark 6:14–16) and eventually that of the Jewish and Roman leaders in Jerusalem.

According to the Synoptic Gospels, Jesus and his disciples made a long journey from Galilee in the north to Jerusalem in the south. They tell us that Jesus undertook this journey with an awareness that it could well end in his suffering and death (see Mark 8:31; 9:31; 10:33–34; Luke 9:51).

According to Mark 11:1–11, Jesus' entry into Jerusalem constitutes a public demonstration. It is carefully scripted to highlight Jesus' identity as a humble king after the pattern set by Zechariah 9:9:"Lo, your king comes to you; triumphant and victorious is he, humble and riding on a donkey, on a colt, the foal of a donkey." And his second public action in Jerusalem— the so-called "cleansing" of the Temple (see Mark 11:15–19)—amounts to a direct and open criticism of those responsible for the administration of the Temple: the chief priests, the scribes, and the elders of the people.

These two public actions also attract the attention of the Roman officials in Judea, especially since they take place at Passover time, which was the traditional Jewish celebration of Israel's miraculous liberation from slavery in Egypt. So dangerous is the situation that the Roman prefect Pontius Pilate comes from his headquarters in Caesarea Maritima to Jerusalem to oversee the crowds who come on pilgrimage for Passover. In this highly charged atmosphere, Jesus makes a very provocative entrance.

That provocative entrance results in Jesus' arrest and trial before the Jewish leaders in Jerusalem (see Mark 14:53–65). The first charge against Jesus (see Mark 14:58) is that he threatened to destroy the Temple and replace it with another "not made with hands" (that is, one made by God). Although Mark dismisses it as a false charge, it does fit with Jesus' action in "cleansing" the Temple (see Mark 11:15–19) and his prophecy about the destruction of the Temple (see Mark 13:2). And the various interpretations given to his charge by other New Testament writers (see Matthew 26:61; John 2:19–22; Acts 6:4) confirm that there was some substance to it. It seems to have been part of Jesus' critical attitude toward the Jerusalem Temple, an attitude shared by other Jews in his time.

The second charge directly concerns the identity of Jesus. According to Mark 14:61, the chief priest asks Jesus:"Are you the Messiah, the Son of the Blessed One?" And when Jesus answers "I am," he went on to identify himself as also the glorious Son of Man (see Daniel 7:13). The irony is that Jesus embraces all these titles—Messiah, Son of God, and Son of Man—

only when they seem most improbable, when he is on trial for his life. But from the perspective of Mark and other New Testament writers, the true nature of Jesus' messiahship and divine sonship becomes clear only in his passion and death.

Jesus suffers under Pontius Pilate. When the Jewish authorities are convinced that Jesus is a blasphemer and a danger to their own security ("There may be a riot among the people," Mark 14:2), they convince the Roman prefect to take charge of Jesus and condemn him to death (see 15:1–20). From Pilate's perspective, Jesus is another in a long line of Jewish religious revolutionaries who fan the fires of Jewish nationalism by evoking visions of a warrior king and judge after the pattern of King David (see *Psalms of Solomon* 17). And so Pilate refers repeatedly to Jesus as the "King of the Jews" (15:2, 9, 12). Of course, Pilate's use of the title is ironic. He intends it as a cruel joke on Jesus and on the Jews, since Jesus never looked less a king. In the eyes of Christian faith, however, Jesus is never more a king than at this moment, as John 18:28–19:16 makes clear.

Pilate condemns Jesus to be crucified, a very painful and public mode of execution inflicted upon slaves and political prisoners. He is crucified along with two "bandits" (*lestai*), who are probably also suspected of being revolutionaries. The Roman policy toward such figures was quick and massive repression before they could gain popular support.

And so Jesus died alone, apart from a few women followers who observed his execution from a distance (see Mark 15:40–41). His male disciples have fled, and Peter has denied him three times. It appears that the Jesus movement has died, along with the death of its principal figure. It appears that the Jesus movement was just another short-lived Jewish religious movement that came and went very quickly. It appeared that the Jesus movement would pass away without leaving a trace. So it seemed.

Possibilities and Problems

While the Church began with the Jesus movement, the Jesus movement itself began in and with Israel as the People of God. The Jesus movement is intelligible only within the context of the history of Israel as God's people as this is portrayed in the Scriptures and against the background of the political circumstances prevailing in first-century Palestine. This means that the Church in the twenty-first century has the obligation to help God's people today to appreciate the specific situation and conditions in which the Jesus movement emerged. As an incarnational religion, Christianity must give continuing attention to the time, place, and circumstances in which the "Word became flesh and lived among us" (John 1:14).

The Church in the twenty-first century also has the mission of keeping alive the values and ideals of Jesus. Its central theme must be the kingdom of God—the affirmation that God reigns over all creation as the kingdom of God, and the hope that all creation soon will acknowledge the sovereignty of God ("Your kingdom come"). From this premise there flow the other special emphases in Jesus' teachings: approaching God as a loving parent, love of God and love of neighbor (including enemies), concern for marginal persons, facing up to radical ethical challenges, and holding out forgiveness as always possible. Just as the Evangelists highlighted these core values of Jesus, so the Church must continue to stress their perduring value. Without a strong connection to these values, there is little or no connection to the Jesus movement.

The gospel passages about Jesus' first disciples remain rich resources for the Church today. The positive and enthusiastic response to Jesus by his first followers remains paradigmatic for all Christians. The ideal of discipleship as being with Jesus and sharing in his ministry of proclaiming the kingdom of God and bringing his healing power to those in need provides the best definition of the vocation of the Christian today. At the same time, the Evangelists' frank admission of the disciples' failures is a sobering challenge to face up to the difficulties involved in following the way of Jesus of Nazareth. Nevertheless, the offer of forgiveness on Jesus' part, even (and especially) in the case of Peter, means that it is always possible to get back on the path of discipleship.

The mystery of the cross is part of the Jesus movement from the start, and must be acknowledged and even embraced by all who seek to carry on that movement. The true nature of Jesus' messiahship is revealed only in his passion and death. The possibility (and indeed the likelihood) of suffering because of one's association with the Jesus movement must be squarely faced.

One problem in carrying on the Jesus movement is the lack of awareness among most Christians regarding their biblical and Jewish heritage. So there is need for ongoing exposure to the treasures of the Hebrew Bible in liturgy and religious education. Without an appreciation of the language and ideas of the Old Testament, Christians cannot appreciate what the New Testament says about Jesus. There is also need for instruction regarding the place of the Jesus movement in the context of first-century Palestinian Judaism. Such a program can help both Jews and Christians better understand what they have in common and where they differ.

While education about the Old Testament and first-century Judaism is important, there does remain the problem of the huge historical and social gap between the world of the original Jesus movement in first-century Palestine and the Church in the world of the twenty-first century. What began as a small renewal movement involving only Jews in the land of Israel has developed into a world religion. What started out as a kind of "reform" Judaism has turned into a separate religion. What took shape among peasants and small businessmen in Galilee is now embraced by peoples of all races and social classes all over the world. The question is, How much of the world of first-century Judaism can and should be transported into the global reality that Christianity has become in the twenty-first century?

And the problems involved in embracing the values of Jesus cannot be passed over in favor of a kind of cultural Christianity handed on from one generation to another. If God is king, then no earthly figure (including oneself!) can be the center of the universe. To love one's enemies often seems impossible, and to show concern for the poor and marginal is far from many persons' minds in the twenty-first century. And to embrace the mystery of the cross and to try to practice the radical teachings of Jesus remain among the most difficult tasks for humans to carry out. Being a member of the Jesus movement has never been easy, and it is not easy today.

For Reflection and Discussion

1. What implications might the original Jesus movement have for relations among the Christian churches and between Christians and Jews today?

2. What values of the Jesus movement are most important for people today? What values are most difficult to transfer?

3. What are the most salient characteristics that might define a member of the Jesus movement today?

chapter two

THE JESUS MOVEMENT CONTINUES

O ne might well have expected that the Jesus movement would die with its principal figure. It was not particularly well organized; its initial phase did not last very long; and the crucifixion of Jesus showed what might happen to those who persisted in continuing the movement. But the Jesus movement did continue—and even flourished. And its continuation is what we call *the Church*.

Why the Jesus movement continued has fascinated theologians and historians, believers and skeptics, for almost two thousand years. Against all human expectations, what started as a small Jewish renewal movement in Galilee developed into a world religion. The New Testament writers attribute this remarkable happening to the power of Jesus' Resurrection and the gift of the Holy Spirit. However, other factors—historical and sociological—surely played an important role. This chapter will consider both the internal (theological) and external (historical and sociological) factors that made possible the survival and flourishing of the Jesus movement. It will conclude with reflections on two basic issues: the relationship between the kingdom of God and the Church, and the question, Did Jesus found the Church?

THE RESURRECTION OF JESUS

According to one of the earliest texts contained in the New Testament (see 1 Corinthians 15:3–5), Jesus who had died and was buried "was raised on the third day . . . and appeared to Cephas [Peter], then to the Twelve." The passage goes on to list further appearances of the Risen Jesus to "more than five hundred brothers," to James, to all the apostles, and to Paul "as to one untimely born." On the basis of these experiences, the early Christians came to believe and proclaim that Jesus had been raised from the dead and was still alive.

The early Christians interpreted these encounters with the Risen Jesus as proof of his resurrection. In some (but not all) Jewish circles, the resurrection of the dead had become an article of faith. Yet even among believers it was assumed that the resurrection would be a corporate or collective event and would take place at the full coming of God's kingdom just before the last judgment (see Daniel 12:1–3). Jesus himself seems to have shared a belief in the resurrection of the dead with the Pharisees over against the Sadducees (see Mark 12:18–27; Matthew 22:23–33; Luke 20:27–40). What was especially surprising about the early Christians' claims regarding the Resurrection of Jesus was their insistence that this resurrection had occurred in the case of one person (Jesus) before the last judgment and the fullness of God's kingdom. Or to put it a way more consistent with early Christian beliefs, the Resurrection of Jesus consti-tuted the beginning of the "end" and the transition to the fullness of God's kingdom: "Christ has been raised from the dead, the first fruits of those who have died" (1 Corinthians 15:20).

The Gospels do not provide a direct description of the Jesus' Resur-rection. Instead, they first narrate accounts about the empty tomb (see Mark 16:1–8; Matthew 28:1–8; Luke 24:1–12; John 20:1–10). While the empty-tomb stories do not prove that Jesus was raised from the dead (his body could have been stolen; see Matthew 28:11–15), the empty tomb is at least the necessary presupposition for the early Christian proclamation that Jesus had been raised from the dead.

The Gospels also present many accounts about the appearances of the Risen Jesus to his followers: to the women who went to the tomb (see Matthew 28:9–10) and the eleven disciples (see Matthew 28:16–20); to the two disciples on the road to Emmaus (see Luke 24:13–35) and the eleven disciples (see Luke 24:36–49); to Mary Magdalene (see John 20:11–18), the disciples (see John 20:19–23), the disciples and Thomas (see John 20: 24–29), and the seven disciples fishing in Galilee (see John 21:1–23); and to the disciples gathered in Jerusalem (see Acts 1:3–11). Mark 16:9–20 seems to be a second-century epitome of appearance stories in the other Gospels.

These encounters with the Risen Jesus changed the lives of those who had originally constituted the Jesus movement. Whereas at Jesus' arrest they all had fled (see Mark 14:50) and Peter had denied that he even knew Jesus (see Mark 14:66–72), now these same people were convinced that Jesus who had died was now alive. Indeed, the dramatic change in Jesus' first followers and their vigorous continuance of the Jesus movement pro-vide the strongest historical evidence for the truth of Jesus' Resurrection. Their experience of Jesus as alive once more gave them the courage and the energy to carry on the movement that Jesus had begun.

Most of the Gospel accounts about the appearances of the Risen Jesus feature the theme of mission. The women are ordered to tell the men that Jesus will meet them in Galilee (see Matthew 28:9–10; Mark 16:7; John 20:17–18); the disciples are told to forgive and retain sins (see John 20:23); and Peter is given a "pastoral" commission ("feed my lambs") in

John 21:15–19. Even more dramatically, the eleven disciples gathered on a mountain in Galilee are commissioned by the Risen Jesus to "make disciples of all nations, baptizing them in the name of the Father and of the Son and of the Holy Spirit, and teaching them to obey everything that I have commanded you" (Matthew 28:19–20). And in Luke 24:47, the eleven disciples are told that "repentance and forgiveness of sins is to be proclaimed in his name to all nations beginning from Jerusalem." In the commissions of the Risen Jesus to his disciples, the Church was born. With the Resurrection of Jesus, the Jesus movement became the Church of Jesus Christ.

THE HOLY SPIRIT

In the New Testament the continuation of the Jesus movement and its development into the Church are attributed to the Holy Spirit. While the major New Testament writers describe this in different ways, they all bear witness to the basic belief that the Holy Spirit was and is at work in the life of the Church.

According to John's Gospel, the Risen Jesus appeared to his disciples on Easter evening when he "breathed on them and said to them, 'Receive the Holy Spirit'" (John 20:22). With these words there is the beginning of the fulfillment of Jesus' promises in his farewell discourses (see John 14–17) about the coming of the Holy Spirit as the "Paraclete." The word *paraclete* refers to a helper, comforter, advocate, or even defense attorney. In John 14:16–17, Jesus speaks of the "Spirit of truth" as "another advocate," suggesting that the Spirit replaces the earthly Jesus and continues his activity after his death and resurrection. One function of the Paraclete is to "teach you everything and remind you of all that I said to you" (John 14:26). Another role of the Paraclete is to testify on behalf of Jesus (see John 14:26), thus fulfilling the role of advocate or defense attorney not only for Jesus but also for his followers. A third function of the Paraclete is to convict or prove the world wrong about sin, righteousness, and judgment (see John 16:8). When Jesus goes, then the Holy Spirit comes (see John 16:7, 13). And when the Spirit comes, the Spirit will "declare to you the things that are to come" and glorify Jesus (see John 16:13–14). From the perspective of John's Gospel, what made possible the continuation of the Jesus movement was the sending of the Holy Spirit, or Paraclete, as a replacement for the earthly Jesus.

In Luke-Acts, the Holy Spirit is a principal figure in the history of salvation. In the infancy narrative (see Luke 1–2), the Holy Spirit is active in inspiring various figures (Elizabeth, Mary, Simeon, Anna) to prophesy and is said to provide the divine agency in the birth of Jesus (see

Luke 1:35). During Jesus' public ministry, he is understood to be the principal (if not the sole) bearer of the Holy Spirit. In his inaugural discourse at Nazareth, Jesus proclaims in the words of Isaiah 61:1–2: "The Spirit of the Lord is upon me because he has anointed me to bring good news to the poor" (Luke 4:18). Throughout his public activity of teaching and healing, Jesus shows himself to be led and empowered by the Holy Spirit. On the cross Jesus is said to have "breathed his last" (Luke 23:46), perhaps a play on the Greek word for "spirit" and "breath" (*pneuma*).

At his Ascension, according to Acts 1:6–11, Jesus promises his disciples: "You will receive power when the Holy Spirit has come upon you; and you will be my witnesses in Jerusalem, in all Judea and Samaria, and to the ends of the earth" (1:8). This verse has been accurately described as the topic sentence or outline for Luke's Acts of the Apostles. It announces the geographical plan of Acts, and it attributes the miraculous spread of the gospel to the agency of the Holy Spirit. On Pentecost the disciples are "filled with the Holy Spirit" (Acts 2:4) and begin to speak in other languages and to prophesy. The power of the Holy Spirit makes it possible for the followers of Jesus to do what he did. In this sense, the early community at Jerusalem enjoys a kind of prophetic succession.

There are three stages in Luke's picture of prophetic succession. In the infancy narrative the Holy Spirit inspires figures who represent the best in the Old Testament period; in Jesus' public ministry he is the vehicle of the Holy Spirit, or the Holy Spirit resides especially and even exclusively in him; and in the time of the Church, the Spirit empowers Jesus' followers to continue the movement that was begun by Jesus. On the basis of Luke-Acts it has become customary to speak of Pentecost as the birthday of the Church. And it is possible to identify Luke's "time of the Spirit" with the "time of the Church," since in his theological perspective they are so closely related. The Holy Spirit is the "soul" of the Church.

While John and Luke relate the gift of the Holy Spirit to particular moments (Easter afternoon, Pentecost), Paul focuses more on what early Christians themselves had experienced. Although this topic is treated in detail in chapter six, it is important to note in this context that Paul assumes that every believing and baptized Christian has received the Holy Spirit: "To each is given the manifestation of the Spirit for the common good" (1 Corinthians 12:7). He goes on to insist that these gifts should be used for the common good to build up the Church as the Body of Christ. In criticizing the Galatians for allowing themselves to be led into following Jewish ways, Paul argues that they have already received the Holy Spirit without the works of the Law or circumcision: "Did you receive the Spirit by doing the works of the law . . . ? Having started with the Spirit, are you now ending with the flesh?" (Galatians 3:2, 3)

16

These three early Christian authors whose writings make up about two-thirds of the New Testament agree that the Holy Spirit was the force that allowed the Jesus movement to continue and made it possible for the Church to flourish. Although they differ about how they present the gift of the Holy Spirit, they agree that the Spirit was given to the followers of Jesus after Jesus' departure. In doing so, they reflect the theological interpretation that was dominant in the early church: the Holy Spirit carries on the work of Jesus in the Church.

EXTERNAL FACTORS

While the New Testament writers emphasize the importance of encounters with the Risen Jesus and the power of the Holy Spirit as major factors in the survival and flourishing of the Jesus movement, some external factors on the historical and sociological levels must also be acknowledged. The spread of early Christianity was greatly facilitated by the Roman Empire and the Jewish Diaspora.

Rome had been expanding its influence and dominion in the Mediterranean world from the third century B.C. onward. Through its alliance with the Maccabees in the mid-second century B.C., Rome gained at least some influence over affairs in the land of Israel. With Roman general Pompey's intervention in the Maccabean dispute over succession in 63 B.C., Rome's role in Palestine became even larger. Herod the Great rose to power by supporting various Roman leaders until he finally managed to convince the emperor Augustus that he could be trusted to keep the peace in Palestine and protect the eastern border of the Roman Empire from Persian attack. At Herod's death in 4 B.C., Galilee was assigned to his son Herod Antipas, and Judea to another son named Herod Archelaus.

Although Herod Antipas held on to power in Galilee until A.D. 37, events in Judea were so fractious that Herod Archelaus was removed in A.D. 6, and Judea came under the direct control of a prefect or governor appointed directly by Rome. The most famous Roman governor of Judea was Pontius Pilate, who served from A.D. 26 to 36. So in the time of Jesus and the early church, the land of Israel was very much part of the Mediterranean world and the Roman Empire.

The dominance of Rome brought with it some external factors that aided the Christian cause. The most obvious factor was peace, or at least relative peace, throughout the Mediterranean world. With the Persians to the east and the barbarians to the north, the Romans carved out for themselves a relatively peaceful sphere around the Mediterranean Sea. Their policy of massive repression toward native rebellions (like those among the Jews) contributed to the real (if strained) atmosphere of peace.

With the military peace under the Romans came relative ease and safety in travel. Travel in the ancient world was always difficult. See Paul's complaints about shipwrecks, hunger, robbers, and cold in 2 Corinthians 11:25–27. But with the work on the road systems, the Romans made it possible to go from one city to another city with less difficulty than ever before. Moreover, through their many campaigns against the pirates, the Romans succeeded in opening the sea-lanes in the Mediterranean to commercial and other traffic. And most of the Roman Empire (apart from the Latin West) used Greek as the language of official communication. And so the peace that the Roman Empire brought, the relative safety in travel, and the widespread use of Greek as the medium of communication greatly facilitated the spread of Christianity throughout the Mediterranean world of the first century A.D.

The word *Diaspora* (from the Greek "scatter, spread over, disperse") is often used to refer to the various Jewish communities scattered over the world (and especially throughout the Roman Empire) outside the land of Israel. There were millions of Jews living in the great cities of the Roman Empire: Alexandria in Egypt, Antioch in Syria, Ephesus in Asia Minor, and Rome itself. In some cities the Jews constituted ten to fifteen percent of the population. These Jewish communities were held together by their national heritage and ancestral religion, which expressed itself in a distinctive religious perspective (monotheism), high ethical standards (the Torah), and certain religious practices (circumcision, food and purity rules, and Sabbath observance) that set them apart from other peoples and groups. And yet these Hellenistic Jews spoke Greek and lived and worked in a world steeped in Greek and Roman culture.

One social and religious institution that held the local Jewish communities together was the synagogue (derived from the Greek word for "assembly, gathering, coming together"). In the first century the synagogue was as much a social institution (like the Irish American Club) as a religious institution. Of course, for Jews there was no strict distinction between their social identity and their religious observances. They expressed their national identity by reading their Scriptures and offering prayers to "the God of the Fathers."

Judaism in general and the synagogue in particular were attractive even to non-Jews. The simplicity of Jewish theology (belief in the one God), the ethical standards (the Ten Commandments), and the many festivals exercised a certain fascination among many in the Greco-Roman world. Some even made a full conversion to Judaism. Others remained in a kind of "associate" status—what Luke in Acts refers to as "God fearers"—perhaps unwilling to take upon themselves the peculiarities of Judaism (circumcision, food and purity rules, Sabbath observance). It is very likely that many of the non-Jews who embraced Christianity were first exposed to the Jewish Scriptures and Judaism through their association with the urban Diaspora synagogues in the Roman Empire. By portraying Paul as going first to the synagogue in any city, Luke in Acts may well reflect the practice of the earliest Christian missionaries.

KINGDOM AND CHURCH

The kingdom of God in its present and future dimensions was the central theological theme of Jesus' preaching and activity. This point is clear from even a casual reading of the Synoptic Gospels (see Mark 1:15). But in John's Gospel Jesus becomes the central theme: "I am the way, the truth, and the life" (John 14:6). And in the Pauline letters and most other New Testament writings, what God has done for humankind through Jesus' life, death, and resurrection (soteriology) becomes the focus of attention. According to a phrase frequently used in New Testament studies, the proclaimer became the proclaimed.

With this shift in focus from God's kingdom to the person of Jesus also comes an increasing interest in the Church. Whereas the word *church* (*ekklesia*) appears only twice in the Gospels (see Matthew 16:18; 18:17), it is a very common term in the rest of the New Testament. Is the Church the same as the kingdom of God? Does the Church somehow replace the kingdom of God? The answers to these questions have an impact on how we look upon the kingdom of God, the work of Jesus, and the Church.

The kingdom of God is not the same as the Church. The kingdom of God is transcendent, eschatological, and universal. The kingdom of God is *transcendent* in the sense that it is God's kingdom; it belongs to God, and its fullness is the work of God. And so Jesus teaches us to pray, "Your kingdom come!" The Church is at least in part the work of believers here and now, and it is the product of human effort under the guidance of the Holy Spirit.

The kingdom of God is *eschatological* in the sense that it will reach its fullness in God's own time, at the end of human history as we know it, on the day of the Lord. The Church is the assembly of believers who await the full coming of God's kingdom, and so it lives primarily in the present but always with an eye toward the future.

And the kingdom of God is *universal* in scope in the sense that at its fullness all creation will acknowledge the sovereignty of God. Then goodness will reign, and sin will be no more ("Your will be done on earth as it is in heaven"). The Church in the present time embraces both saints and sinners; it is not the society of the perfect, however it strives to be such. The kingdom of God is greater than the Church.

While the Church does not replace the kingdom of God, its origin and mission are intimately connected with the kingdom of God. The Church is the community of those gathered in the name of Jesus Christ. It arose from Jesus' proclamation of God's kingdom and has as its mission sharing Jesus' vision of God's kingdom with others. The Church may be described as the fellowship of those who aspire to God's kingdom and are gathered in the name of Jesus Christ and led by the Spirit of God.

The Church is also a sign of the reign of God both in the present and for the future. Just as Jesus' healings and exorcisms pointed toward the inauguration of God's kingdom in his life and ministry, so the good deeds of those who aspire to God's kingdom in the Church point to the decisive change that has taken place in and through Jesus' life, death, and resurrection. The Church is a sign that God's kingdom has been inaugurated in Jesus and will come to its fullness whenever God so wishes ("Your kingdom come").

The task of the Church in the world is to believe, proclaim, and live out the message of Jesus about the kingdom of God. By itself and through its own efforts, the Church does not and cannot bring about the fullness of God's kingdom. In fact, the New Testament writers avoid statements about our building God's kingdom or bringing it about—a silence that reflects sound Jewish and early Christian theology that should be respected. It is not our kingdom to build or to bring about. Moreover, the Church should not make itself the focus of its own preaching. Rather, the New Testament writers make God's kingdom and Jesus central. Again, this is sound theology, and their focus should be respected.

The Church is not the same as the kingdom of God. Nor does it replace God's kingdom. But without the kingdom of God as proclaimed by Jesus, the Church has no identity or reason for existence. The Church consists of those who aspire to God's kingdom as proclaimed by Jesus and who try to live in accord with the ideals and values of Jesus.

DID JESUS FOUND THE CHURCH?

This is not an easy question to answer. But we can say that Jesus came to proclaim the kingdom of God, not to plan out an ecclesiastical organization or institution; that the most decisive events in the origin of the Church were the Resurrection of Jesus and the gift of the Holy Spirit; and that the ministry of the earthly Jesus prepared for important features in the post-Resurrection Church.

In responding to the question "Did Jesus found the Church?" much depends on how the terms are defined. Does *Jesus* refer only to the earthly Jesus during his public ministry? Or does it include his passion, death, and resurrection? Does *found* mean to establish a consciously planned social institution with specific rules and administrative structures? Or does it mean to provide the dynamism and energy (the "Spirit") to inspire others to carry on the movement begun by Jesus? And does *Church* describe a social institution over against other groups and the wider society, an organization with structures that remain unchanged throughout its history? Or does it describe more simply and basically what we have been calling *the Jesus movement?*

According to the first set of definitions, Jesus came to establish an ecclesiastical institution. According to the second set, Jesus, by his life, death, and resurrection, set in motion a movement that developed into the Church. The second set of definitions seems to reflect more closely what really happened. The emergence of the Church from the Jesus movement can be illuminated by two basic sociological concepts: the charismatic prophet, and the routinization of charisma.

A *charismatic prophet* is convinced of a special mission from God and seeks validation only from God. The word *charisma* means "gift" or "grace," and a charismatic prophet receives power as a gift from God. In his role as preacher of the kingdom of God, Jesus fit the profile of a charismatic prophet. His power came not from priestly lineage or knowledge of Scripture or rabbinic ordination but from his own charismatic power, or what the New Testament writers call the Holy Spirit: "They were astounded at his teaching, for he taught them as one having authority, and not as the scribes" (Mark 1:22).

As Jesus attracted disciples to himself, he did not adopt the religious-institutional models that were current in Jewish society in his time. The Jesus movement was not a closed "monastic" community (like the Essenes at Qumran), an exclusive fellowship (like the Pharisees), or a rabbinical academy (like the school of Yohanan ben Zakkai).

Rather, Jesus addressed his proclamation of God's kingdom to all kinds of people (even tax collectors and sinners). He did not confine his activities within the boundaries of a clearly defined organization. Moreover, Jesus showed little concern for establishing the privileges and structural prerogatives of his first followers. What counted most was their willingness to be with Jesus and to share in his ministry and in his cross. They were to adopt his simple lifestyle as they went from place to place and proclaimed the coming of the God's kingdom. They were not appointed to preside over local communities. Instead, they were sent forth as "apostles." Jesus imparted his Spirit to those whom he chose to be his disciples.

While Jesus cannot be said to have designed and set up the religious institution that we call *the Church,* his preaching and other activities before the Resurrection did prepare and provide a basis for the emergence of the

Church after Easter. By his proclamation of God's kingdom in word and deed, Jesus attracted a group of men and women in Israel who set themselves apart by their adherence to Jesus. Moreover, there was a continuity between Jesus' disciples who followed him before his death and resurrection, and those who bore witness to him after his Resurrection. Also, the followers of Jesus carried on his practice of sharing meals with others as a sign pointing toward the coming kingdom of God. And they adopted Jesus' somewhat free attitude toward restrictive interpretations of the Torah by the Pharisees and other Jewish groups. So in their beliefs (about God's kingdom and Jesus as its prophet), personnel (the Twelve, Peter, the women), and practices (shared meals, freedom vis-à-vis Jewish legal traditions), those who gathered around Jesus in the Jesus movement constituted the basis for "the Church."

One of the most famous New Testament passages pertaining to the Church describes Jesus' promise to Peter: "You are Peter, and on this rock I will build my church" (Matthew 16:18). Only here and in Matthew 18:17 does the word for *church* (*ekklesia*) appear in the Gospels. While this text is often cited as proof that Jesus founded the Church and put Peter in charge of it, the promise appears in the context of a prediction about Jesus' death and resurrection (see Matthew 16:21), and is cast in the future tense ("I *will build*"). These factors suggest that the promise to Peter is to be fulfilled after Jesus' death and resurrection. And so this text confirms that what we call "the Church" came to be after (and through) Jesus' death and resurrection.

What was going on here can be described as the "routinization of charisma." This refers to the sociological process by which the prophet (or his disciples) secures the permanence of the prophet's preaching and of the community around him. Part of the process is attending to the structural and economic necessities of the group, and putting people in charge of certain functions (officers). This is what happened as the early church developed. Various structures and offices were devised that served to preserve the charisma of Jesus and to adapt it to new situations throughout the Greco-Roman world. The goal of these structures and offices was to "make routine" (that is, to preserve, channel, and adapt) the impulses set in motion by Jesus the charismatic prophet. In and through Jesus' death and resurrection, the movement that Jesus assembled and animated became the Church.

Possibilities and Problems

The emergence and survival of the Jesus movement and its development into what we call *the Church* constitute a remarkable series of events in human history. That a small Jewish religious reform movement rooted in Palestine under the Roman Empire should become a world religion is in itself quite extraordinary. That the founder of this movement should have been crucified as a political revolutionary ("King of the Jews") and yet proclaimed as still alive by his followers is hard to imagine. And that many people should have accepted the testimony of his followers and come to celebrate Jesus of Nazareth as Son of God and Lord of all creation is truly amazing.

The emergence of the Church is testimony to the power of Christian faith. The internal theological factors that made this development possible—the kingdom of God, the Jesus movement, the Resurrection of Jesus and the appearances to his disciples, and the gift of the Holy Spirit—remind us of the power of the central tenets of Christian faith. While historians and social scientists may profitably look at the early church as objective outside observers, those who take only this perspective miss what was most important and dynamic about the transformation of the Jesus movement into the Church. And if the various churches today wish to make progress in determining what is truly foundational and central to Christian faith, they should look to their common origins in Jesus' proclamation of God's kingdom, the power of his Resurrection, and the gift of the Holy Spirit.

While the external conditions in the Roman Empire that facilitated the growth of the early church do not tell the whole story, they ought not to be neglected either. Christianity is an incarnational religion: "The word became flesh and lived among us" (John 1:14). One must acknowledge that the relative peace and safety brought about by the Roman Empire aided greatly the spread of the gospel from Palestine throughout the Mediterranean world. One must also acknowledge the debts that Christianity owes to Jewish institutions like the synagogue and to the Jewish religious tradition for its theological concepts and terms. Nevertheless, it is intriguing that Christianity survived and flourished whereas, in much the same circumstances, its rivals, such as the Isis cult and Mithraism, died off.

Likewise, sociological concepts that illumine the survival of the Jesus movement and the development of the early church ought not to be neglected. The interpretation of Jesus as a charismatic prophet fits the evidence that we have about him and links him to other figures who fit the type in other times and places. And the notion of the routinization of charisma helps us understand how the work of a great leader was carried on even after his death, and how institutions were developed in order to preserve, channel, and adapt the impulses that the great leader set in motion. Whatever else it is, the Church is a social institution and, at least to some extent, it proceeds according to the laws of institutional development. And so if we wish to understand the Church in antiquity and today, we need to analyze it in the light of sociological concepts that have proved their explanatory value in other contexts.

The various theological and historical topics covered in this chapter reveal that the emergence of the Church was a gradual and complex development. And this complexity raises the question about specifying the precise moment when the Church was born. Was it with the call of the first disciples, the promise to Peter, the appearances of the Risen Jesus at Easter, or the outpouring of the Holy Spirit on Pentecost? No one of these events explains everything, and yet each one is an important part of the process.

Also, the acknowledgment of Christianity's debts to the Roman Empire and to the Jewish synagogue as well as the celebration of Christian faith as incarnational pose the challenge of determining what in early Christian experience is essential and what is accidental or time-conditioned only. The world in which the gospel was first inculturated was the Mediterranean world of the first century A.D. As Christians in different parts of the increasingly global society of the twenty-first century try to inculturate the gospel, they come up against the problem of deciding how far they can go and remain genuinely Christian. Moreover, they have the obligation to discern what may be a good inculturation from a bad one. And they may find that this was as much a problem for Christians in the first century as it is for people in the twenty-first century.

Likewise, however illuminating some sociological concepts may be for understanding the early church, an excessive reliance on them can lead to a neglect of the theological elements that are at the heart of Christian faith, and so to a kind of reductionism that views the early Christian movement as completely explicable in human terms. For example, some scholars explain the appearances of the Risen Jesus totally in terms of "cognitive dissonance," by which humans customarily make the best out of a bad situation, especially when their fondest hopes have been disappointed or frustrated. They also point to the psychological conflicts that Jesus' first followers had in coming to face their teacher's horrible death and their own cowardice before it. In this sense, the argument goes, Peter's experience of the Risen Jesus was wish fulfillment or a hallucination by which Peter dealt with or worked out his own feelings for having denied Jesus.

But these approaches are extreme and generally are used by people with little sympathy for traditional Christian faith. They are by no means the necessary consequences of the social scientific study of the Bible. In fact, our understanding of life in the early church has been greatly enriched by recourse to modern sociology, as will become clear in the chapters that follow.

For Reflection and Discussion

1. How would you answer the question, "Did Jesus found the Church?"

2. How would you explain the statement, "Jesus proclaimed the kingdom of God, and what came forth was the Church"?

3. To what extent might sociological concepts help in understanding the early church? What might be their limitations?

chapter three

WHAT EARLY CHRISTIANS
BELIEVED ABOUT JESUS

The biblical words for "faith" (*'emunah* in Hebrew, *pistis* in Greek) refer most basically to faithfulness or fidelity in the sense of putting one's trust in God. The biblical model of faith is Abraham: "And he believed the LORD; and the LORD reckoned it to him as righteousness" (Genesis 15:6). But biblical faith is more than emotion. It also has content. In the New Testament, the center of faith is what God has done for humankind in the life, death, and resurrection of Jesus.

One way of gaining access to what the earliest Christians believed about Jesus is through the creedal formulas and hymnic fragments that have been preserved in the New Testament writings. These materials are generally put forward as affirmations about which the writer and the addressees can agree. They serve as "common ground." They presumably express the faith of the wider community of believers and so represent the "tradition" of what was still a very young movement. In that sense, they convey authoritative teaching.

The method by which these creedal statements and hymnic fragments are isolated is called source criticism. Just as form criticism enables us to identify the literary forms and historical settings in which early traditions about Jesus' words and deeds circulated before their inclusion in the Gospels, so source criticism is a tool for determining when a literary work incorporates pre-existent material.

Sometimes an author will announce that he is quoting a tradition, as when Paul in 1 Corinthians 15:3 says: "For I handed on to you as of first importance what I in turn had received." In other cases there may be at least a clue that traditional material is being used, as in the Pastoral Epistles where traditional statements are introduced or concluded by a formula such as "the saying is sure and worthy of full acceptance" (1 Timothy 1:15).

Where there is no explicit statement or formula to indicate the incorporation of traditional material, the best guide is unusual vocabulary that differs from what appears in the context. The occurrence of unique words and phrases can serve to mark a passage as an "odd block." Likewise, when the content of the whole statement does not fit the context except for the one point that is being developed (as in Galatians 3:28 and

Philippians 2:6–11), then there is some likelihood that a creedal statement or hymnic fragment may be present.

These precious witnesses to early Christian beliefs about Jesus are most prominent in the Pauline letters, both in those letters that were written directly by Paul and in those that were written in his name (Colossians, Ephesians, Pastorals). Some hymns preserved in the Gospels of Luke and John provide further early testimony about Jesus' origins and significance.

PAUL'S LETTERS:
THE POWER OF JESUS' DEATH AND RESURRECTION

The center of Paul's theology is what God has done for us in Jesus' death and resurrection. Indeed, it is common to describe Paul's Christology as a soteriology, since it focuses on the saving significance (the meaning of *soteriology*) of the Christ event. The key terms of Paul's theology—justification, redemption, salvation, sanctification, and so on—are different ways of approaching and expressing what God has done for us in Christ. Paul shows remarkably little interest in the sayings and deeds of Jesus. For him the decisive moment in the history of salvation is Jesus' death and resurrection (which he took as one event).

Although it is principally through Paul that this soteriological Christology became an integral part of Christian faith, Paul did not invent it. It was already traditional, it would seem, from the earliest days of Christian faith. The antiquity of this interpretation of Jesus' death and resurrection is suggested by several pre-Pauline confessions of faith (see Galatians 3:28; 1 Corinthians 15:3–5; Romans 1:3–4; 3:25–26) and an early hymn (Philippians 2:6–11).

One the most famous verses in Paul's letters is Galatians 3:28: "There is no longer Jew or Greek, there is no longer slave or free, there is no longer male and female; for all of you are one in Christ Jesus." It appears in the context of Paul's long and complicated biblical argument that the real children of Abraham are people of faith, and not necessarily Jews alone. In the logic of Paul's argument, only the part that says, "... there is no longer Jew or Greek" is relevant. Likewise, the rhythmic flow (three pairs plus a reason why) suggests that this traditional statement was intended to cap off Paul's argument. The point of the saying is that "in Christ Jesus," the ethnic (Jew/Greek), social (slave/free), and gender (male/female) distinctions that do so much to divide people are no longer important. What is important is being "in Christ." While these distinctions may not disappear entirely (see 1 Corinthians 11:2–16; Philemon), they are not what really matter in light of the Christ event. It is very likely that Galatians 3:28 was a slogan or saying connected with the rite of baptism in which believers were formally incorporated "in Christ Jesus." It reflects the early Christian belief that Jesus' death and resurrection brought about a unity and equality that transcends ethnic, social, and gender differences among humans.

First Corinthians 15:3–5 has already been cited as an early creedal formula. At the beginning of a lengthy reflection on Christ's Resurrection and our resurrection, Paul quotes the "gospel" that he proclaimed to the Corinthians when he brought them to Christian faith as being exactly the same as what he himself had received. Since Paul turned to Christian faith shortly after Jesus' death (three to six years afterward), what Paul cites here must be a very early tradition. The focus of that tradition is Jesus' death and resurrection: ". . . that Christ died for our sins in accordance with the scriptures, and that he was buried, and that he was raised on the third day in accordance with the scriptures, and that he appeared to Cephas, then to the twelve."

Besides the factual narration of Jesus' death, burial, and resurrection, there are two important points of theological interpretation in 1 Corinthians 15:3–5. The first point is that Jesus died "for our sins"—both on account of our sins and to wipe away or atone for our sins. The phrase suggests that Jesus' death was interpreted as an expiatory sacrifice undertaken "for us." The second point is conveyed by the phrase that appears twice: ". . . in accordance with the scriptures." This indicates that Jesus' death and resurrection was willed by God as God's will was expressed in the Old Testament. Thus Jesus' death appears as the perfect sacrifice for sins because it was willed by God and so was acceptable to God. The wiping away of past sins makes possible a new beginning—life in the Spirit (see Romans 8).

In introducing his Letter to the Romans, Paul includes a description of Jesus as one "who was descended from David according to the flesh and was declared to be Son of God with power according to the spirit of holiness by resurrection from the dead, Jesus Christ our Lord" (Romans 1:3–4). This statement is generally identified as a pre-Pauline creedal statement on the basis of its peculiar way of referring to the Holy Spirit ("the spirit of holiness") and what appears to be its peculiar adoptionist Christology. On its surface, the statement suggests that Jesus became the Son of God only with his Resurrection from the dead. It is sometimes put forward as evidence for "adoptionism"—the idea that God fully adopted Jesus as his Son only at his Resurrection (as in Romans 1:3–4) or at his baptism (as in Mark 1:9–11). This notion, however, runs counter to Paul's own theology in which Jesus was and is the Son of God always. The key word is *declared*. Paul could use this formula because, at least in its present context in Romans, it served to highlight the Resurrection of Jesus as his vindication as God's Son. Whatever the original theology of the creedal statement was, it now emphasizes Jesus' earthly descent from King David and his Resurrection as the affirmation and revelation of his divine sonship.

Having established in Romans 1:18–3:20 that all persons—Gentiles and Jews alike—needed the revelation of God's righteousness in Jesus, Paul begins his meditation on righteousness through faith after the example of Abraham by referring to an early Christian interpretation of Jesus' death as a redemptive sacrifice: ". . . whom God put forward as a sacrifice of atonement by his blood effective through faith. He did this to show his righteousness, because in his divine forbearance he had passed over the sins previously committed" (Romans 3:25–26). Again the peculiar (especially cultic) vocabulary marks this as a pre-Pauline piece. Paul does not much develop elsewhere the death of Jesus in terms of Old Testament sacrifices (compare Hebrews). This traditional confession, however, is heavily dependent in its terms and concepts on Leviticus 16:13–15, which describes the sacrifice made by the Jewish high priest on the Day of Atonement. It reflects an interpretation of Jesus' death on the cross as the one sacrifice that truly takes away sins. Since it is God's own sacrifice ("whom God put forward"), it is an acceptable and effective sacrifice for sins. It is generally agreed that Paul inserts into this traditional statement the phrase "effective through faith" to make his main point that faith is the way by which humans gain access to the atoning sacrifice that is the death of Jesus.

Thus far, with the help of four pre-Pauline confessions of faith, we have gained access to some very early Christian beliefs about Jesus. His death and resurrection (taken as one event) was "for our sins" and "in accordance with the scriptures" (1 Corinthians 15:3–5); his death was an effective sacrifice for sins (see Romans 3:25–26); his Resurrection was the moment of his vindication and revelation as the Son of God (see Romans 1:3–4); and through him, ethnic, social, and gender differences have been broken down (see Galatians 3:28).

A more extended statement of early Christian beliefs about Jesus appears in what seems to have been an early Christian hymn preserved in Philippians 2:6–11. Again, the vocabulary and poetic style (parallelism, rhythm) mark this passage as a foreign body in Paul's letter. Paul quotes it to encourage the Philippians to imitate the humility of Jesus ("he humbled himself," 2:8) in accepting and serving one another. It appears as part of a moral exhortation. But while it may have moral implications, the pre-Pauline hymn was primarily concerned with Christology—exploring the identity of Jesus and the significance of his death and resurrection.

The first stanza (see Philippians 2:6–8) in the pre-Pauline hymn concerns the abasement of Jesus as God's Servant. It begins by describing Jesus as being "in the form of God" (Philippians 2:6a). Whether this refers to Jesus' pre-existence as the Son of God or to Jesus as an Adam figure in the image and likeness of God (see Genesis 1:26–27) is a matter of dispute among exegetes. The main point, however, is that Jesus did not "hold on to" or "exploit" (another exegetical dispute) his equality with God. Rather, he humbled himself (the basis for Paul's use of the hymn in the hortatory context) first in the Incarnation ("being born in human likeness") and then in his death on the cross ("became obedient to the point of death"). The latter point is underlined by what seems to have been Paul's editorial addition: ". . . even death on a cross" (Philippians 2:8). In his abasement, Jesus showed himself to be the "Servant" or "Slave" in his perfect service of God and of humankind.

The second stanza (see Philippians 2:9–11) concerns the exaltation of Jesus as God's Servant. Here the Resurrection of Jesus is depicted in terms of an exaltation: "Therefore God also highly exalted him" (Philippians 2:9). In exalting Jesus, God also gave Jesus the right to bear his own divine name of "Lord" (*Kyrios*; see Romans 1:4). The result of Jesus' exaltation is a kind of cosmic liturgy in which all creation acknowledges the lordship of Jesus ("every knee should bend") and proclaims Jesus as "Lord." The imagery here is appropriate for describing what is hoped will happen when God's kingdom comes in its fullness ("Your will be done on earth as it is in heaven," Matthew 6:10). And since the Resurrection was understood to belong to the complex of eschatological events (resurrection, last judgment, rewards and punishment, the fullness of God's kingdom), it was not inappropriate that the Resurrection of Jesus should be celebrated in these terms.

The hymn preserved in Philippians 2:6–11 is a very important witness to what early Christians believed about Jesus. As in the pre-Pauline creedal statements, the center of attention is Jesus' death and resurrection, with some allusion also to his Incarnation. The principal titles create a paradox: "Slave" (*doulos*) and "Lord" (*Kyrios*). While Jesus' death on the cross appears as the low point, his abasement yields to vindication and exaltation in the Resurrection, which in turn sets off the cosmic celebration of the lordship of Jesus.

PASTORAL EPISTLES: "THE SAYING IS SURE"

The Pastoral Epistles—1 and 2 Timothy and Titus—offer advice about Christian life and church discipline. They are addressed to two of Paul's most prominent co-workers, and seek to promote church order in local communities. They emphasize the role of church leaders ("pastors") in these local communities. On the basis of their language and style, theology, and historical setting, they are generally attributed to disciples or admirers of Paul in the late first century A.D. Those who defend their direct Pauline

authorship place them in the last years of Paul's apostolic career
(A.D. 61–63).

One way in which the Pastorals promote church order and support
local church leaders is by citing traditional confessions of faith. These summaries express what early Christians believed about Jesus and provide a
theological basis on which all can agree. Some of them are introduced or
followed by the tag "the saying is sure," which marks them off as traditional and authoritative statements. Others display a poetic structure with
parallelism and/or rhythm that suggest ease of memorization and repetition. Of course, these statements are now preserved in some of the latest
documents in the New Testament (or at least in the Pauline corpus), and
so the creedal statements in the Pastorals are not necessarily as early as
those in the uncontested letters of Paul. And in some of them, there are
elements of Paul's own theology (see Titus 3:4–7). Nevertheless, the traditional confessions of faith in the Pastorals offer precious insights into what
early Christians believed about Jesus.

The first summary of Christian faith in the Pastorals is marked off by
a solemn introduction: "The saying is sure and worthy of full acceptance"
(1 Timothy 1:15a). This introduces the summary about the purpose of
Jesus' mission in the world: "Christ Jesus came into the world to save sinners" (1:15b). In its present context, the saying is part of the theme of Paul
as the converted sinner—the one who, despite his wickedness in persecut-
ing the church, has become the object of God's mercy. The saying itself
continues the pre-Pauline and Pauline emphasis on Jesus' death as being
"for us" and "for our sins," while stressing salvation as the positive result of
Jesus' death and resurrection. The epithet "Christ Jesus" shows that "Messiah (*Christos* in Greek) has become part of Jesus' proper name.

A second creedal formula appears in 1 Timothy 2:5–6 and stresses the
role of Jesus in the economy of salvation: "... there is one God; there is also
one mediator between God and humankind, Christ Jesus, himself human,
who gave himself as a ransom for all." This saying now appears in the
context of teaching about God's desire for everyone to be saved and to
come to the knowledge of the truth. It serves to base this teaching on the
unique role of Jesus as the "one mediator" between God and humankind,
and insists that he could play this role effectively because he himself was
human. As mediator, Jesus made it possible for humans to return to God
through his sacrificial death, which is here described in terms of a "ransom" (*antilytron*; for similar terms see Matthew 20:28; Mark 10:45; Luke
1:68; 2:38; 24:21; Acts 7:35; Hebrews 9:12; 1 Peter 1:18). This creedal
statement specifies Jesus' role as mediator between God and humans, and
celebrates the liberating effects of Jesus' death and resurrection under the
image of "ransom" or "redemption."

A third creedal summary in 1 Timothy concerns the incarnation and exaltation of Jesus: "He was revealed in flesh, vindicated in spirit, seen by angels, proclaimed among Gentiles, believed in throughout the world, taken up in glory" (1 Timothy 3:16). This statement is put forward as the definition of "the mystery of our religion"; that is, the definitive revelation of God's plan. It consists of three short couplets, with each of the six members containing one verb in the Greek aorist passive tense. Behind the passive verbs is the implication that God is the real agent in the revelation. The first couplet ("He was revealed in flesh, vindicated in spirit") refers to the Incarnation of Jesus (see John 1:14) and to his Resurrection (understood as God's vindication of Jesus). The second and third couplets form an ABB'A' structure (chiasmus) in which the exaltation of Jesus is celebrated in heaven ("seen by angels . . . taken up in glory") and is preached to all people on earth ("proclaimed among Gentiles, believed in throughout the world").

The traditional confession preserved in 2 Timothy 2:11–13 is introduced by the formula "the saying is sure." It appears as part of Paul's instruction to Timothy to "share in suffering like the good soldier of Christ Jesus" (2:3). In words reminiscent of Matthew 10:32–33 and Luke 12:8–9, it promises a share in Jesus' eternal life to those who remain faithful to him in their sufferings: "If we have died with him, we will also live with him; if we endure, we will also reign with him; if we deny him, he will also deny us; if we are faithless, he remains faithful" (2 Timothy 2:11–13). This saying links the sufferings of faithful Christians to the sufferings of Jesus and promises them a share in his glorious Resurrection. The interesting twist comes at the end where the last member breaks the pattern of expectations and insists on the faithfulness of Jesus even in the face of the faithlessness of humans.

The formula "the saying is sure" appears as a tag at the end of Titus 3:4–7, although this saying seems less a traditional confession of faith than a combination of Paul's favorite terminology ("works of righteousness," "justified by his grace"), early Christian vocabulary ("the water of rebirth and renewal by the Holy Spirit"), and the characteristic phraseology of the Pastorals ("when the goodness and loving kindness of God our Savior appeared"). While this may not be a pure example of an early Christian confession of faith, it does convey some central tenets regarding the significance of Jesus: The manifestation (Incarnation) was an act of God's goodness; the salvation effected by Jesus was due to God's mercy, not to human achievements; we become part of this central mystery in baptism where the Holy Spirit is poured out on us; and now being in right relationship with God (justification), we can become heirs of the promises made to God's people and can legitimately hope for eternal life.

Examination of the traditional confessions of Christian faith in the Pastoral Epistles shows a strong continuity with the pre-Pauline and Pauline traditions regarding Jesus. The focus is Jesus' death and resurrection and its significance "for us" (salvation, redemption, hope for eternal life). Attention is given to both the Incarnation and the exaltation of Jesus. And a link is made between his sufferings and those of his faithful followers.

OTHER EARLY TRADITIONS ABOUT JESUS

In New Testament epistles that are more or less related to the Pauline corpus, there are passages that seem to incorporate early traditions about the significance of Jesus. In most cases, however, there are no tags like "the saying is sure" to mark off the passages as traditional pieces. Also, the vocabulary and poetic literary style do not always make evident the presence of early Christian traditions about Jesus. Nevertheless, the five examples treated in this section at least have about them the "ring" of tradition and serve to confirm some of the perspectives found in the traditions contained in Paul's letters and the Pastorals.

The second half of the Letter to the Ephesians begins with Paul's exhortation to maintain "the unity of the Spirit in the bond of peace" (Ephesians 4:3). Although written in Paul's name and sometimes described as a compendium of Paul's theology, the Letter to the Ephesians is generally regarded as having been composed around A.D. 80 by a disciple or admirer of Paul as a revised and expanded version of the Letter to the Colossians. While the first half of the letter is mainly concerned with theological topics, the second half reflects on their implications for Christian life. The exhortation to "the unity of the Spirit" is confirmed by the use of what may well have been a set piece connected with Christian baptism (see Galatians 3:28): "There is one body and one Spirit, just as you were called to the one hope of your calling, one Lord, one faith, one baptism, one God and Father of all, who is above all and through all and in all" (Ephesians 4:4–6). The sevenfold repetition of "one" and the concluding doxology give the impression of its being a liturgical piece. At the center is the confession of Christ Jesus as the "one Lord" who gives meaning and coherence to all the other members.

A second possible christological tradition in Ephesians is introduced by a formula that indicates that it is a quotation: "Therefore it says . . . " (5:14a). The problem is that the origin of this quotation is not clear, and there is no obvious candidate in the Old Testament for it. The source may well be an early Christian hymn or confession of faith. In Ephesians 5:14 it appears as part of an exhortation to put aside pagan ways of life: "Sleeper, awake! Rise from the dead, and Christ will shine on you." The text uses an early Christian image for death ("sleep") as a help toward stimulating Christians to act in ways that are appropriate for those who, through baptism, already share in the power of Jesus' Resurrection. It promises to those who "wake up" that the Risen Christ will shine his light of glory upon them. It is thus a description of Christian life after incorporation into the Christ event through baptism.

The letter known as 1 Peter is, of course, attributed to the apostle Peter (although it is generally regarded as coming from the Petrine circle in Rome around A.D. 80). But scholars have often pointed to what they regard as elements of Pauline theology in 1 Peter. Or perhaps it would be more accurate to say that elements of early Christian theology appear in the writings attributed to Paul and Peter.

The reflection on Christ as the Suffering Servant of Isaiah 52: 13–53:12 that appears in 1 Peter 2:21–25 contains what may well be another piece of early Christian tradition: "He himself bore our sins in his body on the cross, so that, free from sins, we might live for righteousness; by his wounds we have been healed" (1 Peter 2:24). This rich sentence takes up the early Christian interpretation of Jesus' death as an effective sacrifice for sins that brings about freedom from the power of sin and freedom to live a righteous life. It makes the connection between the Christ event and the life of the Christian, and places Jesus' death at the center of the economy of salvation.

A similar statement appears in 1 Peter 3:18: "For Christ also suffered for sins once for all, the righteous for the unrighteous, in order to bring you to God." This formulation of the saving significance of the Christ event again takes Jesus' death as a sacrifice for sins, identifies Jesus as the righteous Sufferer (see Wisdom 2), and views his sacrificial death as opening up to sinful humankind (the "unrighteous") access to God. The text is an excellent summary of the "Pauline" theology of justification.

Even further removed in language, style, and theology from Paul is the Letter to the Hebrews. In fact, this work is a sermon ("my word of exhortation," 13:22) written by a skilled rhetorician about Jesus' death as an atoning sacrifice for sins and about Jesus as the perfect High Priest who willingly offered himself as a sacrifice. In his prologue (see 1:1–4) the author describes Jesus in terms appropriate to Wisdom personified: "He is the reflection of God's glory and the exact imprint of God's very being, and he sustains all things by his powerful word" (1:3). The language here is very similar to what appears in the Book of Wisdom (a first-century B.C. Jewish composition) in its meditation on the nature of Wisdom (portrayed as a feminine figure!): "For she is . . . a pure emanation of the glory of the Almighty . . . a reflection of eternal light, a spotless mirror of the working of God, and an image of his goodness. . . . She reaches mightily from one end of the earth to the other, and she orders all things well" (Wisdom 7:25–26; 8:1). In the rest of Hebrews, the author does not develop in any detail the theme of Jesus as the Wisdom of God. This is another indication that here in the prologue he is citing an early Christian tradition. While Jesus' death and resurrection remains the focus of Christian faith in Hebrews (as in Paul's letters, the Pastorals, Ephesians, and 1 Peter), the author does introduce a christological theme—Jesus as Wisdom personified—that is developed in two great early Christian hymns preserved in the New Testament.

JESUS AS THE WISDOM OF GOD

The description of Jesus as Wisdom personified in Hebrews 1:3 evokes two substantial presentations of this same theme in what appears to have been two early Christian hymns now preserved in Colossians 1:15–20 and John 1:1–18.

These two passages must be read against the background of the personifications of Wisdom in various Old Testament and early Jewish texts. In Proverbs 8:22–31, Wisdom speaks in the first person about her role before and during creation. In keeping with the feminine gender of the Hebrew noun for "wisdom" (*hokmâ; sophia* in Greek is also feminine), Wisdom is portrayed as female. She claims that God created her "at the beginning of his work" (Proverbs 8:22), that she was present when God "established the heavens" as a kind of master-builder or guardian for creation (8:27, 31), and that she continues her work of "rejoicing in his inhabited world and delighting in the human race" (8:31).

The portrayal of Wisdom as a female person who is pivotal in God's plan for creation is taken up in several early Jewish works. In Sirach 24, for example, Wisdom, who was present at creation, finds a permanent home in the Jerusalem Temple: "In the holy tent I ministered before him, and so I was established in Zion" (Sirach 24:10). She is also equated with the Torah: "All this is the book of the covenant of the Most High God, the law that Moses commanded us" (Sirach 24:23). In the Wisdom of Solomon, the figure of Wisdom functions as a kind of world soul that continues to animate and guide God's creation: ". . . she pervades and penetrates all things . . . while remaining in herself, she renews all things" (Wisdom 7:24, 27). A very different approach to Wisdom appears in *1 Enoch* 42:1–3, where she cannot find a place to dwell on earth (though Iniquity does!) and so she returns to her home in heaven. To obtain wisdom, one must (like Enoch, see Genesis 5:24) be granted heavenly visions or even trips (mystical ascents) to heaven.

Much of what is said about Wisdom in these Jewish texts is repeated with reference to Jesus in Colossians 1:15–20, at least in the first half of the passage (see 1:15–17). The Letter to the Colossians seems to have been composed in Paul's name shortly after his death to play down the attractions of some form of esoteric Judaism in western Asia Minor by insisting on the perfect sufficiency of Jesus' death and resurrection in bringing about right relationship with God. It presents Jesus as the Wisdom of God and celebrates his primacy in the order of creation and in the order of redemption.

The "base" text for the Letter to the Colossians is an early Christian hymn about Jesus as the Wisdom of God that is quoted in 1:15–20. The first half of the hymn (see 1:15–17) describes Jesus in terms of the Jewish tradition about Wisdom personified. There is no hesitation or embarrassment about transferring what had been said about a female figure to the male Jesus of Nazareth. In the order of creation, Jesus is said to be "the image of the invisible God, the firstborn of all creation" (1:15), who was present at creation ("before all things") and continues to hold all things together.

The second half (see Colossians 1:18–20) insists that the same Jesus who was first in the order of creation is also the first in the order of redemption. Here the language and ideas reflect early Christian beliefs about Jesus. He is "the head of the body, the church." He is "the firstborn from the dead," and so in his Resurrection is the hope of resurrection for all believers. In him "the fullness of God was pleased to dwell"—a powerful statement about the Incarnation. And his death on the cross was God's way of reconciling all creation to himself: ". . . by making peace through the blood of his cross" (1:20). The emphasis on Jesus' incarnation, death, and resurrection is not surprising. What is new here is the idea of the Church as the Body of Christ.

The Prologue to John's Gospel (see 1:1–18) is one of the most famous and influential passages in the Bible. It celebrates Jesus as the "Word" of God. In this context, "Word" seems to be a synonym for "Wisdom," and what is said about Jesus as the Word of God stands in the tradition of the personification of Wisdom in Jewish and early Christian texts. The Word is said to have been with God before creation and to have been instrumental in the process of creation: "He was in the beginning with God. All things came into being through him, and without him not one thing came into being" (John 1:2–3). These statements establish Jesus' identity as the Wisdom of God.

The distinctly Christian theological claim comes later in the text: "And the Word became flesh and lived among us" (John 1:14). Jesus is God's Wisdom incarnate. What God wants to say to humankind is present in the person of Jesus. He is both the revealer and the revelation of God. This is the central insight of John's Gospel.

One of the peculiar features of John's Gospel is that after 1:1–18, there is no explicit reference to Jesus as the Word of God. This apparent silence is a good reason to suspect that the Prologue represents an early Christian hymn, and so can be viewed as a "foreign body" in the Fourth Gospel. But from the perspective of theology, the idea of Jesus as the Word of God is fundamental to the whole of John's Gospel. As the Word and Wisdom of God, Jesus reveals who God is and what God wills for us. And in his life, death, and resurrection, Jesus is the revelation of what God wants us to be.

In these two Wisdom hymns we see how early Christians took up themes associated with personified Wisdom in Jewish theology, and adapted and developed them to express their beliefs about Jesus of Nazareth. In doing so they laid the foundation for the fuller and more comprehensive (than what is found in the confessional statements and hymns) portraits of Jesus that appear in the Gospels. They suggest that Jesus the wisdom teacher whose incarnation, death, and resurrection constitute the pivotal events in salvation history is the Wisdom of God not only personified but even incarnate.

HYMNS IN LUKE'S INFANCY NARRATIVE

The focus of Luke 1–2 is the greatness of Jesus even from his conception, birth, and infancy. The Lukan accounts about John the Baptist and Jesus regarding the announcements of their births and their actual births show that while John is great, Jesus is even greater. These narratives are interrupted and enriched by poetic pieces that are commonly designated by the first words in their Latin versions: the *Magnificat* (see Luke 1:46–55), the *Benedictus* (see 1:68–79), and the *Nunc Dimittis* (see 2:29–32).

While some scholars attribute these poetic pieces directly to Luke the Evangelist, most view them as Jewish Christian hymns written in Hebrew or Aramaic and translated into Semitic or Septuagintal Greek. Or they may have been directly composed in this kind of Greek. It is even possible that purely Jewish compositions have been lightly edited for Christian purposes and inserted into Luke's infancy narrative.

These hymns string together Old Testament words and phrases in what is sometimes called the anthological style. This mode of composition is prominent in the Qumran scrolls and in other Jewish writings of the first century. It is based on the insight that creativity consists in using old materials (biblical terms and images) in new contexts and new combinations. These hymns celebrate the Christ event as the fulfillment of Scripture and of Israel's hopes. They may well reflect the consciousness and worship of the early Palestinian Christian community.

Taken on its own, the *Magnificat* (see Luke 1:46–55) is not particularly

"Christian." Its biblical model is the Song of Hannah in 1 Samuel 2:1–10. After praising God (see 1:46b–47), the speaker explains ("for") that God has exalted the lowly (see 1:48a, 49) in such a way that all "generations" (1:48b, 50) shall remember. Then in 1:51–53 the speaker reflects on God's ways in dealing with the proud, the powerful, and the rich: God puts down the mighty and raises up the lowly. Finally, in Luke 1:54–55, the speaker applies this dynamic to God's dealings with Israel ("to Abraham and to his descendants forever").

When placed in the mouth of Mary (although some manuscripts attribute it to Elizabeth), the *Magnificat* becomes a celebration of the Christ event. In its Christian context, the hymn praises God for the salvation that comes with the birth of this child Jesus to a seemingly insignificant woman in Palestine. It celebrates the Christ event as another example of how God works in using weak human instruments to put down the mighty and raise up the lowly. It praises the God of Israel for being faithful to the promises now being fulfilled in the person of Jesus.

The *Benedictus* (see Luke 1:68–79) is attributed to Zechariah, the father of John the Baptist. While its literary occasion is the birth of John, its real focus is John's role in preparing the way for the Lord: "And you, child, will be called the prophet of the Most High; for you will go before the Lord to prepare his ways" (Luke 1:76). It focuses in turn on God (see 1:68–70), God's people (see 1:71–75), and the child (see 1:76–79). Its progress of thought revolves around the themes of God's intervention (see 1:68, 71b, 74a, 78–79), salvation (see 1:69, 71a, 74b–75, 77), and word/prophet (see 1:70, 72–73, 76). In 1:76–79 it specifies the role of John the Baptist as preparing the way of the Lord, proclaiming forgiveness of sins, and awaiting the day of the Lord. In the Lukan context, the "Lord" is Jesus. And so in the Lukan framework, the *Benedictus* celebrates the Christ event as the decisive intervention of God, the beginning of the process of salvation, and the fulfillment of God's promises to Israel.

The witness of Simeon in the *Nunc Dimittis* (see Luke 2:29-32) is a pastiche of words and phrases from Second Isaiah prepared for in 2:25 by the phrase "the consolation of Israel" (see Isaiah 40:1). Simeon says that he can now die at peace because in this child he has seen the fulfillment of God's promises to Israel. The salvation promised to Israel by Second Isaiah is now being fulfilled in the person of Jesus. The hymn is made up of motifs that are prominent in Isaiah 40–55: seeing salvation (see Isaiah 40:5), the presence of all peoples (see 52:10), light to the Gentiles (see 42:6; 49:6), and glory for Israel (see 46:13).

Whether these three hymns were composed by Jews, Jewish Christians, or Luke himself is hard to know. In their present context in Luke's infancy narrative, however, they celebrate the birth of Jesus as God's intervention in history in order to bring salvation to his people and so to fulfill God's promises to Israel. As such they provide evidence for early Christian reflection on the significance of Jesus from the time of his conception and birth. They proclaim Jesus as "the consolation of Israel."

Possibilities and Problems

Since the Church is first of all the community of those who gather around Jesus, believe in him, and follow his way, it is important to know what his first followers held about him. With the help of early Christian confessions of faith and hymns, we have been able to discern something of what early Christians believed about Jesus. What emerges as being of greatest importance is the centrality of his death and resurrection (understood as one event) and its effects on humans (soteriology). This was not perceived as an isolated historical event. Rather, it was believed to exercise effects on others in the depths of their lives by enabling them to live in freedom from the powers of sin and death, in right relationship with God, and in the hope of sharing Jesus' own eternal life with God. Jesus' death and resurrection is the focus of the earliest creedal formulas and hymnic fragments, and is the core of Christian faith in every age.

The same Jesus whose death and resurrection has saving significance is also celebrated as Wisdom incarnate. While Jesus is correctly regarded as a wisdom teacher (besides being a prophet and a healer), the early Christians who gave us the New Testament saw in him more than a wisdom teacher. Rather, what was said about personified Wisdom in the Jewish tradition was predicated of Jesus by early Christians. The Prologue to John's Gospel went even further in affirming that in Jesus the Word of God became flesh, and in depicting him as the revealer and the revelation of God. The identification of Jesus as the Wisdom of God in turn gave special prominence to his wisdom teachings that were being gathered in the traditions that were later incorporated in the Gospels.

The early confessions insist that Jesus' death and resurrection was "according to the scriptures." Although sometimes it is hard to discern which Scriptures are meant, it is an article of early Christian faith that Jesus stands in continuity with the history of his people Israel. Likewise, the hymns that appear in the Lukan infancy narrative with their rich biblical language serve to situate Jesus in the context of God's saving intervention on behalf of his people.

Perhaps the biggest problem posed by early Christian beliefs about Jesus for Christians today concerns the interpretation of his death as a sacrifice for sins. The affirmation of Jesus' death as "for our sins" is an early and profound element in Christian faith. However, most Americans and

Europeans have no experience and no understanding of sacrifice as a religious reality. At best we may work with a "spiritual" notion of sacrifice or make some connection with the "sacrifice of the Mass." Moreover, many people today (especially women) resent the concept of sacrifice because they feel that it has been used to make them take on unwelcome and unnecessary duties and burdens in their lives. But for people all over the Greco-Roman world in the first century A.D., sacrifices of animals and produce were part of their everyday experience. In fact, Christianity's success in promoting the death of Jesus as the one perfect sacrifice for sins (see Hebrews) is largely responsible for the cessation of other sacrifices—and thus our current difficulty in comprehending Jesus' death as a sacrifice for sins.

A second problem encountered in these early Christian witnesses to Christian faith is due to their concentration on Jesus' death and resurrection. Where do the teachings of Jesus fit in? How important are they? Why do Paul and the other New Testament writers (apart from the Evangelists) quote these teachings so infrequently? Indeed, without the Gospels, we would know very little about the wisdom of Jesus. Here the early Christian hymns about Jesus as the Wisdom of God can provide a bridge between beliefs about Jesus and the wisdom that he himself taught.

A third problem is this: How literally are we to take the traditions associated with Jesus as personified Wisdom? This question raises especially the issue of Jesus' pre-existence. Are we to assume that Jesus really existed before creation? Or is this simply part of the imaginative tradition from Proverbs 8 and other Jewish texts that Wisdom existed with God before God began to create the world? Although orthodox Christian faith takes these statements literally, the topic has been debated since patristic times and is part of the current debate about doing Christology from "above" or "from below."

For Reflection and Discussion

1. What are the principal beliefs about Jesus in the earliest Christian sources? How do they compare with the classic Christian professions of faith (the Apostles' Creed, the Nicene-Constantinople Creed, etc.)?

2. How would you explain to someone today the meaning of the affirmation "Christ died for our sins"?

3. What in early Christians' beliefs about Jesus stands within Judaism, and what seems to go beyond Judaism?

chapter four

HOW EARLY CHRISTIANS WORSHIPED

The New Testament is best viewed as a witness to the religious experiences of the early Christians. The heart of that experience was the belief that Jesus of Nazareth is both the revealer and the revelation of God. This belief was expressed in baptism as the sacrament of Christian initiation, and by participation in communal worship and the Lord's Supper as the sacrament of ongoing Christian life.

No New Testament text provides an exact description of an early Christian worship service. But there are enough allusions to allow us to learn about some important features associated with baptism and the Eucharist, or the Lord's Supper, as well as the community meetings held in private homes. What we learn can help the churches today to recover some of the vitality of early Christian experience and worship, and to recognize that the first Christians faced some of the same problems that confront Christians in the twenty-first century.

BAPTISM AS INITIATION INTO CHRIST

Baptism was the ritual by which those who had come to believe in Jesus and sought to follow his way became members of the Body of Christ, the Church. The Greek word *baptisma* derives from the verbs *bapto* and *baptizo*, which mean "dip" or "immerse." These terms may also carry the sense of drowning or sinking. The words are associated with water—a natural element that conveys the symbolism of life (life being impossible without water), cleansing or purification, destruction (by flood or violent storm), and death (by drowning). The richness and ambivalence of water as a symbol fit perfectly with early Christian beliefs about Jesus' death and resurrection and the possibility of participating in its effects (soteriology).

Some precedents for Christian baptism can be found in the Old Testament. Priests were expected to practice water purifications before carrying out rituals in the Tent of Meeting or the Temple (see Exodus 40:12, 30–32). And on the Day of Atonement the high priest bathed before putting on his priestly garments and performing the sacrifices (see Leviticus 16). Likewise, the Torah mandated ritual washings to end the uncleanness brought about by contact with unclean objects or corpses (see Leviticus 11:24–40; 14:1–8; 15:1–13; Numbers 19:1–24).

Further preparations for Christian baptism can be found in Judaism in Jesus' time. Many ritual baths (*miqwa'ot*) have been discovered in the course of archaeological excavations in Israel. The Pharisees promoted a program of "priestly" holiness for all Israel, and so they sought to extend the priestly practices of ritual purity beyond those priests who served in the Temple. The Essene community at Qumran devised an elaborate system of water channels to carry on their regimen of ritual purification. They also made a link between external washings and the state of one's soul: "And when his flesh is sprinkled with purifying water and sanctified by cleansing water, it shall be made clean by the humble submission of his soul to all the precepts of God" (1QS 3:8–9). There may also be some influence of "proselyte baptism," whereby a female convert to Judaism underwent ritual immersion and a male convert underwent both circumcision and ritual immersion (see *b.Yebamot* 46a–47b). But how early this practice came into Judaism is a matter of long-standing debate.

The most obvious precedent for early Christian baptism was the baptism practiced by John the Baptist. Although it is possible that John had been a member of the Qumran community or a related group in the area (see Luke 1:80), he gave a new and distinctive twist to the ritual purifications practiced by Jews in the first century. His baptism was a once-for-all-time ritual that symbolized spiritual and moral conversion in preparation for the kingdom of God and "the Stronger One" (see Mark 1:7). Jesus himself underwent this baptism (see Mark 1:9–11), and apparently many other Jews did also (see Mark 1:5 and Josephus, *Antiquities* 18.116–119). Indeed, it is possible that Jesus himself baptized others (see John 3:22, 26; 4:1).

Early Christian baptism, however, was distinctive in several respects. First, Christian baptism was "in the name of Jesus." The association of baptism with the name of Jesus is assumed by Paul (see Romans 6:3; 1 Corinthians 1:13, 15; Galatians 3:27) and mentioned also in Acts (see 2:38; 8:16; 10:48; 19:5). This formula seems to have been even more original than the trinitarian baptismal formula in Matthew 28:19. The idea is that through baptism, one belongs to Jesus (see 1 Corinthians 1:10–17), confesses Jesus as Lord (see 1 Corinthians 12:3; Romans 10:9), and moves from the dominion of darkness to the kingdom of God's beloved Son (see Colossians 1:13).

A second distinctive element in Christian baptism is the connection with the gift of the Holy Spirit, a connection affirmed in the account of Jesus' own baptism by John when the Holy Spirit descended upon him (see Mark 1:10). While the fullness of the Holy Spirit is reserved for the kingdom of God, baptism is understood as bringing "the first fruits of the Spirit" (Romans 8:23) and as the "down payment" or "first installment" of what will be in the future (see 2 Corinthians 1:22; 5:5; Ephesians 1:14). Although some texts in Acts (see 8:14–17; 19:1–7) suggest a separation between water baptism and the gift of the Holy Spirit, the overwhelming thrust of the New Testament is insistent that the two belong together.

The distinctive Christian theology of baptism as participation in Jesus' death and resurrection is expressed most directly by Paul in Romans 6:3–4: "Do you not know that all of us who have been baptized into Christ Jesus were baptized into his death? Therefore we have been buried with him in baptism into death, so that, just as Christ was raised from the dead by the glory of the Father, so we too might walk in newness of life." Baptism in water, with its symbolism of both death and life, means sharing in the Christ event and in its effects or benefits (freedom, justification, sanctification, salvation, etc.).

There is no direct description of the ritual of baptism in the New Testament. From what is said in passing, however, one can infer that some kind of catechesis preceded baptism (see 1 Corinthians 15:1–8; Hebrews 6:1–2), that baptism was administered by someone other than the person to be baptized (see 1 Corinthians 1:14–17), that immersion in water was the usual method of baptizing (see Romans 6:1–11; but see *Didache* 7:3), and that the person was baptized "in the name of Jesus" and later in the name of the Father, Son, and Holy Spirit. The baptismal ceremony may have included hymns, confessions of faith, questions about the candidate's fitness, and the imposition of hands (see Acts 8:16–17; 19:6). Candidates for baptism were normally adults. Whether infants or young children were baptized cannot be proved (or disproved) from the New Testament. The strange practice of baptism on behalf of the dead (see 1 Corinthians 15:29), while not condemned by Paul, ran counter to his insistence on baptism as involving walking "in newness of life" (Romans 6:4).

The Lord's Supper and Early Christian Life

Besides baptism, the most prominent ritual practiced by early Christians was the Lord's Supper, or Eucharist. While baptism served as the rite of Christian initiation, the Lord's Supper was the rite of ongoing Christian life. Whereas baptism was a once-in-a-lifetime experience, the Lord's Supper could be repeated throughout one's life. It was not so much a rite of passage as it was the means by which Christian life could be sustained and nourished.

Meals were a prominent feature in Old Testament religion. From Abraham's hospitality to the three mysterious visitors in Genesis 18 to early Jewish apocalyptic speculations about God's kingdom as a great banquet, the motif of the meal is a recurrent biblical feature. The Passover meal first celebrated in Egypt and repeated every year is a household ritual (see Exodus 12). God's covenant with Moses on Mount Sinai is ratified with a meal (see Exodus 24). The sacrifices offered in the Temple often involved a meal, especially in the case of thanksgiving sacrifices (see Leviticus 7:12–15). And Wisdom issues an invitation to all who are "simple" to join in the banquet at her house (see Proverbs 9). While no one of these biblical precedents explains everything about Jesus' Last Supper and the rite of the Lord's Supper, each one adds a dimension within the early Christian ritual.

The most obvious precedents for the Lord's Supper are the meals that were characteristic of Jesus' public ministry and his Last Supper. Jesus' meals with marginal people are among the best attested and most certain features of his life. Very early in his public ministry, according to Mark, the scribes of the Pharisees asked in a critical way: "Why does he eat with tax collectors and sinners?" (Mark 2:16) In Matthew 11:19 Jesus contrasts himself with the ascetic John the Baptist, and says that "the Son of Man came eating and drinking." He goes on to repeat the charge that his opponents were making about him: "Look, a glutton and a drunkard, a friend of tax collectors and sinners!"

These meals shared by Jesus with marginal persons were enacted parables of the kingdom of God. Jesus preached a gospel of repentance, forgiveness, and conversion (see Mark 1:15) against the horizon of the kingdom of God. In apocalyptic Jewish circles it was customary to picture God's kingdom as a great banquet (see Luke 14). The Qumran community interpreted and structured its meals as anticipations of the meal to be celebrated in God's kingdom. What was unusual and shocking about Jesus' meals was their inclusiveness; they were open to people who were engaged in occupations or practiced lifestyles that made unlikely their presence at the messianic banquet. Nevertheless, such persons were welcomed at Jesus' meals and presumably at God's own final banquet.

It is in the context of Jesus' meals with marginal people as anticipations of the kingdom of God that we should understand the accounts about the multiplications of the loaves and fishes (see Mark 6:30-44 and 8:1–10 and parallels) as well as the meals shared by the Risen Christ with his disciples (see Luke 24:13–49; John 21:9–14). And it is in this context that we should interpret the Last Supper of Jesus as well as the early Christian rite of the Lord's Supper, or Eucharist.

The earliest New Testament document that contains a description of the Lord's Supper is Paul's First Letter to the Corinthians (around A.D. 55–56). Paul refers to the Lord's Supper twice, each time in an effort to call the Corinthian Christians to greater communal unity. At the end of his advice about eating food associated somehow with the worship of pagan gods, Paul first reminds the Corinthians about what they do when they celebrate the Eucharist together: "The cup of blessing that we bless, is it not a sharing in the blood of Christ? The bread that we break, is it not a sharing in the body of Christ?" (1 Corinthians 10:16) Just as in baptism the early Christians came to share in Jesus' death and resurrection, so in the Eucharist they continue their profound participation in the Christ event. Paul goes on to call them to greater unity by appealing to the one bread that they share: "Because there is one bread, we who are many are one bread, for we all partake of the one bread" (10:17).

Likewise in 1 Corinthians 11:17–34, Paul uses the tradition about the Lord's Supper in 11:23–26 to convince the Corinthians to end certain abuses that had crept into their community meetings (of which the Lord's Supper was a part). Apparently the rich and influential members were inviting their friends and social peers to come early for a "good meal," while the poor and socially inferior were expected to arrive later for the celebration of the Lord's Supper. Paul regarded such economic and social factionalism as inimical to the life of the Christian community.

In the middle of his criticism of the Corinthians' behavior, Paul reminds them about what it is that they really do at the Lord's Supper. He introduces his description as a tradition that goes back to Jesus himself: "For I received from the Lord what I also handed on to you. . . ." According to this tradition, at the Last Supper Jesus took a loaf of bread, gave thanks to God, broke the bread, and said: "This is my body that is for you. Do this in remembrance of me" (1 Corinthians 11:24). Not only does Jesus identify himself with the broken bread (thus foreshadowing his death) but he also hints that his death has significance as a sacrifice ("for you") and that this ritual is to be repeated by his followers as a memorial of him.

According to 1 Corinthians 11:25, Jesus' words over the cup took place "after supper," perhaps an allusion to the Passover celebration. These words identify the cup as "the new covenant in my blood," probably an allusion to the covenant meal at Sinai in Exodus 24, where Moses sprinkled blood upon the people: "See the blood of the covenant that the Lord has made with you in accordance with all these words" (Exodus 24:8). And again there is a directive to "do this, as often as you drink it, in remembrance of me." The saying over the cup also situates Jesus' impending death in the context of a sacrifice ("in my blood").

To the words of Jesus over the bread and the cup, Paul (or more likely, his tradition) adds a directive that links the Lord's Supper to the Second Coming of Jesus and the fullness of God's kingdom: "For as often as you eat this bread and drink this cup, you proclaim the Lord's death until he comes" (1 Corinthians 11:26). The celebration of the Lord's Supper is also a sign of hope for the eschatological banquet ("Our Lord, come! = Maranatha," see 1 Corinthians 16:22).

If we step back from this extraordinarily rich text preserved in 1 Corinthians 11:23–26, we can see in it very clearly the many dimensions of the Lord's Supper. It is a meal shared with Jesus' friends. It is a meal hosted by Jesus for sinners and marginal people (since at it Jesus prophesies that his disciples will betray him). It involves participation in Jesus' suffering and death. It is at once a Passover celebration, a covenant meal, a sacrifice, a memorial, and Wisdom's banquet. And it looks forward to the banquet to be shared in the fullness of God's kingdom and at the glorious return of Jesus.

Another tradition about Jesus' Last Supper appears in Mark 14:22–25 and Matthew 26:26–29. Luke 22:14–20 appears to combine the Pauline and Markan/Matthean traditions in a somewhat confusing way. John's Gospel contains no explicit narrative of Jesus' Last Supper, although the bread of life discourse in John 6 seems to allude to the Eucharist at several points. The Markan/Matthean tradition consists of Jesus' words over the bread ("Take; this is my body") and over the cup ("This is my blood of the covenant which is poured out for many"). While in Mark's chronology the Last Supper is a Passover meal, in John's different chronology and from the perspective of historical likelihood, it was more likely a meal with Passover themes celebrated before the actual festival began (like a Christmas party before December 25). The Markan/Matthean tradition includes Jesus' interpretation of the broken bread and the shared cup as representing his imminent death, the theme of sacrifice ("poured out for many"), and the covenant ("my blood of the covenant"). This tradition also includes a saying about the meal as an anticipation of the banquet in God's kingdom: "Truly I tell you, I will never again drink of the fruit of the vine until that day when I drink it new in the kingdom of God" (Mark 14:25).

The version in Matthew 26:26–29 is basically the same as that in Mark 14:22–25, although the addition of the instruction before the words over the cup ("Drink from it, all of you") is generally taken as further evidence for the liturgical use of the text. The version in Luke 22:14–20 contains the basic elements from both traditions, but in an unusual order: kingdom and cup sayings (see 22:16–18), bread saying (see 22:19), and cup saying (see 22:20). Moreover, some manuscripts omit 22:19b–20. Some scholars explain the Lukan version as an attempt to align the Last Supper more closely with the order of the Passover meal ("I have eagerly desired to eat this Passover with you before I suffer," 22:15). Others regard it as a deliberately confusing way to avoid making too public what had become the ritual of ongoing Christian life. In either case, the Lukan version adds the theme of memorial ("in remembrance of me") and underlines the connection with Passover ("to eat this Passover with you").

While the story of Jesus' Last Supper is recounted by the Evangelists as part of their passion narratives, there are elements in these accounts that suggest liturgical usage—an impression already well established by 1 Corinthians 11:23–26. The "Last Supper" turned into the Lord's Supper, or Eucharist; it became the ritual at which Christians retold the story of Jesus' Last Supper and did what Jesus did at the Last Supper. No New Testament book provides an exact description of this ritual, but we may assume that it contained a retelling of the Last Supper narrative along with a sharing of the bread ("Take") and the cup ("Drink from it, all of you"). We do not know who presided at this rite, although it is likely that they were people who were recognized as leaders within the community. We do know that the Last Supper narrative evoked the great themes of the biblical tradition: Passover, covenant, sacrifice, vicarious suffering, Wisdom's banquet, memorial, and hope for the fullness of God's kingdom. And we do know that the Lord's Supper took place in the context of the community meeting or assembly (see 1 Corinthians 11:17–34).

The House Church

Where did early Christians meet for worship? It seems to have been at the private homes of the relatively well-to-do members. The earliest Christians did not have a system of animal or produce sacrifices, and so there was no need for a temple. Nor did they have the membership necessary for erecting separate buildings ("churches"). The closest analogies were Greco-Roman clubs or voluntary associations and Jewish synagogues (provided we bear in mind that "synagogue" first of all meant "gathering" or assembly, and only later came to refer to a building).

The early Christians called their gathering or assembly the *ekklesia*, perhaps to distinguish their group from the Jewish *synagoge*. The word *ekklesia* derives from the Greek "called out," and it was originally used in connection with citizens who had been "called out" to represent themselves and their city in political matters. Rejecting the political nuances, the early Christians used *ekklesia* in a religious context with reference to their experience of having been called by God out of the darkness of their former lives and into the light of Christ and the life of discipleship (see 1 Peter 2:9–10). The term *ekklesia* expressed the early Christians' consciousness of their divine election and their mission.

Those who made up the *ekklesia* were a mixture of Jews and Gentiles, slaves and free persons, and males and females (see Galatians 3:28). What brought these people together was their experience of a call from God in

Christ that allowed them to transcend their ethnic, social, and gender differences. According to Paul, "not many of you were wise by human standards, not many were powerful, not many were of noble birth" (1 Corinthians 1:26). But Paul may be indulging in some rhetorical exaggeration here, and we need not imagine that the earliest Christians were drawn exclusively from the lower classes or were slaves. For example, Erastus seems to have been the treasurer of the city of Corinth (see Romans 16:23). Also, understanding Paul's letters and other documents that became part of the New Testament canon demanded some familiarity with Greco-Roman rhetoric, and in particular with the Jewish Scriptures in their Greek version. Moreover, in 1 Corinthians 1:16, Paul had just referred to his having baptized "the household of Stephanas," a person of sufficient economic and social status to preside over a household.

In the Greco-Roman world a "household" (*oikia*) extended beyond the nuclear family. It consisted not only of the owner's extended family but also of servants and slaves who performed the household tasks and worked in what we might call small businesses or "cottage industries" associated with the household. The household was a patriarchal institution ruled over by the male head of the family (*paterfamilias*). There were, however, certain spheres of household life over which women had authority (see Proverbs 31). For an insight into the everyday life and relationships of these people, see the "household codes" in Colossians 3:18–4:1 and Ephesians 5:21–6:9.

Paul's letters provide occasional references to the "house churches" as the assemblies of early Christians gathered at the houses of the wealthier members. The controversy over the proper celebration of the Lord's Supper glimpsed in 1 Corinthians 11:17–34 illustrates the problematic side of this institution. The householder might naturally favor his own social and economic peers to the detriment of the less fortunate or prominent members. Whatever the problems that arose, it appears that the earliest Christians generally met in private homes. In both 1 Corinthians 16:19 and Romans 16:5, Paul sends special greetings and praise to Prisca and Aquila, a married couple whom Paul describes as his co-workers. At the same time, he sends greetings to the "the church at their house."

A particularly interesting test for the house church appears in Paul's Letter to Philemon. Paul had brought Philemon to Christian faith. Philemon had a slave named Onesimus who had run away from Philemon's household and eventually found his way to Paul in prison (probably at Ephesus). Paul then brought Onesimus to Christian faith. Paul's letter to Philemon is a request that Philemon accept Onesimus back into his household "no longer as a slave but more than a slave, a beloved brother" (v. 16). The letter that Paul wrote to Philemon was to be read publicly in "the church in your house" (v. 2). Those who hosted the "church" were Philemon, Apphia (probably Philemon's wife), and Archippus. In the letter Paul deliberately puts Philemon "on the spot"; he not only directs that the letter be read publicly but also uses financial imagery to suggest that Philemon is in Paul's debt (see vv. 18–21) and promises a personal visit (v. 22) to see how things worked out.

The house churches were small. It has been estimated that a household could accommodate forty to fifty people. On the positive aside, the house church promoted a strong sense of community ("the family of Jesus") and broke down social barriers (which were very prominent in Mediterranean societies). On the negative side, the success of the early Christian mission led the local community to outgrow the ideal of one house church in a city and to divide up and meet in several different locations. This may explain the factionalism that Paul sought to combat in 1 Corinthians. Moreover, the household was very much a hierarchical and patriarchal institution in which the *paterfamilias* was the ultimate authority. The community was expected to accept the hospitality of the householder and to abide by the rules that he laid down. While women exercised authority in certain areas, they were under the ultimate authority of the husbands, fathers, and even sons. Also, while early Christians may have assented to the proposition that "all of you are one in Christ in Jesus" (Galatians 3:28), the more wealthy and prestigious among them probably found this matter hard to practice (as 1 Corinthians 11:17–34 demonstrates).

The house church was a necessary but transitional step in the history of the early church. While it had many attractive features, it should not be romanticized or held up as the only model for today. In fact, it was the victim of the success of the early Christian mission and the sociological laws of group formation. But the fact remains: The household was the place where the first Christians met, prayed, and celebrated the Lord's Supper.

THE CHRISTIAN ASSEMBLY

What happened when the *ekklesia* gathered? The New Testament provides no detailed description. The most sustained treatment appears in 1 Corinthians 11–14, but there Paul is more concerned with correcting abuses than with giving an objective picture.

If (as seems likely) the early Christian assembly was influenced by the practice of Jewish synagogues, we can assume that there were readings from Scripture (the Old Testament in its Greek version), some reflection or homily, and prayers of petition (at least the Lord's Prayer).

In 1 Corinthians 14:26, Paul adds to the picture when he writes: "When

you come together, each one has a hymn, a lesson, a revelation, or an interpretation." He insists that "all things be done for building up" and gives
instructions on how these different elements can be shared so that they
will indeed edify others.

From various references in Paul's letters, we get the impression that
these were read aloud before the community so that all might profit from
the apostle's wisdom (see Philemon, the responses to questions in
1 Corinthians, etc.). And it is likely that there was a collection, especially
to benefit the "saints" in the mother-church at Jerusalem (see
1 Corinthians 16:2; 2 Corinthians 8:1–9:15). And of course there was
the celebration of the Lord's Supper (see 1 Corinthians 11:17–34). Other
rituals such as "ordination" and anointing the sick may well also have been
part of the community assemblies. Whether baptism was performed in this
setting or outside by rivers and streams is hard to know.

Likewise, it is hard to know when these meetings took place. Given
the setting presupposed in 1 Corinthians 11:17–34 and the large number
of items on the agenda, one can assume that these gatherings generally
took place in the evening after supper. And given the prominence of Sunday as the day of Jesus' Resurrection, it is likely that Sunday was the
appropriate day for such meetings.

An interesting description of an early Christian assembly comes from
an unlikely source: Pliny, the Roman governor of Bithynia (in northern
Asia Minor) in the early second century. In his letter (see *Epistles* 10.96) to
the Emperor Trajan, Pliny reports what was learned about the Christians
and their assemblies with the aid of torture inflicted upon two female
slaves who held the title of "deaconess." Pliny states that the Christians
"were in the habit of meeting on a certain fixed day before it was light."
The day was very likely Sunday. The timing near dawn may reflect
Jewish practice (like the Qumran Essenes) or (more likely) be tied to the
celebration of Jesus' Resurrection from the dead. Pliny goes on to report
that the Christians "sang in alternate verses a hymn to Christ as to a god"
(see Philippians 2:6–11; Colossians 1:15–20; John 1:1–18). Next he speaks
about a "solemn oath" (*sacramentum*) that the Christians swore to avoid
wicked deeds such as fraud, theft, and adultery (perhaps the Ten Commandments). Finally, he notes that "it was their custom to separate, and
then reassemble to partake of food—but food of an ordinary kind." It is
hard to escape a reference to the bread and wine of the Lord's Supper here.

Pliny's report came from a situation far removed from Paul's churches
in date (about fifty years later) and place (northern Asia Minor). But apart
from the question of timing (morning versus evening), there is a nice fit
between what can be inferred from Paul's letters and what Pliny's infor-
mants told his torturers. From Pliny's report, the early Christian meetings

seem harmless. They sing songs, promise to do good and avoid evil, and share a simple meal of ordinary food. Nevertheless, Pliny calls Christianity a "depraved and excessive superstition" and a "contagious superstition," and writes to the emperor for advice on how to deal with it.

In 1 Corinthians 11–14, Paul devotes four chapters to correcting abuses associated with the Christian assembly. The major themes in his pastoral advice are orderliness, edification, and unity.

When treating the role of women in the Christian assembly (see 1 Corinthians 11:2–16), Paul assumes that women pray and prophesy in public (see 11:5), notwithstanding 14:33b–35, which is most likely the quotation of a Corinthian slogan that Paul rejects in 14:36. Here Paul's concern is order in the assembly and, in particular, that in their hairstyles (or head coverings) the men should look like men and the women should look like women.

The socioeconomic and community problems associated with the Lord's Supper (see 1 Corinthians 11:17–34) have already been treated in this chapter. Paul's concern was that the practice of the elites in eating and drinking beforehand was disrupting the unity and orderliness of the Lord's Supper ("one goes hungry and another becomes drunk," 11:22).

The problem treated at greatest length by Paul in 1 Corinthians 12–14 seems to have been occasioned by Christians who spoke in "tongues." By glossolalia, or speaking in tongues, here we are most likely to understand not speaking in foreign languages (as in Acts 2) but rather unintelligible noises ("sighs too deep for words," see Romans 8:26) as part of being under the influence of the Holy Spirit. Those who possessed this "spiritual gift" or charism were apparently putting themselves forward as paragons of spirituality.

Paul's criticism of glossolalia is that it fails to build up others and the community as a whole. Without interpretation, speaking in tongues remains inaccessible and useless to others. In his critique, Paul insists that all the spiritual gifts are for the edification of others: "To each is given the manifestation of the Spirit for the common good" (1 Corinthians 12:7). When Paul lists the various charisms, he puts speaking in tongues at the bottom (see 12:10, 28). He calls on all the Corinthians to recognize the primacy of love in Christian life (see 13:1–13), and shows why prophecy is superior to glossolalia: "Those who prophesy speak to other people for their upbuilding and encouragement and consolation" (14:3). He emphasizes the need for interpreting tongues and counsels that "if there is no one to interpret, let them be silent in church and speak to God" (14:28). But Paul does not forbid speaking in tongues. Rather, his point is that "all things should be done decently and in order" (14:40).

The Corinthian assembly was a lively and enthusiastic event. And one

of Paul's arguments for greater unity and order was to consider what outsiders or unbelievers might say if they entered such a meeting: "Will they
not say that you are out of your mind?" (1 Corinthians 14:23). In his
criticisms, Paul provides a theological foundation for Christian life and
worship according to which each Christian has been gifted by the Holy
Spirit and so has a duty to use those gifts for building up the Body of
Christ.

Possibilities and Problems

It took some time for the Church to emerge as a religious institution
separate from Judaism. At the start it perceived itself and was perceived by
others as an exotic form of Judaism. And yet, as our discussions of baptism
and the Lord's Supper show, it offered a new and distinctive way to God—
through Jesus Christ—right from the beginning. To be baptized in Christ
Jesus and in the name of Jesus involved participation in his death and
Resurrection. To celebrate the Lord's Supper "in memory of me" meant
that throughout one's life as a Christian it is possible to be part of the great
history of salvation by means of incorporation into Jesus. What brought
the early Christians together was not race or social status or gender. It was
the experience of God in Christ Jesus.

The problems associated with the house churches and the community
assemblies, whatever their negative features were, bear witness to a religious movement that was full of vitality and enthusiasm. Through their
new experience of God in Christ and their membership in the *ekklesia*,
the early Christians found themselves "born again" and eager to share
their faith with others. To be part of this movement was a new and excit-
ing experience for them. And so it is not surprising that they made mistakes in judgment and in action. Paul's insistence on orderliness and unity
was necessary because these people took their new faith so seriously.

The fact that early Christians met in private houses reminds us that
"the Church" is not simply a building. Rather, the Church is first of all a
community of believers gathered in the name of Jesus. The gifts that God
has given its members are not for their self-esteem or fame but for the
common good and for building up the Body of Christ. While it was inevi-
table that "the Church" would outgrow the house church as its primary
setting, there is always the need to work at establishing and nurturing the
sense of identity and community that the house church fostered among
the first Christians.

The main problem is how little we really know about early Christian
religious experience and worship. While Paul and other New Testament
writers do allude to baptism and the Lord's Supper as part of their teach-

ings about faith and unity, they felt no need to spell out the details of time and place, rituals and formulas, and so on. They could assume that their readers knew these matters from their own experience and did not need detailed descriptions. But there is so much that we in the twenty-first century would like to know about early Christian life and worship.

A consequence of our lack of full knowledge about these matters has been the tendency for various Christian movements and traditions to emphasize certain elements to the exclusion of others. For some Christians, for example, the high point of their religious experience is speaking in tongues. Some traditions only celebrate the liturgy of the word (Scripture readings, sermon, and prayers), while others have given little attention to the word in their zeal for celebrating the Lord's Supper. Still other groups make the community meeting (silence and sharing) into their primary sacrament. Each of these practices has a basis in the New Testament. But no one of them reproduces the worship adopted by the first Christians. Recognition of this problem can promote humility within the churches today and foster greater efforts at church unity.

Another problem is the tendency to idealize or romanticize the religious experiences and formulas of the first Christians. While in some respects the formative years of the Church represent a "golden age" for experiencing the Spirit of Jesus and for mission, we cannot overlook the conflicts and problems that arose: factionalism, pride in exotic spiritual gifts, allowing social differences to direct church life, and so on. That their problems remain our problems is both sobering and encouraging.

For Reflection and Discussion

1. In what sense is baptism an initiation into the death and resurrection of Jesus? How are faith and baptism related?

2. In what sense is the Lord's Supper a sharing in Jesus' death and resurrection and in the great events of salvation history?

3. Are there any points of contact between the problems encountered by the first Christian communities and those encountered in your experience of church life? What is the same and what is different?

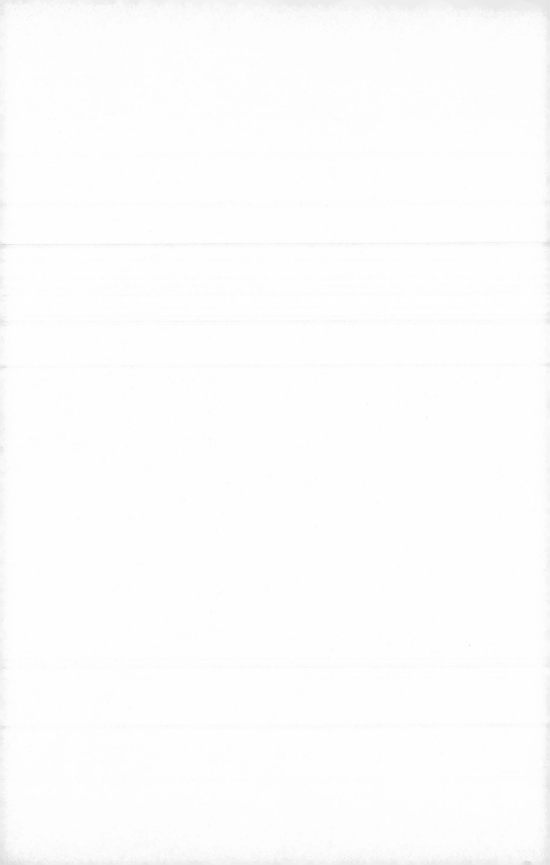

chapter five

PAUL ON THE CHURCH

Paul's letters (from the fifties of the first century A.D.) are the earliest complete documents in the New Testament. Paul was once a vigorous opponent and even a persecutor of the Jesus movement. But his experience of the Risen Jesus on the Damascus Road (see Acts 9, 22, 26) changed everything. At some point between A.D. 33 and 36, Paul moved from Pharisaic Judaism to Jewish Christianity (or perhaps more accurately, Christian Judaism). While the Gentile mission of the Church was not begun by Paul (see Acts 10–11), Paul's experience of the Risen Jesus also involved a special call to bring the gospel to non-Jews. According to Galatians 2:9, Paul's calling was later ratified by the "pillar apostles" (James, Cephas = Peter, and John) in Jerusalem.

In his work as an apostle, Paul's practice was to arrive at a new site without a church, preach the gospel there, found a Christian community, and move on to repeat the process. The house church became the center for the local community. Paul worked with a team of "co-workers," the most prominent being Timothy and Titus. He also developed a network of communication among his converts and co-workers (see Romans 16). His project of collecting funds for the Christian community in Jerusalem (see 1 Corinthians 16:1–4; 2 Corinthians 8–9; Romans 15:25–27) reminded his Gentile converts of the Jewish roots of their new faith and was intended to promote unity among the local churches.

Paul's letters (except Romans) were a means of keeping alive communication between the founding apostle and the communities that he had founded. These letters were written between A.D. 51 and 58. In them Paul was usually responding to problems or questions that had arisen after he had moved on to another missionary foundation. This is certainly the case with 1 Thessalonians, Galatians, Philippians, Philemon, and 1 and 2 Corinthians. The Letter to the Romans is different, however. Paul had not founded the Christian community in Rome, nor had he ever visited Rome. In writing to the Roman Christians, Paul was introducing himself and his gospel in preparation for a short stay there on his way to Spain after taking the proceeds of the collection to Jerusalem (see Romans 15:22–29). He may also have been indirectly addressing the divisions between Jewish Christians and Gentile Christians at Rome.

Thus far we have used Paul's letters as sources of information about early Christian beliefs and religious experiences. The focus has been on the pre-Pauline traditions preserved in Paul's letters. Now we turn to what Paul himself says about the Church as the Spirit-led community, the charismatic community, and the Body of Christ. While Paul did not necessarily create these images of the Church, he did develop them and gave them theological depth and practical relevance.

It is important always to recognize the "occasional" character of Paul's letters. Paul the apostle was a pastoral theologian. In other words, Paul developed his theology as he was responding to the spiritual needs and questions of other Christians. He did not set out to write an ecclesiology. He was not a professor of theology or a philosopher. At the same time, Paul the pastoral theologian was something of a pioneer. Writing some twenty-five years after Jesus' death, Paul was often forced to bring his theological vision to bear in areas and matters where there were no precedents. It is in the framework of Paul the pioneering pastoral theologian that we need to read his great statements about the Church as the Spirit-led community (see Romans 8), the charismatic community (see Romans 12:1–8), and the Body of Christ (see 1 Corinthians 12–14).

THE SPIRIT-LED COMMUNITY

According to 1 Corinthians 12:7, every Christian is a gifted or graced person, and has the duty to use those gifts for the good of others: "To each is given the manifestation of the Spirit for the common good." The origin of these gifts is the Holy Spirit. The Christian is the conduit or instrument of the power of the Risen Christ. The power of Christ made manifest in the present—between Jesus' death and resurrection and the fullness of God's kingdom—is what we call the Holy Spirit.

For Paul, each and every Christian is a bearer of the Holy Spirit. The Spirit dwelling within each Christian is the force that expresses itself in the Christian community. And the power of the Holy Spirit is at the root of life in the Christian community.

Paul's reflection on life in the Spirit in Romans 8 is foundational for understanding his vision of Christian life and of the Church as the Spirit-led community. His Letter to the Romans is a sustained reflection on the revelation of God's righteousness in Jesus' death and resurrection, and on faith as the means by which we participate in the benefits of the Christ event (see Romans 1:16–17).

Paul first establishes that everyone—Jews and Gentiles alike—needed the Christ event to make possible right relationship with God (see Romans 1:18–3:20). Next, in 3:21–4:25, he shows that faith after the example of Abraham is the way by which Jewish and Gentile believers can participate in the benefits of the Christ event. Then in Romans 5–7 Paul considers how the Christ event has made possible freedom from domination by Sin, Death, and the Law. These three powers are depicted as enslaving humans before and apart from Christ. But their domination has been ended through Jesus' death and resurrection.

Romans 8 is a positive reflection on Christian life lived in freedom and under the guidance of the Holy Spirit. It is the life of the "spirit" (that aspect of the human person that is open to God) with the guidance of the Holy Spirit (the Spirit of God and of the Risen Jesus). It concerns Christian life as being in the spirit/Spirit (see 8:1–11), "sonship" (see 8:12–17), living in hope (see 8:18–30), and God's victory "for us" (see 8:31–39).

Being in the spirit/Spirit (Romans 8:1–11): Basic to Paul's understanding of the Church is the Holy Spirit's relationship to God and Christ and to human persons. Through the Holy Spirit, the Risen Lord manifests his presence and power in the world. The power of the Holy Spirit creates the Church as the earthly sphere of God's authority in opposition to the flesh.

Paul uses the opposition of flesh versus spirit to describe two ways of life. Those who live in the "flesh" close themselves off from the Holy Spirit and are under the dominion of Sin and Death. Those who are in the "spirit" are open to God's Holy Spirit and so can live in the freedom that is appropriate to the children of God. By sending his Son Jesus "in the likeness of sinful flesh" (that is, as a human being), God has made it possible for all humans to live in the "spirit" under the guidance of the Holy Spirit. Those who continue to live in the flesh are in revolt or rebellion against God, and set their minds on "the things of the flesh" (which is death). But those who live according to the spirit/Spirit find life and peace, and please God.

Those who are in Christ Jesus are in the Spirit. Note the different ways of talking about the Holy Spirit in Romans 8:9–11: the Spirit, the Spirit of God, the Spirit of Christ, the Spirit of him who raised Jesus from the dead, and his Spirit. These terms are used interchangeably to refer to the abiding presence of God and Christ in Christians (and so in the Church). Walking in the Spirit now is in turn the anticipation of the fullness of resurrected life with God. In summary, the present manifestation of the freedom won by Christ is life lived by those who are in the Holy Spirit. By faith and baptism every Christian is a bearer of the Holy Spirit and must walk in the Spirit.

"Sonship" (Romans 8:12–17): Those who are in the Spirit must live according to the Spirit and not according to the flesh. Being in the Spirit demands appropriate action. Otherwise it can be lost. But those who let

themselves be directed by the Holy Spirit deserve to be called children of God and can share in Jesus' own divine "sonship" (see 8:14). Because they experience themselves as children of God through the Holy Spirit, they too can share in Jesus' relationship of intimacy with God and can address God as "Abba, Father." Indeed, the status of Christians as God's children is brought to consciousness through the Holy Spirit and is dependent on Jesus' own sonship: "if children, then heirs, heirs of God and joint heirs with Christ" (8:17a). But Paul qualifies the divine "sonship" of Christians by linking it to Jesus' death and resurrection: "if, in fact, we suffer with him so that we may also be glorified with him" (8:17b). In summary, life in the Spirit as God's children must be proved daily in actions, and links God's children not only to the glorious Risen Christ but also to the suffering Christ ("provided we suffer").

Living in Hope (Romans 8:18–30): Paul insists that being in the Spirit and being children of God are not yet the fullness of God's kingdom. The best is yet to come. And so, in comparison with that blessed future, the sufferings of the present are like nothing (see 8:18). He foresees a kind of cosmic liberation in which all creation will participate. In the meantime, the whole world awaits the definitive revelation of God's children with a mixture of resigned futility and eager longing (see 8:19–21).

Hope is the attitude that should characterize the Christian in the present. While Christians have received "the first fruits of the Spirit," they must recognize that the present manifestations of the Holy Spirit are not the whole story (see 8:22–25). Even in the case of prayer (see 8:26–27) it is the Holy Spirit who supplies the dynamism for prayer and serves as the mediator between God and those who pray: "the Spirit intercedes for the saints according to the will of God." Prayer then is the experience of both the presence of the Holy Spirit and the incompleteness of life in the Spirit in the present.

The section closes in 8:28–30 with the affirmation that everything is proceeding according to God's plan to vindicate those who love God. Just as God initiated the process of salvation, so God will bring that process to its fitting conclusion. In summary, the present manifestations of the Holy Spirit are both the first fruits and the signs of hope for the fullness of God's kingdom.

God's Victory for Us (Romans 8:31–39): The final part of Paul's reflection on life in the Spirit is as much a celebration as it is an argument. He first establishes that God is "for us" with reference to God's willingness to give his Son "for all of us" (8:32). Again, Jesus' death and resurrection are placed at the center of God's plan for the redemption of all creation. Since God is on our side and Christ Jesus intercedes for us (see 8:33–34), then nothing can separate us from the love of God (see 8:35–39). Therefore, Christians can live in the present with the full confidence that in Jesus' death and resurrection God's victory over Sin and Death has already been won. Their hope is enriched by an assurance about the outcome. And so sufferings in the present time are not of ultimate significance. In summary, for those who are in the Spirit, the present is a time of confident waiting because God's victory is assured and nothing can separate us from God's love.

In his reflection on life in the Holy Spirit, Paul never mentions the Church. Nevertheless, what Paul says about life in the spirit/Spirit in Romans 8 is foundational for his understanding of the Church. Those who have experienced the Spirit of God in Christ constitute the Church. The Holy Spirit supplies the energy and inspiration for every aspect of Christian life. The marvelous things that Christians are empowered to do, both as individuals and as a community of faith, are the first fruits of the Holy Spirit and the signs that point to an even more glorious future. When Paul, in Romans 8:14, says that "all who are led by the Spirit of God are children of God," he is describing those who make up the Church.

THE CHARISMATIC COMMUNITY

According to Paul, every Christian is a bearer of the Holy Spirit and is led by the Spirit. The actions of individual Christians and of the Christian community are expressions of the Spirit. The various ways in which the activities of the Spirit are expressed are called *charisms*.

The Greek word *charisma* means "gift." It is related to the term *charis*, which means "grace." To speak of the Church as the "charismatic community" means that it is the assembly of graced persons. "Charism" describes the individuation of grace, how each Christian responds to grace. The charisms are God's actions through human persons for the upbuilding of the community of faith. Charism is not the same as church office—but, ideally, appointment to church office should be the recognition of the person's charism, and the actions of office holders should be the actualization of the *charis* given to them.

The Church as the charismatic community is rooted in Jesus and in the Holy Spirit. One way to describe Jesus, as we have seen, is to classify him as a charismatic prophet, one whose source of power and basis of authority came not from humans but from God. The extraordinary power of Jesus was made manifest in his teachings and healings as well as in his freedom toward the Jerusalem Temple and the interpretation of the Old Testament Law. His disciples saw themselves as sharing in Jesus' charismatic power and freedom. The Resurrection of Jesus was viewed as the greatest act of divine power. His followers believed that even after death, Jesus was still alive, and that his life was available to them through the Spirit of Jesus or the Holy Spirit.

For Paul and other early Christians, the Holy Spirit as the power of the Risen Christ was the life-force of the Church. Both the apostle and the community are subject to the Holy Spirit. The Church as the charismatic community is the realm of the Holy Spirit in which each member can find salvation and serve others. Thus the charisms are the unfolding of the Holy Spirit's power in the many members of the body of the Church.

The Pauline images of the Church as the charismatic community and as the Body of Christ are closely related. And so the most extensive treatments of them—Romans 12:1–8 and 1 Corinthians 12–14—consider both images together. Here, for purposes of clarity, these images are treated in turn, though in fact they cannot be separated.

In dealing with the charisms, Paul makes an important qualification regarding their meaning and exercise. In its common usage, as popularized by sociologist Max Weber, *charism* refers to the free and unbridled exercise of spiritual power. Weber's classic examples of charismatic leaders were the Old Testament judges (such as Gideon and Samson). But Paul uses the concept of *charisma* as an ordering principle, when he insists that the charisms exist not for the glorification of their recipients but, instead, are directed toward the service of others and the building up of the community as a whole.

Paul's teaching on the charisms in Romans 12:1–8 is part of the introduction to his exhortation about the behavior of Christians in everyday life. In this introduction he lays the theological foundations for his practical advice. In 12:1–2 he insists that everyday life is the arena in which Christians worship God, and that the whole of Christian life can and should be the worship of God. And he appeals to Christians to discern God's will in the present as befits their status as persons living in the "age to come" (as opposed to "this world") by way of anticipation.

Paul then prefaces his advice about spiritual humility and sober judgment by appealing to his own charism as an apostle: "For by the grace given to me I say to everyone among you . . ." (Romans 12:3). Next in 12:4–5 he appeals to the image of the Church as the Body of Christ as a reminder that Christians are to use their gifts in the service of the community, not as the occasion for personal pride.

Paul's basic doctrine of the charisms is stated in Romans 12:6a: "we have gifts that differ according to the grace given to us." First, Paul affirms *1)* that all Christians have "gifts" (*charismata*). These gifts are the unfolding of Christ's power in individual Christians within the context of the Church.

As a gifted person, each Christian deserves honor and respect within the community. Second, these gifts are different (*diaphora*). Several examples of the different gifts appear in 12:6b–8, but here Paul's point is to encourage Christians to recognize the variety of their gifts and not always to seek the more extraordinary and exotic gifts (like speaking in tongues). Third, these gifts are "according to the grace given to us." This is an example of the theological or divine passive construction that is very common in the New Testament. The assumption is that God is the source of all these gifts, and since they are God's gifts to give, no one should become proud over them or boast about them.

What really counts about the charisms according to Paul is the use to which they are put in the community. They are not the same as natural abilities or human talents. Rather, in the exercise of the charisms, it is God acting through the Holy Spirit in individual Christians for the community and for the good of others.

The list of charisms that Paul provides in Romans 12:6b–8 underlines their variety and usefulness to the community as a whole. Here there is no apparent hierarchy of importance, and the emphasis is on activity rather than on office. *Prophecy* refers to speaking the words given by the Holy Spirit about God's will for the present situation or for the immediate future. *Ministry* describes actions that serve the needs of fellow believers or the community's life (e.g., acts of hospitality, care for the unfortunate, deeds of charity). *Teaching* involves the transmission of the community's authoritative traditions (pertinent Old Testament texts, sayings of Jesus, summaries of faith) and insight into their relevance for the present situation. *Exhortation* is most likely public utterance providing encouragement, advice, or moral guidance. *Giving* probably refers to sharing food, possessions, or money within the community "with generosity." The *leader* (Greek *ho proistamenos*) can mean "one who presides or rules" in the sense of managing worship or other community affairs, or "one who cares for others" in the sense of championing the causes of those with no one else to speak and act for them. *Compassion* may allude to acts of mercy in general and perhaps to almsgiving in particular.

What Paul says about the charisms in Romans 12:1–8 is a summary of what he wrote at much greater length in 1 Corinthians 12–14. His teaching is neatly summarized in 1 Corinthians 12:7: "To each is given the manifestation of the Spirit for the common good." He provides two lists of charisms. The first list (see 1 Corinthians 12:8–10) stresses the activities in which the charisms are expressed: the utterance of wisdom, the utterance of knowledge, faith, healing, the working of miracles, prophecy, the discernment of spirits, tongues, and the interpretation of tongues. The second list (see 12:28) mixes what seem to be offices and activities: "And God has appointed in the church first apostles, second prophets, third teachers; then deeds of power, then gifts of healing, forms of assistance, forms of leadership, various kinds of tongues." These two lists seem to embody a kind of hierarchy that runs from ministries of the word that build up the community to speaking in tongues which, without interpretation, is useless to others.

According to 1 Corinthians 12–14, there are criteria for assessing the charisms. First, the manifestations of the Holy Spirit must be consistent with the Christian confession "Jesus is Lord" (12:3). Second, the proof of truly spiritual persons is the spirit of love in which they act. If the charismatics lack love, they do themselves and their community no good (see 13:1–13). And third, the various manifestations of the Holy Spirit must serve and build up the community (see 14:1–40). If these manifestations destroy the unity of the congregation, cause harm to its members, or leave outsiders bewildered, they should be ignored or rejected.

THE BODY OF CHRIST

In the midst of his instruction about the charismatic community in Romans 12:1–8, Paul appeals to the image of the body: "For as in one body we have many members, and not all the members have the same function, so we, who are many, are one body in Christ, and individually we are members one of another" (12:4–5). The "body" image is a simple analogy that anyone can understand. The human body has many parts; these parts all have different functions; and the ideal is that all these parts work together for the common good. When applied to the Christian community, the point is that, to function effectively, all the charismatic persons must perform their different functions together and in concert.

Paul's most important theological qualification to the body analogy comes with his insistence that "we, who are many, are one body *in Christ*." It is Christ who makes this body possible. This body is not merely a collection of individuals joined together, but rather individual believers have been called by Christ to constitute his body. And with the aid of the image of the Body of Christ, Paul urges individual Christians not to take pride in their gifts (*charismata*) but to realize that these gifts are to used in the service of the Body of Christ.

Paul's statement about the Body of Christ in Romans 12:4–5 is a summary of an idea that he develops at length in 1 Corinthians 12–14. The church at Corinth in Greece that Paul had founded was threatened by deep divisions. According to 1 Corinthians 1:10–17, the Corinthians were divided into parties or factions according to the major figures who administered their baptisms: Paul, Apollos, Peter, and "Christ." According to 1 Corinthians 11:17–34, the celebration of the common meal or the Lord's Supper was being pulled apart by factions formed along social and economic lines.

The attitudes toward the charisms and the conduct arising out of the charismatic experiences also constituted a threat to the unity of the Christian community at Corinth. The root of the problem was the excessive value being placed on "knowledge" and "wisdom" by those who were especially proud of their spiritual gifts (see 1 Corinthians 1:10–4:21). The wave of spiritual enthusiasm led to all kinds of questionable behavior in the area of sexuality (see 5:1–7:40) and in eating meat that had been sacrificed to pagan gods (see 8:1–11:1). It also resulted in an overemphasis on speaking in tongues, which in turn brought about disorder in the Christian assembly (see 11:2–14:40). Even the understanding of the Resurrection had become muddled through the perception among some that the fullness of the Resurrection had already occurred in them (see 15:1–58). Rather than expressing their unity in the Spirit of Jesus, the Corinthian charismatics expressed their lack of faith, hope, and love. Rather than building up the community, they posed a threat to the community.

In 1 Corinthians 12–14 Paul is dealing with abuses that have come to the fore in the assemblies of the Christian community. In particular, he is trying to counter the overemphasis on the more exotic spiritual gifts such as speaking in tongues. And so Paul argues that the many gifts must contribute to the unity of the body (see chapter 12), that love is the greatest and most abiding of the charisms (see chapter 13), and that all things done in the assembly should be carried out decently and in order (see chapter 14).

In the course of treating the proper use of the "spiritual gifts" (pneumatika), Paul invokes at some length the image of the Church as the Body of Christ (see 1 Corinthians 12:12–31). In 12:12 Paul presents his basic point much as he does in Romans 12:4–5: "For just as the body is one and has many members, and all the members of the body, though many, are one body, so it is with Christ." Paul seems to assume that his readers are already familiar with the notion of the Body of Christ. Perhaps it was part of Paul's own preaching. Scholars have sought its roots in the image of the city as the "body politic" in Greco-Roman philosophy, in the idea of the universe as a gigantic body, in the notion of Adam as the archetype of all human persons, and in the Hebrew notion of corporate personality. But perhaps the comparison is so obvious that the search for precedents is futile.

Whatever the origins of the body image may be, Paul uses it to explain why and how the different members can exist and work together. According to 1 Corinthians 12:13, what made all these different people—

Jews and Greeks, slaves and free, male and female—into one body was their baptism into Christ Jesus and their "drinking of the one Spirit." The body came into existence not from the independent decisions of its members but from their relationship to Christ and to the Holy Spirit. The Church is the means by which Christ reveals himself in the world through the Spirit. Fellowship (*koinonia*) in the Church is first of all relationship to Christ and to the Holy Spirit, and secondarily relationship to other Christians. In other words, Paul's ecclesiology is a consequence of his Christology and pneumatology.

In 1 Corinthians 12:14–21, Paul begins by stating his basic thesis: "the body does not consist of one member but of many." The rest of this section appears to be directed toward those who may seem to have weaker gifts or inferior tasks. Just because a foot is not a hand or an ear is not an eye does not mean that the foot or the ear should dissociate themselves from the body (see 12:15–16). Indeed, a body that consisted of a single organ such as an eye or an ear would be a monstrosity (see 12:17–19). As human experience shows, the various parts of the body need one another in order for the whole body and each of its parts to function properly (see 12:20–21).

The next section (see 1 Corinthians 12:22–26) seems to be directed to those with "superior" gifts. They are reminded that the apparently weaker and less honorable parts of the body are indispensable to the good order of the body (see 12:22–25). In fact, there seems to be a natural adjustment (by way of clothing or special care) made in favor of the less-esteemed parts of the body. Indeed, there is a sympathetic relationship among all the members of the body in both pain and pleasure: "If one member suffers, all suffer together with it; if one member is honored, all rejoice together with it" (12:26).

By way of conclusion in 1 Corinthians 12:27–31, Paul applies the image of the body to the problem of the charisms in the Corinthian assembly. He begins with a summary in the form of direct address ("Now you are the body of Christ") and insists that Christ makes the body. The list of charisms that follows begins with three classes of persons (apostles, prophets, teachers) who exercise the ministry of the word, moves into various activities (deeds of power, gifts of healing, forms of assistance, forms of leadership), and places speaking in tongues at the end.

So as a means of putting order into the chaos of the charismatic community at Corinth, Paul appeals to the metaphor of the body. He insists that Christ forms this body, and that the charismatics all have the same Spirit as the source of their powers and so should work together for the common good.

Possibilities and Problems

There are other important images of the Church in Paul's letters. For example, in 1 Corinthians 3:16, Paul writes: "Do you not know that you are God's temple and that God's Spirit dwells in you?" See also the next chapter for the Church as "the people of God." But the three images treated in this chapter—the Church as the Spirit-led community, the charismatic community, and the Body of Christ—are closely related and fundamental to Paul's understanding of the Church. The ways in which Paul appeals to these images in the course of his arguments and exhortations suggests that he had developed them in his preaching ministry or perhaps was also using ideas that had become part of Christian preaching in general. Nevertheless, the powerful presentation of these images in Paul's letters has made them into the foundations of New Testament ecclesiology.

The idea of the Church as the Spirit-led community links the Christ event (especially Jesus' death and resurrection), the Holy Spirit, the religious experiences of individual believers, and the Church. The Holy Spirit continues the work of Jesus in new peoples and in new places. The Church is made up of those who have experienced God in Christ Jesus through the Holy Spirit. That experience of God impels them to come together to form the Church of Jesus Christ. The Church then is not simply a club, a social or political institution, or a voluntary association (although it has elements of all of these). What unites believers in the Church is their experience of God as the Father of Jesus—an experience that is facilitated through the Holy Spirit.

From the Church as the community of persons led by the Holy Spirit, it follows that each and every Christian is a gifted or charismatic person. Here Paul's decisive contribution is his insistence that the charisms are to be used for the service of others and for building up the Christian community. The exercise of the charisms should foster order within the community rather than disorder, rivalry, or competition. While Paul's caveat was necessary in the Corinthian situation, it need not obscure his emphasis on the gifts of the Holy Spirit as integral to Christian life. Christians today need to be shaken out of their passivity so they can recognize the presence of the Holy Spirit in their lives and appreciate the gifts that God has given them for building up the Body of Christ.

The image of the Church as the Body of Christ rests on an analogy that probably every coach of an athletic team or every director of a play has used. The image of the body encourages both individual responsibility and corporate concern. But Paul's distinctive contribution lies in his insistence that Christ makes the body, that it is Christ's initiative that transforms all these disparate persons into the Body of Christ, and that Christ enables them to work effectively together.

When these three master images of Pauline ecclesiology are disregarded, the Church runs the risk of turning into an all-too-human institution. Without constant attention to the experience of God in Christ through the Holy Spirit, the Church can become a philosophical school at best and just another political force at worst. The leaders in the churches must always try to bring their people to prayer and to all other means that may facilitate openness to God and the experience of the Holy Spirit. The primary concern of the Church must be to help God's people to deepen their relationship with God and with one another in light of that primary relationship. This is spirituality in its broadest and most profound sense.

As the example of the Corinthian Christians shows, a charismatic community without a strong sense of communal responsibility runs the risk of degenerating into a spiritual "free for all." That is why Paul's emphasis on using the Spirit's gifts for the common good is so important. And that is why the image of the charismatic community needs to be linked to those of the Spirit-led community and the Body of Christ.

The image of the Church as the Body of Christ, when properly understood, can help in achieving a balance between the divine and the human aspects of the Church while encouraging individual and communal responsibility. One set of problems emerges when the image is used only in the framework of organizational efficiency without recourse to the spiritual foundations on which the Church is built. Another set of problems comes when the divine aspect is so stressed that it becomes impossible to question church structures, officials, and policies that may be all too human. Just as Christ is both human and divine, so the Body of Christ is both human and divine.

For Reflection and Discussion

1. In what sense is the Holy Spirit the link between Jesus and the Church? What implications does this have for understanding the Church and Christian life?

2. When you look at your own local Christian church, what evidence—positive and negative—do you find for its identity as a charismatic community?

3. What makes your church into the "Body of Christ" and more than just another voluntary association?

chapter six

THE CHURCH AND THE PEOPLE OF GOD

The images of the Church as the Spirit-led community, the charismatic community, and the Body of Christ are essential for understanding the nature of the Church according to Paul. These images are not mutually exclusive. There can be no question of choosing one and ignoring the others. Indeed, they work together and are so tightly linked that no one of them stands alone. They all are aspects or facets of the great mystery of salvation in Christ Jesus.

The three images treated in the preceding chapter focus on the Christ event (Jesus' death and resurrection) and its consequences for believers: the experience of the Holy Spirit, the exercise of the charisms, and incorporation into the Body of Christ. The image treated in this chapter—the Church as the People of God—places the Church in the wider context of the history of salvation beginning with the Old Testament. It concerns the ways in which Paul and other early Christians struggled with the possibilities and problems associated with their continuity and discontinuity with Israel as the People of God.

The topic of the Church and the People of God will be approached here first by looking at some key Old Testament texts that establish the outlines of biblical Israel's understanding of itself as God's people. Then we will focus on New Testament texts (especially 1 Peter 2:9–10 and Galatians 3:6–29) that illustrate why and how early Christians (even those not Jews by birth) understood themselves as the People of God in continuity with ancient Israel. Finally, with reference to Romans 9–11, we will consider the relationship between the Church and Israel, with particular attention to those in Israel who do not accept Jesus as their Messiah and Lord. For fuller treatments of these matters, see my books *God's People in Christ: New Testament Perspectives on the Church and Judaism* (Philadelphia: Fortress, 1980) and *Paul on the Mystery of Israel* (Collegeville, MN: Liturgical Press, 1992).

OLD TESTAMENT PERSPECTIVES

In Genesis 12:1–3 God's first words to Abraham are the promises that God will "make of you a great nation" and that "in you all the families of the earth shall be blessed." So from the start of Israel's history according to the

Old Testament, there is the twofold conviction that God has chosen Israel to be a special people and that this special people has significance for all the nations of the world. The history of salvation begins with God's call to Abraham.

The early Christian practice of making creedal summaries was based on models found in the Old Testament. Israel's description of itself as the People of God in Deuteronomy 26:5–11 is generally recognized as an early liturgical confession used in the context of offering the "first fruits" of crops to God (see 26:10–11). It is connected with the Feast of Weeks (or Pentecost), which was based on an old Canaanite agricultural festival. As with other agricultural festivals on the Canaanite calendar, ancient Israel reinterpreted this feast in terms of its own historical experiences. The confession in Deuteronomy 26:5–11 can be regarded as reflecting the core beliefs of Israel as God's people.

The confession begins in 26:5 with the journey of the patriarch Jacob to Egypt to escape famine in Canaan ("a wandering [or perishing] Aramean was my ancestor") and the growth of his descendants in Egypt ("there he became a great nation, mighty and populous"). Then, in 26:6–7, it tells about the Egyptians' harsh treatment of Israel and Israel's cry for help based on the beliefs that God hears prayers and does intervene in history. According to 26:8–9, God answered Israel's prayer in two mighty acts: the Exodus from Egypt, and the gift of the land of Canaan. And so in 26:10–11, the offering of the first fruits of the spring harvest at the Feast of Weeks is a symbolic acknowledgment of God's gracious activity. It is fitting to present these token gifts to God as the source of all good gifts. Israel's confession of faith in Deuteronomy 26:5–11 shows that Israel recognizes itself as a people especially gifted by God (particularly in the Exodus and in the gift of the land) and views its history as the record of its encounter with Yahweh and its response to this encounter.

The source of Israel's status as God's people is God's gracious choice. This recognition preserves the biblical concept of the chosen people from degenerating into a crude nationalism or the ideology of a super-race. The meditation on Israel as God's elect people in Deuteronomy 7:6–9 comes between God's promise to clear the land of "seven nations mightier and more numerous than you" (7:1) and the appeal to observe God's commandments (see 7:10–11). Israel is addressed as "a people holy to the Lord your God" (7:6). In Hebrew and other languages, *holy* has the sense of being "set apart" and regarded as special to God. In fact, in the biblical perspective, persons and objects are "holy" insofar as God (the all-holy one) makes them holy. Israel is holy because "the Lord your God has chosen you out of all the peoples on earth to be his people, his treasured possession" (7:6).

The passage goes on in 7:7–8a to remind Israel that its status as God's people is due not to its own merits ("it was not because you were more numerous than any other people") but to God's love for and fidelity to Israel ("because the Lord loved you and kept the oath"). The proof of God's love and fidelity was the Exodus from Egypt: "the Lord has brought you out with a mighty hand and redeemed you from the house of slavery, from the hand of Pharaoh king of Egypt." The God who saved his people from slavery remains "the faithful God who maintains covenant loyalty with those who love him and keep his commandments" (7:9). In this context, keeping God's commandments is a fitting response to God's love.

Biblical Israel's understanding of itself as God's people is not a crude nationalism. Rather, its election was initiated by God and provided the framework for observing God's Law. And its election was for the purpose of glorifying God and being God's light to the nations.

An important source of biblical Israel's knowledge of God was reflection on its own history. Psalm 98 illustrates this point. The ending of this psalm (see Psalms 98:7–9) suggests that it was used at the fall new year festival that coincided with the beginning of the rainy season in Israel: "Let the sea roar . . . let the floods clap their hands." The renewal of the earth's fertility is then associated with God's coming as the one who "will judge the world with righteousness and the peoples with equity." The preceding stanza (see 98:4–6) is a call to praise God in all the ways that were imaginable to people in biblical times: "joyous song . . . the lyre and the sound of melody . . . trumpets and the sound of the horn."

Nevertheless, the psalm that celebrates God's power made manifest in nature takes as its starting point God's power made manifest in Israel's history (see Psalms 98:1–3). The references to "his right hand and his holy arm" and to "his victory" allude to the exodus event where God served as Israel's defender and protector. The Exodus is taken as proof of God's fidelity: "He has remembered his steadfast love and faithfulness to the house of Israel" (98:3). By revealing "his vindication in the sight of the nations," God has made Israel known among the nations. And this same God who saved his people from slavery in Egypt can be relied on to remain faithful to his people in the generations to come.

The religion of biblical Israel was not based on the cycle of nature or worldly wisdom or mystical experiences or philosophical ideals. Rather, it was rooted in the conviction that the God who creates all things chose this people as his own and rescued them from slavery in Egypt—and that this same God will remain faithful to this people in the future.

One of the most prominent concepts in the religion of biblical Israel is the *covenant*. The concept derives from treaties made between masters (suzerains) and servant chiefs (vassals) in the ancient Near East. One of the great covenant texts that pertains to Israel as the People of God is Joshua 24. In the first section (see 24:2–13), Joshua recounts God's mighty acts on Israel's behalf from Abraham to the gift of the land.

Then in the light of God's benefactions to Israel, the people are challenged in Joshua 24:14–15 to renew their covenant relationship with God and to choose once again to "revere the Lord, and serve him in sincerity and faithfulness." In the context of the covenant, Israel is being asked to reaffirm its servant-master relationship with God and to put away all other gods. When Joshua asserts that he and his household will serve the Lord (see 24:15), the people make the same response: "We also will serve the Lord, for he is our God" (24:18). They do so on the basis of what God had done for Israel in the past by rehearsing the events associated with the Exodus and the conquest of the land (see 24:16–18).

The God of biblical Israel is the God of the covenant. The closest thing to a definition of God in the Bible comes in Exodus 34:6–7, where everything hinges on God's covenantal relationship with his chosen people: "The LORD, the LORD, a God merciful and gracious, slow to anger and abounding in steadfast love and faithfulness, keeping steadfast love for the thousandth generation." Because this God has taken the initiative and remained faithful to his promises, Israel can recognize itself as the People of God. Having come to know and love this God in the great events of its national story, God's people promises to respond in steadfast love by keeping God's commandments. Israel's election is based on God's initiative, is proven in the great events of the people's history, and expresses itself in the context of the covenant.

THE PEOPLE OF GOD IN 1 PETER 2:9–10

One of the great contributions of the Second Vatican Council to modern ecclesiology was its emphasis on the Church as the People of God. This image of the Church is appealing for several reasons. It expresses the historical and dynamic nature of the Church as a "pilgrim" people. It underlines the continuity between the Old Testament People of God and the church in the New Testament. And it preserves the communal dimension of Christian life.

It may seem surprising, however, that the New Testament directly addresses Christians as the People of God only in one text. While the identity of the Church as the people of God may be the assumption or background of many New Testament writings, this identification is made explicit only in 1 Peter 2:10: "Now you are God's people."

By what logic can the Church call itself the People of God? And what implications does this title have for understanding the Church? The logic is simple enough: insofar as Jesus has fulfilled the hopes of his people Israel (the Old Testament People of God), the people who gathered around him, whether they be of Jewish or Gentile origin, constitute the People of God. The Jewishness of Jesus is the link between the two Testaments and the basis of the biblical claims to be the people of God. Moreover, as the People of God, the Church has been given the prerogatives of biblical Israel and the structure of its faith. Its election has been initiated by God; its mission is carried out in the course of salvation history; and its existence is lived out in the context of the covenant.

The clearest statement of the Church's identity as the People of God appears in 1 Peter 2:9–10. The passage begins by applying to the Church the titles that were applied to biblical Israel at Mount Sinai according to Exodus 19:1–6: "But you are a chosen race, a royal priesthood, a holy nation, God's own people." This text uses the categories of race, priesthood, nation, and people to describe the unity brought about in Jesus Christ. And it uses phrases taken from the beginning of the "Book of the Covenant" (see Exodus 19–24), in which Israel enters into its covenantal relationship with God. The effect of these biblical epithets being applied to the Christian community is to suggest that in Christ a mixed group of Jews and Gentiles form a "chosen race," that in Christ the Church's mission is to serve God as God's own royal priesthood, that in Christ the Church becomes suffused with the holiness of God, and that through Jesus the Jew the Church has become God's own people.

The mission of this people formed by and around Jesus is to "proclaim the mighty acts" of God. Just as the Old Testament People of God never ceased to proclaim the Exodus and the gift of the land as the mighty acts of God *par excellence*, so God's people in Christ must continually proclaim Jesus' life, death, and resurrection as the mighty acts of God.

What has happened to these people is explained in terms of two familiar New Testament patterns for describing conversion. The first pattern captures their movement from darkness to light: "who called you out of darkness into his marvelous light" (1 Peter 2:9b). This imagery expresses not only their intellectual illumination but also the moral transformation that had come over the new Christians. The second pattern concerns their movement from being "no people" to being God's people: "Once you were not a people, but now you are God's people" (2:10a). The imagery here captures the communal aspect of Christian faith and the experience of being bound together into a spiritual unity as God's own people in Christ. The whole experience is attributed to the mercy or compassion displayed by God: "once you had not received mercy, but now you have received mercy" (2:10b).

The startling nature of these claims about the Church as the People of

God comes into even sharper focus when we look at the historical and literary context in which they appear. Few interpreters today regard 1 Peter as having been composed directly by the apostle Peter. Many suppose, however, that it came from a "Petrine circle" (with some connections to the Pauline school) at Rome between A.D. 70 and 90. It addresses a group of predominantly Gentile-Christian communities (see 1:18; 2:10) in northern Asia Minor (see 1:1). The uses of the word *Dispersion* (or *Diaspora*) in the address identifies the addressees in a literary pattern that is appropriate to Israel as God's people. In that framework, those Jews who live outside the Holy Land are said to be in the Dispersion or Diaspora. Here, however, the title *Diaspora* is applied to Gentile Christians.

The Christians addressed in 1 Peter are said to be in "exile" (1:17) and to be "aliens and exiles" (2:11). In their part of the Roman Empire these new Christians were very much a religious and social minority. Their refusal to slide back into pagan ways made them targets for social ostracism and perhaps even for organized persecution. The letter known as 1 Peter sought to remind them of their place in salvation history, to believe that their good example would impress others, and to look to the example of the suffering Christ to make their own difficult situation bearable and plausible.

What made such community consciousness possible was baptism. The First Letter of Peter is so full of references to baptism that it has often been described as a baptismal homily or catechesis: "new birth into a living hope" (1:3); "you have been born anew" (1:23); "like newborn infants . . . you may grow into salvation" (2:2); and so on. What makes possible the application of Israel's titles as God's people to the Christian community is faith in Christ as the "living stone" (2:4; see Psalms 118:22 and its uses in Matthew 21:42; Mark 12:10–11; and Luke 20:17). Being part of God's people comes with incorporation into Christ through baptism. Now Jesus Christ creates the People of God out of those who are baptized in his name.

THE PEOPLE OF GOD IN GALATIANS 3

Galatians 3:28 ("There is no longer Jew or Greek . . . slave or free . . . male and female") is one of the most quoted verses in the New Testament today. As we have seen, it probably originated as a baptismal slogan ("for all of you are one in Christ Jesus"). Its current popularity rests mainly on the part that says, "There is no longer male and female." But in the context of Paul's letter to the Galatians, the key phrase was, "There is no longer Jew or Greek."

Galatians 3:6–29 is significant for understanding the Church as the

People of God because it explains how Jews and Gentiles constitute God's people in and through Christ, and because it reflects on the relationship between Israel as God's people and the Church as God's people in Christ. The point of Paul's argument comes at 3:29: "And if you belong to Christ, then you are Abraham's offspring, heirs according to the promise." The real children of Abraham are those who display faith after the pattern of Abraham.

Paul wrote his letter to the Galatians in the mid-fifties of the first century A.D. He had brought Christianity to the Galatians and moved on to other missionary activities. Then it appears that other Jewish-Christian missionaries came to Galatia in Asia Minor (present-day Turkey) and tried to convince Paul's Gentile converts that in order to be real Christians they had to undergo circumcision and observe the Jewish laws about foods, Sabbaths, and so on. Paul perceived their program to be a betrayal of his gospel, and so he wrote to the Galatians to explain why they should disregard the advice of the other Jewish-Christian missionaries, and remain faithful to the gospel that he had preached.

After expressing his amazement at what was happening among the Galatians (see 1:1–9), Paul presents a personal and historical defense of the gospel that he had preached as revealed by the Risen Christ and approved by the chief apostles (see 1:10–2:21). Then, after reminding the Galatians that they had received the Holy Spirit without embracing the Law (see 3:1–5), Paul appeals to various Old Testament texts to show that Christians are heirs to the promises made to Abraham and that Gentile Christians share in these promises by their faith and not by the observance of the Law (see 3:6–4:31). Finally, Paul exhorts the Galatian Christians not to lose their freedom in Christ with regard to circumcision (see 5:1–12), to act in accord with the "law of Christ" (5:13–6:10), and to live in Christ as "the Israel of God" (6:11–18). So Galatians 3:6–29 is part of a letter that concerns how non-Jews can be part of the People of God, in which the opponents are other Jewish-Christian missionaries, and that contends that baptism into Christ makes one part of God's people and heirs to the promises made to Abraham.

Paul's argument about the true children of Abraham in Galatians 3: 6–29 is a *tour de force* in which Paul tries to show that he can outdo his opponents at biblical interpretation—although his argument is often subtle and complicated. Its starting point in 3:6 is Genesis 15:6: "Abraham believed God, and it was reckoned to him as righteousness." His basic thesis is that people of faith are the children of Abraham, and Abraham is the model for those who believe: "so, you see, those who believe are the descendants of Abraham" (3:7). His conclusion is that faith and baptism into Christ allow non-Jews to become children of Abraham and heirs of the promises made to Abraham: "If you belong to Christ, then you are Abraham's offspring, heirs according to the promise" (3:29).

Between stating his thesis in 3:6–7 and drawing his conclusion in 3:27–29, Paul first develops an argument based on various Old Testament texts to confirm his point that people of faith are children of Abraham (see 3:8–14). He cites:

- Genesis 18:18 (or 12:3) in Galatians 3:8 to show that all nations are blessed in Abraham

- Deuteronomy 27:26 in Galatians 3:10 to indicate that all who rely on the works of the Law are under a curse

- Habakkuk 2:4 in Galatians 3:11 to prove that justification comes through faith

- Leviticus 18:5 in Galatians 3:12 to suggest that faith and the Law are not the same

- Deuteronomy 21:23 in Galatians 3:13 to affirm that Christ in his death on the cross redeemed us from the curse of the Law

Then in 3:15–16 Paul notes that the promise was made to "Abraham and his offspring" in Genesis 13:15; 17:8; and 24:7. In the Old Testament the word *seed* (or *offspring*) is a collective noun that refers to all the descendants of Abraham. But Paul insists on the singular grammatical form of the noun in both Greek and Hebrew (*seed* rather than *seeds*) and argues that *seed* must refer to one person (who is Jesus Christ). The implication is that those who are "in Christ" share in the promise made to Abraham and to Christ as his "seed."

Those who read all these Old Testament quotations in their original historical settings may come away baffled by Paul's arguments. But Paul read these texts from the theological perspective that Christ is the key to the Scriptures and that the Scriptures were talking about Christ. In this context *faith* means the fidelity displayed by Abraham and by Christ, as well as faith in the efficacy of Jesus' death and resurrection to make possible right relationship with God. The *nations* refers to non-Jews who became part of God's people in and through Christ. The *law* refers to the use of the Mosaic Law as a means of establishing one's own righteousness apart from the Christ event. And the *offspring* of Abraham means Christ and those who are "in Christ." Paul makes all these interpretive moves on the basis of his fundamental principle that Christ is God's way of solving the mysteries of Scripture and of making intelligible the religious heritage of God's people.

"Why then the Law?" Paul has already begun to answer his own question (see Galatians 3:19) by noting that the covenant, the promise, and the inheritance promised to Abraham preceded the giving of the Law to Moses by 430 years, and so the latter cannot be used to nullify the former. Having established the superiority of the promise to Abraham over the Law given to Moses, Paul goes on in 3:19–20 to assert that the Law was secondary to the promise ("it was added"), provisional until Christ came ("until the offspring would come"), and inferior to the promise ("ordained through angels by a mediator"). The phrase "because of transgressions" may mean that the Law serves to specify sins and even tempt one to sin.

Next, in Galatians 3:21–22, Paul indicates that by making people conscious of the pervasive character of sin, the Law had the effect of showing the necessity of the Christ event, faith as the principle of right relationship with God, and faith as the means of becoming part of God's people in Christ. Finally, in 3:23–26, Paul uses the image of the Law as the "disciplinarian" (*paidagogos*)—a slave who was charged with leading children to and from school and with supervising their conduct while they were still minors. Paul's point is that with the coming of Christ we no longer need such an overseer "for in Christ Jesus you are all children of God through faith" (3:26).

What emerges from Paul's long and complex argument in Galatians 3 is the conviction that belonging to Christ by faith and baptism makes one part of the people of God and an heir to the promise made to Abraham. Christ is the key to unlocking the mysteries of Scripture. Christ does what the Law of Moses cannot do—bring about right relationship with God. And Christ makes it possible for non-Jews to become children of Abraham and so members of the People of God.

THE MYSTERY OF ISRAEL IN ROMANS 9–11

Paul's most extensive reflection on God's plan for the history of salvation appears in Romans 9–11. There he considers the Church composed of Jews and Gentiles as God's people, and speculates about God's purposes for those Jews who have not accepted the gospel. Paul's reflection represents his mature attempt to articulate what God was doing with Jewish Christians like himself, Gentile Christians, and other Jews. Rather than present a full exposition of this complicated text, here we will ask and answer five questions that are pertinent to the theme of the Church as the people of God in Romans 9–11.

First, by what right does the Church, composed of Jews and Gentiles, take to itself the privileges of Israel as God's people? Those privileges are listed in Romans 9:4 and include the adoption, the glory, the covenants, the gift of the Law, worship, the promise, the patriarchs, and the Messiah. Paul will claim later, in 11:29, that "the gifts and the calling of God are irrevocable." The Church can claim these gifts because the real descendants of Abraham are "the children of the promise" (9:8), people of faith after the pattern of Abraham. So the Church composed of Jews and Gentiles has a right to the privileges of God's people because they are the real children of Abraham. The promise made to Abraham has reached fulfillment in Christ, and those who are "in Christ" share in it.

Second, how can Gentiles be considered part of God's people? In Romans 9:24–29 Paul appeals to various Old Testament texts (see Hosea 2:25; 2:1; Isaiah 10:22–23; 1:9) to argue that the present, though provisional, goal of salvation history is the Church as the collective of Jews and Gentiles. He takes the biblical references to "not my people" and "not my beloved" in Hosea to mean the Gentiles who have accepted the gospel and so can now be called "the children of the living God." So Paul appeals to the Old Testament to show that the inclusion of Gentiles in God's people was part of God's plan. And he uses the passages from Isaiah to suggest that only a "remnant" (the Jewish Christians) need be part of God's people.

Third, has God rejected his people Israel and so been unfaithful to his promises? Paul's answer is "no!" While part of Israel may have rejected the gospel, other Jews like Paul himself have accepted the gospel and so function as the remnant within Israel. Paul could not imagine the People of God without an organic relationship to Israel as the historic People of God.

Fourth, what is the significance of the Jewish rejection of the gospel and the Gentile acceptance of it? According to Romans 11:14–15, the partial Jewish rejection of the gospel has inspired the possibility of preaching the gospel to non-Jews. And Paul develops the idea that acceptance of the gospel by non-Jews will make the rest of Israel jealous, so that eventually Israel, too, will embrace the gospel.

How all these entities fit together in salvation history—Christian Jews (like Paul), Gentile Christians (like most of Paul's converts), and other Jews—is explained in Paul's image of the olive tree in Romans 11:17–24. In the Old Testament (see Hosea 14:6; Jeremiah 11:16), the image of the olive tree sometimes serves to describe Israel as God's people. In Paul's application of it, Jewish Christians like himself serve as the root of the olive tree. He reminds his Gentile Christian readers that "it is not you that support the root, but the root that supports you" (Romans 11:18). Paul goes on to explain that Gentile Christians have been grafted into the olive tree by God's grace—and it was their faith that made the grafting successful. At the same time, other natural branches (Israelites by birth) have been cut off "because of their unbelief" (11:20). And yet Paul does not regard either the grafting in of non-Jews or the cutting off of Jews as absolutely definitive. This point leads to the final question.

Fifth, will all Israel finally be saved? Having reflected at length on the working out of God's plan and the history of salvation, Paul at last reveals in Romans 11:25b–26a what he calls a "mystery": "a hardening has come upon part of Israel, until the full number of the Gentiles has come in. And so all Israel will be saved."

Paul first explains the partial Jewish rejection of the gospel in terms of the Old Testament motif of the obtuseness or "hardening" of God's people toward the word of God. The key text is Isaiah 6:9–10, which in turn is taken up in many New Testament writings to explain the rejection of Jesus' teachings (see Matthew 13:14–15; Mark 4:12; John 12:40) and of Paul's proclamation of the gospel (see Acts 28:26–27) by their fellow Jews.

The idea of a full or fixed number of Gentiles coming into God's people fits with Old Testament hopes that Gentiles will join with Israel in acknowledging the sovereignty of the God of Israel (see Isaiah 2:2–4; Zechariah 8:20–23). To this concept, Paul adds the notion that when the quota is reached, then Israel's spiritual obduracy will cease.

"And so all Israel will be saved." In Paul's revelation of the "mystery" of salvation, the hardening of part of Israel and the inclusion of Gentiles among God's people are elements in the process leading to the salvation of all Israel. However, Paul's statement leaves some questions unanswered. First, who is "all Israel"? Is it each and every Jew or is "Israel" taken collectively or is the Church now viewed as "the Israel of God"? Second, does Israel's salvation come only with the fullness of God's kingdom (see Romans 11:15) or before that? Third, is Israel's salvation brought about directly by God or through the missionary efforts of the church? And fourth, is God's way of salvation for "all Israel" an explicit acceptance of the gospel, or does God have another way?

These difficult questions have been debated by biblical scholars and theologians for many years. But the problems that Romans 11:25–26 raises need not distract from the clarity of Paul's basic message. The inclusion of non-Jews in God's people is a miracle of God's grace. The root of God's people, however, remains Israel as the historic people of God. The acceptance of the gospel by Jews like Paul means that Israel's obduracy is not total. And Paul fully expects that in the end "all Israel will be saved."

Possibilities and Problems

Attention to the theme of the Church as the People of God in Scripture reveals some of the ways in which early Christians struggled with expressing their identity and their relationship to biblical Israel in particular. Besides the passages treated in this chapter (see 1 Peter 2:9–10; Galatians 3:6–29; Romans 9–11), one could also reflect on Ephesians 2, according to which Christ has "broken down the dividing wall" between Jews and Gentiles (see 2:14) and created "in himself one new humanity in place of the two, thus making peace" (2:15). Or one could consider how the author of Hebrews used Old Testament figures and institutions to highlight the saving significance of Jesus' death and resurrection. Or one could also look at the claim in Matthew 21:43 that "the kingdom of God will be taken away from you and given to a people that produces the fruits of the kingdom." The issue of the Church's continuity and discontinuity with Israel was one of the most important theological and pastoral concerns for early Christians. And it remains important for the Church of the twenty-first century.

From the various approaches to the issue of the Church as the People of God in the New Testament, what emerges most clearly in the pertinent texts is the absolute centrality of Jesus Christ in dealing with the question. The Church is God's people *in Christ*. It is through Jesus the Jew that Christians can be said to be God's people in continuity with the biblical People of God and to be genuine children of Abraham. Through baptism in the name of Jesus, it has become possible for non-Jews to be part of God's people.

Also, reflection on the Church as the People of God can help Christians clarify their thinking about the most important questions in Christian-Jewish dialogue today. Jews often challenge (and with good reason) Christians for calling themselves the "new Israel" or the "true Israel" without grasping the implications of their statements. The texts treated in this chapter can introduce some clarity and precision into Christian reflection about the Church's place in the history of salvation and with reference to biblical Israel as the People of God.

One set of problems associated with Christian claims to be God's people in continuity with biblical Israel came with the success of Gentile Christianity and the gradual disappearance of the various forms of Jewish Christianity. This development has led in some Christian circles to a disregard of the Jewish roots of Christianity and even to anti-Judaism. In this perspective, the Old Testament is at best a collection of types and allegories that point toward Christ, and Judaism is regarded as a historical curiosity rather than a living religion.

A traditional Christian way of dealing with the disappearance of Jewish Christianity and the devaluation of Judaism is often described as *supersessionism*. The term refers to the Christian claim that the Church has superseded Judaism in every respect and so has rendered Judaism no longer significant in the history of salvation. Those who take this view need to read again Romans 9–11 and take seriously Paul's affirmation that "all Israel will be saved" (11:26a). Without attention to the Jewishness of Jesus and the "mystery" of the history of salvation (see Romans 11:25b–26a), the Church of the twenty-first century runs the risk of repeating theological and practical errors that have been a source of shame throughout Christian history.

Another "problem" is posed by the absolute centrality of Christology in the New Testament understanding of the Church as God's people in Christ. Of course, for the New Testament writers and for most Christians, this is not so much a problem as it is a principle of faith. But for those who seek to develop a Christology that is more sensitive to the context of religious pluralism in the twenty-first century, the pivotal significance of Jesus may present a real obstacle. And it is hard to find a way to remove this obstacle—if one wants to do so—without compromising the plain teaching of the New Testament. The New Testament claims that the Church is God's people in and through Christ.

For Reflection and Discussion

1. What implications does the Old Testament theme of the People of God have for the structure and practice of Christian faith?

2. How would you explain to a Jewish friend that the Church is the People of God through Jesus Christ?

3. What in Paul's reflection on the mystery of Israel in Romans 9–11 do you find most convincing, and what do you find most problematic?

chapter seven

PAUL'S LEGACY:
THEOLOGY, NARRATIVE, AND PRACTICE

Of the twenty-seven books that comprise the New Testament, thirteen are letters that are attributed to Paul. And more than half of the Acts of the Apostles is concerned with Paul's missionary activities. Moreover, the earliest complete documents in the New Testament are the undisputed Pauline Epistles: 1 Thessalonians, Galatians, 1 and 2 Corinthians, Philippians, Philemon, and Romans. These letters come from the period between A.D. 51 and 58. And thus they have been the major sources in our description of church life in earliest Christianity.

The legacy of Paul is also well represented in the New Testament. It appears in Acts and also in the six letters written in Paul's name by disciples and admirers: Colossians, Ephesians, 2 Thessalonians, and the three Pastoral Epistles (1 and 2 Timothy, Titus). The "Deuteropauline" writings can help us trace the legacy of Paul as it worked itself out from around A.D. 60 to the end of the first century. What emerges, however, is not simply the legacy of one man (Paul) but also, and especially, the development of the churches that Paul founded into what is sometimes called the "great" or "catholic" (in its sense of "universal") Church.

After looking at some "ecumenical" (in its sense of "worldwide") dimensions of Paul's missionary activity and theology, this chapter will consider Paul's legacy as it pertains to the development of the Church in the New Testament. It will explore how Paul's legacy regarding the Church is expressed in terms of theology (Ephesians), narrative (Acts), and practice (Pastorals).

ECUMENICAL DIMENSIONS IN PAUL'S ECCLESIOLOGY

When Paul used the term *church* in his undisputed letters, he was generally referring to a community in a specific locale (at Corinth, Rome, Jerusalem, etc.). Each community was regarded as the Body of Christ and so as complete in itself. And yet there are dimensions in Paul's missionary practice and theology that point in the direction of a bond among the local communities and a certain kind of universal outlook.

Paul's missionary practice was motivated by the conviction that he had a special mission or calling to bring the gospel to non-Jews. He was convinced that non-Jews, or Gentiles, could share in the benefits of Jesus' life, death, and resurrection, and could be part of God's people in Christ. And so he sought to preach the gospel where it had not yet been heard. And yet, after his preaching had some effect and the local communities could survive without his physical presence, Paul moved on to begin once again the missionary process somewhere else. The result was a whole series of new church foundations that were linked by their history to the apostle Paul and his gospel.

Paul kept in touch with these various communities by sending personal emissaries to them (Timothy, Titus, Silvanus, etc.) and by corresponding with them. His letters were an important way of staying in contact with his converts, of answering their theological and practical questions, and of giving them advice as new crises arose. In his letters Paul insisted that the most important factor in these people's lives was their faith in God and in the gospel of Jesus Christ. He taught them that in Christ their social, ethnic, and gender differences had lost their ultimate importance. And so he counseled Philemon to accept his slave Onesimus back "no longer as a slave but more than a slave, a beloved brother" (Philemon 16). And Paul insisted that a collection be taken up among his churches for the community at Jerusalem (see 1 Corinthians 16:1–4; 2 Corinthians 8–9; Romans 15:25–27). The idea behind this project was that Christians in one place were responsible for the welfare of those in another, especially those of the "mother church" in Jerusalem. These elements in Paul's missionary practice point beyond isolated local communities as being the whole story about the Church.

Many elements in Paul's theology also supported and inspired the move toward viewing the Church in more universal terms. The starting point, of course, was the tendency in Second Temple Judaism to view the God of Israel as the one God of all the universe, as the Creator and Lord beside whom there is no other God (see Deuteronomy 6:4–5). Another one of Paul's theological insights was that all humans—Gentiles and Jews alike—stood in need of salvation (see Romans 1:18–3:31). From human experience and from Scripture, he argued that "all, both Jews and Greeks, are under the power of sin" (Romans 3:9), and that "all have sinned and fall short of the glory of God" (3:23).

In this framework of the one God of all and the need of all humankind for redemption, Jesus appears not only as the Messiah of Jewish expectations but also as the new or second Adam whose life and work have significance for all humankind. Just as in the first Adam, as the representative human being, all have sinned, so in Christ, as the second or new Adam, right relationship with God (justification) and salvation are now possible for all. And the lordship that the Risen Christ now exercises is universal in scope and extends to all creation: "so that at the name of Jesus every knee should bend, in heaven and on earth and under the earth, and every tongue should confess that Jesus Christ is Lord to the glory of God the Father" (Philippians 2:10–11).

The idea of the "church universal" is based primarily on belief in the universal sovereignty of God and the universal significance of Christ. In this context, ecclesiology is a consequence of theology and Christology. The Church is the assembly of those who are "in Christ." It is made up of those who believe that God can and does accomplish what God wishes for humankind in and through Jesus Christ. And this assembly not only includes different kinds of persons (Jew and Greek, slave and free, male and female) but also has communities in many different places bound together by their faith in Christ Jesus.

THEOLOGY: EPHESIANS

The Epistle to the Ephesians purports to be a letter from Paul in prison (like Philippians, Philemon, Colossians, and the Pastorals). But most New Testament scholars today regard it as an essay written by a Jewish-Christian disciple or admirer of Paul around A.D. 80. Although the author stands firmly within the tradition of Pauline theology, even a cursory reading of the text in English reveals striking differences in tone and expression from Paul's undisputed letters. Moreover, the phrase "in Ephesus" is absent from some manuscripts, and there is little in the document that refers to a concrete situation.

The reasons for doubting the direct authorship of Ephesians by Paul include differences in vocabulary and style, in the use of theological terms and concepts, and in the historical situation presupposed by the document. Ephesians gives the impression of being an essay rather than a real letter. One scholarly theory views it as an epitome or compendium of Paul's theology adapted for circumstances in the late first century A.D. and serving as the preface to a collection of Paul's letters. However dubious this theory may be, it has the merit of underlining both the links of Ephesians to Paul and its differences in form and content.

What we call the Letter to the Ephesians begins with a salutation (see 1:1–2), a blessing (see 1:3–14), and a thanksgiving (see 1:15–23). Next there is a theological reflection (see 2:1–3:21) on the reasons for blessing and thanksgiving: salvation in Christ, unity in the Body of Christ, and the mystery of God's plan in bringing Jews and Gentiles together in Christ. Then in 4:1–6:9 there is an exhortation about church unity, living as the new humanity, the contrast between the old and the new life, and so on. It concludes with a call to stand firm in the spiritual battle (see 6:10–20) and a postscript (see 6:21–24).

With regard to our understanding of the Church in the New Testament, Ephesians provides an important bridge between Paul's own letters and the development of the "great" or "catholic" Church. Following the letter to the Colossians (which was used as a source), the author of Ephesians emphasizes the cosmic Christ reigning over all creation (see Colossians 1:15–20) and serving as the head of the body (which is the Church). The writer was concerned with the Church as a whole (and not just local communities) and as the new humanity through which the Risen Christ is at work in the world. He stresses the apostles and the prophets as the foundation of the Church, and the importance of the teaching charisms in building up the Body of Christ. He also describes the union between Christ and the Church with the help of two powerful image patterns: head/body and husband/wife.

The theological contributions of Ephesians to understanding the Church in the New Testament come in five areas: the Church as the place of Christ's power and authority (see 1:20–23), the Church as the Body of Christ and the People of God (see 2:11–22), the apostles as the foundation of the Church (see 3:1–13), the role of the charisms in the Church (see 4:7–16), and the relationship between Christ and the Church (see 5:21–33). All these topics were treated in some fashion by Paul. But each receives a somewhat different treatment from the author of Ephesians.

First, the Church according to Ephesians 1:20–23 is the place of Christ's power and authority (*exousia*). The passage comes as the conclusion to the long benediction-thanksgiving in chapter 1. Drawing on the language of Psalm 8:6 ("You have given him dominion . . . ") and 110:1 ("Sit at my right hand . . . "), it first shows in 1:20–22a how God's power and authority have been made manifest in Christ by his Resurrection from the dead ("he raised him from the dead"), by his exaltation to God's right hand ("seated him at his right hand in the heavenly places"), and by granting him lordship over all creation ("far above all rule and authority . . . he has put all things under his feet").

Then in Ephesians 1:22b–23 the author connects the lordship of Christ over all creation with the Church. The language is taken from the second half of the hymn about Christ as the Wisdom of God found in Colossians 1:18–20. He first identifies Christ as "the head over all things," thus introducing the head/body distinction that is especially prominent in Ephesians 4:15–16 and not found in Paul's undisputed letters. Then he attributes a central place to the Church ("for the church") in the cosmic reign of Christ. Finally, he insists that Christ's power and presence as the head of the body fill the Church: "which is his body, the fullness of him who fills all in all." And so according to Ephesians 1:20–23, the Church is the place in which the reign of the Risen and exalted Christ over all creation is made actual and manifest.

Second, the Church according to Ephesians is the Body of Christ and the People of God. Chapter 2 deals with the reconciliation of sinful humankind to God through Christ (see 2:1–10) and the inclusion of non-Jews in the Body of Christ and the People of God (see 2:11–22). After describing the state of spiritual death in which humans found themselves before and apart from Christ (see 2:1–3), the passage in 2:4–10 celebrates what God "who is rich in mercy" has done for us "in Christ Jesus." The result, according to 2:11–22, is that Gentiles and Jews are now one in Christ. This unity has been made possible through Christ from whom there came about "one new humanity" (2:15), "one body" (2:16), and "one Spirit" (2:18).

The reflection on the one People of God in Ephesians 2:11–22 is addressed to "you Gentiles by birth" (2:11). It first reminds them that when they were without Christ, they were "aliens from the commonwealth of Israel and strangers to the covenant of promise, having no hope and without God in the world" (2:12). Through Jesus' death and resurrection, it has become possible for Jews and Gentiles to constitute one people. Whereas in Romans 11 Paul used the organic image of the olive tree to explain this unity, the author of Ephesians speaks about Christ having broken down the dividing wall ("the hostility between us") and abolishing "the law with its commandments and ordinances" (2:14–15). He goes on to insist that through Christ's body on the cross it is now possible for Gentiles and Jews to come together as the one Body of Christ.

In addition to the images of the Church as the one new humanity, the one body, and the one Spirit, in Ephesians 2:19–22 the author introduces the image of the Church as God's "holy temple." Without its own public building or a sacrificial system, the Church forms a spiritual building. It has the apostles and the prophets as its foundation (compare 1 Corinthians 3:11) and Christ Jesus as its cornerstone or capstone (see Ephesians 2:20). Unlike a material building, this temple can "grow" precisely because it is the Body of Christ (see 2:21–22). This "temple" is a people made into one body through Christ.

Third, the Church is "apostolic" in the sense that it is founded upon the apostles. In the literary framework of Ephesians, Paul writes from prison as the apostle *par excellence* who is suffering for preaching the gospel. As the apostle Paul has been granted the revelation of a great "mystery" (compare Romans 11:25–26), "the Gentiles have become fellow heirs, members of the same body, and sharers in the promise in Christ Jesus through the gospel" (Ephesians 3:6). The revelation concerns the Church as the one

Body of Christ and the one People of God. The mission of Paul the apostle is to make this mystery known to the Gentiles (see 3:8–9). Moreover, it is the mission of the Church to reveal "the news of the boundless riches of Christ" not only to the human race composed of Jews and Gentiles but even to "the rulers and authorities in the heavenly places" (3:10). The Church is the means by which the gospel is to be proclaimed to all the universe. And the Church is apostolic in the sense that it carries on the mission of the apostles in proclaiming the gospel.

Fourth, the function of the charisms is to build up the unity of the Body of Christ and the People of God. In Ephesians 4:1–16 the author lays a theological foundation for his ethical exhortations in the rest of the epistle. Paul begins by appealing to his status as a "prisoner in the Lord" that the readers make "every effort to maintain the unity of the Spirit in the bond of peace" (4:1, 3). He then drives home his point by setting forth the ideal of "one body and one Spirit . . . one hope of your calling, one Lord, one faith, one baptism, one God and Father of all" (4:4–6).

In Ephesians 4:7 there is a version of Paul's basic teaching on the charisms (compare Romans 12:3–8; 1 Corinthians 12:1–11): "But each of us was given grace according to the measure of Christ's gift." This formulation emphasizes Christ as the source of the charisms, and in 4:8–10, Psalm 68:18 is used to underscore that point: "he gave gifts to his people." The gifts listed in 4:11 ("some . . . apostles, some prophets, some evangelists, some pastors and teachers") are actualized in individuals or even offices, and all are related to doctrine or the ministry of the word. The immediate purpose of these gifts is to work for building up the Church as the Body of Christ (see Ephesians 4:12–13). The ultimate goal is to "grow up in every way into him who is the head, into Christ" (4:15). Again, Christ is the "head" of the body—the source of its gifts (charisms), and the origin and goal of its unity.

Fifth, the relationship between Christ and the Church is like that between husband and wife. Ephesians 5:21–33 is an expansion of part of the household code in Colossians 3:18–19. But the author of Ephesians is more interested in Christ and the Church than in husbands and wives. He repeats some basic points that he has already made: "Christ is the head of the church, the body of which he is the Savior" (5:23); and "we are members of his body" (5:30). And he adds other important perspectives in the course of developing the analogy: the Church is the object of Christ's love ("Christ loved the church," 5:25); his self-sacrifice was undertaken on behalf of the Church ("gave himself up for her," 5:25); he initiates what comes about in baptism ("by cleansing her with washing of water by the word," 5:26); and marital unity reflects the even greater unity that binds Christ and the Church ("this is a great mystery, and I am applying it to

Christ and the church," 5:32). The relationship between Christ and the Church is so close that it is portrayed in terms of the marriage relationship and can even provide the model for intimacy between husbands and wives.

NARRATIVE: THE ACTS OF THE APOSTLES

The Acts of the Apostles tells the story of the growth of the early church from Jesus' Resurrection and Ascension to shortly before Paul's death at Rome in A.D. 62. As part of the Christian canon of Scripture, Acts has become the "official" narrative about the early church. It is by all measures a great story, and it is very well told by the same author who wrote Luke's Gospel (see Luke 1:1–4; Acts 1:1–2).

Luke composed Acts as a second volume to his Gospel. He wanted to show how the great apostles Peter and Paul carried on Jesus' mission under the guidance of the Holy Spirit, and how non-Jews came to embrace the gospel and became part of God's people. Acts contains many precious historical details, and it is the only connected and coherent narrative of the history of the early church that we have.

But how much of Acts is history, how much is story (literary creation), and how much is theology? This is a hard question to answer, and scholars have been debating it for centuries. On this issue, as on many other issues in Luke-Acts, it is possible to read the evidence in many different ways. Luke is always something of a chameleon. It is a tribute to his skill as a writer that some two thousand years later scholars are still arguing about his real positions on Judaism, women, rich and poor, and many other topics.

What is beyond scholarly argument is that Acts is the canonical narrative of earliest Christianity and that its influence on Christians throughout the centuries has been enormous. Here we will focus on five areas in which Luke's story of the early church has shaped and continues to shape our understanding of the Church: mission, the Holy Spirit, Christian preaching, community life, and the Jerusalem "council."

First, with regard to mission, Acts continues the story begun in Luke's Gospel. There Jesus went from place to place and proclaimed the good news of God's kingdom. He called disciples and sent them out to continue his mission, and he showed particular concern for outcasts and marginal people. At his Ascension, the Risen Jesus commissions the disciples to be his "witnesses in Jerusalem, in all Judea and Samaria, and to the ends of the earth" (Acts 1:8). This is the topic sentence or outline of the whole book.

In the first part of Acts (see 1:1–8:4) Luke tells the story of the Christian community in Jerusalem—how the apostles and other disciples received the gift of the Holy Spirit, how they proclaimed the gospel and attracted converts to "the way," and how they suffered persecution and even martyrdom in the service of the Christian mission. Next, in 8:5–40, Luke shows how the gospel was carried to other parts of Judea and to Samaria. Then, in 9:1–14:28, he treats the conversion of Paul who is called to be the apostle to the Gentiles, and explains how non-Jews like Cornelius came to embrace the gospel and how Paul and Barnabas had their greatest success outside the land of Israel among Gentiles. Their success in turn led to the "council" held in Jerusalem (see 15:1–35), where the apostles made a decision about the terms on which non-Jews might be accepted into the Christian community.

In the second half of Acts (see 15:36–28:31), the central character is Paul. In 15:36–20:38 Paul conducts missions in various cities throughout Asia Minor and Greece. His usual pattern is to go first to the local Jewish synagogue, where he generally encounters an unfavorable reception (after the pattern set by Jesus in Luke 4:16–30). Then he moves out to non-Jews in the area and has great success. His decision to bring the proceeds of the collection to the community at Jerusalem leads to his arrest (see Acts 21:1–22:21)—and this in turn provides the occasion for Paul to bear witness to his gospel before Roman officials and others. Because Paul claims to be a Roman citizen, he is sent off to Rome for trial. There, under house arrest, he continues to exercise an active and effective ministry: "He lived there two whole years at his own expense and welcomed all who came to him, proclaiming the kingdom of God and teaching about the Lord Jesus Christ with all boldness and without hindrance" (28:30–31). From start to finish, the Acts of the Apostles underlines the missionary aspect of the Church.

Second, the Holy Spirit is the force that empowers the Christian mission and facilitates the growth of the Church. Acts is sometimes called the "Book of the Holy Spirit," because it tells how, after Jesus' departure at the Ascension, the Spirit enabled weak human instruments like Peter and Paul to touch the minds and hearts of persons throughout the Mediterranean world. In Acts 1 the Holy Spirit serves as the intermediary between the Risen Jesus and the apostles (see 1:2), the force behind the Christian mission (see 1:5, 8), and the inspiration behind the Old Testament Scriptures (see 1:16). The Holy Spirit is the principle of continuity for the three great periods in Luke's schema of salvation history: the Old Testament, Jesus, and the Church.

The most spectacular and important manifestation of the Holy Spirit comes at Pentecost (see Acts 2). Luke portrays the coming of the Spirit upon the apostles and other disciples (including Mary and other women; see 1:14) as shown forth in their ability to communicate the gospel to people who spoke languages other than Aramaic (or

Hebrew). The Spirit also empowers Peter to proclaim the gospel without fear—an amazing transformation in light of his betrayal of Jesus in Luke 22:54–62.

Throughout Luke's story of the spread of the gospel, he emphasizes that the apostles speak through the inspiration of the Holy Spirit (e.g., Acts 4:8; 7:55; 13:9), and that the Holy Spirit is the ultimate author of the Old Testament Scriptures (e.g., 1:16; 28:25). To become a Christian means to receive the Holy Spirit. And in some peculiar incidents (see 8:14–17; 19:1–7), Luke opposes any attempt to separate receiving the Holy Spirit from water baptism. The decision reached at the Jerusalem council is cast in terms of a collaboration between the apostles and the Holy Spirit: "For it seemed good to the Holy Spirit and to us . . . " (15:28). Acts is the "Book of the Holy Spirit," since in it the Holy Spirit makes the Church grow and even flourish.

Third, the many speeches in the early parts of Acts (see 2:14–42; 3:12–16; 4:24–30; 5:30–42; 10:34–43; 13:16–44) have set the pattern for Christian preaching throughout the centuries in content and even style. For example, in his speech at Pentecost in Acts 2:14–42, Peter announces that the "last days" have come (the reason for the quotation of Joel 2:28–32 [3:1–5] in Acts 2:17–21), quotes various biblical texts (Joel 2: 28–32; Psalms 16:8–11; 110:1) to show that they have been fulfilled in Jesus, proclaims the death and resurrection of Jesus ("God raised him up, having freed him from death," 2:24) as the core of Christian faith, and issues a call to repent and be baptized in order to receive the benefits of the Christ event—the forgiveness of sins and the gift of the Holy Spirit (see Acts 2:38). An exception to this pattern is Paul's speech on the Areopagus (see 17:22–31) where he appeals mostly to the sophisticated religious sensibilities of the Athenians and introduces references to resurrection and judgment only at the end. Whether Luke intends this as a positive example of inculturation or as a negative example of failed preaching (the results were meager; see 17:32–34), is a matter of ongoing dispute.

In one sense these are Luke's speeches. Following the practice of historians in antiquity (see Thucydides, Livy, etc.), Luke presents what the speakers would have said or should have said on the occasion. That helps explain their similar language and style. But these speeches also echo the concerns of the earliest Christian confessions of faith (e.g., 1 Corinthians 15:3–5): Jesus as the fulfillment of the Old Testament Scriptures, the centrality of Jesus' death and resurrection, the return of Jesus and the last judgment, and repentance and baptism as the proper response in the present. In that sense, the speeches in Acts represent the concerns of early Christian preachers, and tell us what they regarded as the most important doctrinal elements.

Fourth, Luke's idealized portrait of community life in the church at Jerusalem (see especially the summaries in Acts 2:42–47 and 4:32–35) has functioned as a prototype for many Christian religious movements (especially those of an enthusiastic bent). Luke paints a picture of people touched to the core of their being by their experiences of the Holy Spirit. In response, they devote themselves "to the apostles' teaching and fellowship, to the breaking of bread and the prayers" (2:42). Their unity in heart and soul leads them to share their material goods: "no one claimed private ownership of any possessions, but everything they owned was held in common" (4:32).

Their practice as described by Luke was not exactly communism or even the "monastic" community of goods practiced by the Qumran Essenes. As the contrasting examples of Barnabas (see Acts 4:36–37) and of Ananias and Sapphira (see 5:1–11) show, those who owned property would sell it off as needs arose within the Christian community, and were expected then to hand over the proceeds to the apostles for distribution by them. Whether this idyllic form of existence was ever really practiced or was Luke's ideal scenario projected back onto the life of the earliest Christians is another matter of long-standing debate. But one can say with certainty that Luke's narrative of the life of the earliest church at Jerusalem has served as a model that various groups (Franciscans, Mennonites, Pentecostals) have tried to follow or adapt throughout Christian history. It seems to be almost irresistibly attractive.

A fifth area in which Luke's narrative of the early church in Acts has greatly influenced church life throughout the centuries is his presentation of the "council" of Jerusalem in Acts 15. Whether this meeting is properly called a "council" and whether it happened exactly as Luke describes it are matters of dispute. Nevertheless, the account in Acts 15 has served as the model for Christian discernment and decision making as well as the prototype for church councils and other meetings.

The main issue at the Jerusalem council was the conditions under which non-Jews might be invited to full fellowship with Jewish Christians. Some Jewish Christians contended that Gentiles had to be circumcised, and had to take on all the obligations of the Torah (see Acts 15:1, 5). First, according to Luke, Peter resists this narrow position (see Acts 10–11) and argues that all—Jews and Gentiles alike—"will be saved through the grace of the Lord Jesus Christ" (15:11). Next, Paul and Barnabas point to the "signs and wonders that God had done" (15:12) in the course of their ministry among Gentiles, presumably as proof of God's favor toward Gentile Christians. Finally, James proposes as a compromise that these Gentiles need not become Jews in the fullest sense but that they should observe certain laws that were regarded as incumbent upon non-Jews as the "sons of Noah": "to abstain only from things polluted by idols and from fornication and from whatever has been strangled and from blood" (15:20, 29; see Exodus 34:15–17; Leviticus 18:6–23; 17:10–16).

How exactly the apostles arrived at this decision is not made explicit. But in the letter issued by the council, there is a statement prefacing the decree to the effect that "it has seemed good to the Holy Spirit and to us to impose on you [Gentiles] no further burden than these essentials" (15:28). The decree is to be promulgated to the Gentile Christians in Antioch (where the matter had become critical), Syria, and Cilicia (see 15:23) by a letter and by the emissaries Judas Barsabbas and Silas along with Paul and Barnabas.

According to Acts 15, a controversial issue was resolved by a gathering of the apostles in which there was free and open discussion among them. The decision was made with reference to and under the guidance of the Holy Spirit. And it was promulgated in a written document and by representatives sent forth from the apostles. Whatever the precise details behind the text may have been, the text as it now stands has been enormously influential in Christian history.

PRACTICAL ADVICE: THE PASTORAL EPISTLES

The letters known as the Pastorals are addressed to Timothy and Titus as the chief "pastors" at Ephesus and Crete, and largely concern their "pastoral" duties. The transformation of Timothy and Titus from being the apostle Paul's co-workers into local pastors is indicative of the change in perspective that these writings represent. The age of the great apostles traveling from place to place, founding new communities, and then moving on seems to be over. Now what is needed most are local leaders (bishops and deacons) who will protect and nurture the communities that had come into existence through the work of the apostles. The Pastorals provide practical advice for such local leaders, and about the communities that they are to guide.

The Pastorals are written in Paul's name and contain many of the great themes of Pauline theology. But most New Testament scholars today regard them as having been composed by a disciple or admirer of Paul in the late first century A.D. Their vocabulary and style as well as their theological emphases are different from those of Paul's undisputed letters. Moreover, the historical situations that they imply fit better in the late first century than in the decade of the fifties.

The Pastorals provide wise practical advice for church leaders, especially stressing the important role of local church leaders. Following the format adopted in the two previous sections, we will look at five areas in which the Pastorals make important contributions to understanding the Church in the first century and in the twenty-first century. They concern true and false teaching, the Church and the world, bishops and deacons, the Church as the household of God as well as the pillar and bulwark of truth, and charism and ministry. The main guide here will be 1 Timothy (since there is much repetition in the Pastorals), although some related texts in the other two letters will be considered.

First, the Pastorals make a sharp distinction between true and false teachings. After the usual epistolary introduction in 1 Timothy 1:1–2 ("Paul . . . to Timothy . . . grace, mercy, and peace"), the writer charges Timothy to oppose those who promote a "different doctrine" and occupy themselves with "myths and endless genealogies that promote speculations" (1:3–4a). The precise nature of this "different doctrine" is not entirely clear, although it does seem to have connection to "gnostic" themes and to the Old Testament Law ("desiring to be teachers of the law"). Perhaps it was some gnostic form of Jewish Christianity.

What is clear is the assumption that there is a sharp line dividing true teaching (orthodoxy) and false teaching (heresy). The false teaching is characterized as "meaningless talk" (1:6), while the "divine training" known by faith has as its goal love that proceeds from "a pure heart, a good conscience, and sincere faith" (1:5). Those who are faithful to Paul's gospel will act properly, since sound doctrine expresses itself in sound actions. In this context, the proper function of the Old Testament Law is to make righteous persons cognizant of sin and to convict evildoers of their sins. "Sound" teaching promotes health of mind and spirit, and this sound teaching has been entrusted to the apostle Paul (the basis for the idea of the "deposit of faith"). And so 1 Timothy 1:3–11 is evidence for consciousness of a sharp division between what would later be called orthodoxy (the gospel, apostolic teaching, sound doctrine, the deposit of faith) and heresy (meaningless talk, misunderstanding of the function of the Law).

Second, the Church envisioned in the Pastorals is not some small apocalyptic sect waiting for "this world" to pass away. Rather, it is an entity (however small) within the Roman Empire, one that promotes cooperation with the state and adopts many of the cultural assumptions of the Greco-Roman world. Therefore Christians are not only allowed but even encouraged to make "supplications, prayers, and intercessions . . . for kings and all who are in high positions" (1 Timothy 2:1–2). The idea behind this directive is that cooperation with the Roman officials will allow Christians to "lead a quiet and peaceable life in all godliness and dignity" (2:2b). This teaching is rooted in Paul's instructions in Romans 13:1–7 (see 1 Peter 2:13–17). At the same time there is the expectation that the exemplary lives led by Christians will bring others to inquire about the Christian faith (which is summarized in 1 Timothy 2:5-6) and embrace it. This is the missionary strategy of good example.

The impulse toward social conformity also finds expression in the instruction about women in 1 Timothy 2:9–15. There are indications that women were prominent in supporting the heterodox teachers (see 2 Timothy 3:6), and that the opponents forbade marriage (see 1 Timothy 4:3). In this situation, the author insists on modesty in attire and in action for women, their subordination to their husbands, and the importance of bearing children. The ideal for Christian women is "faith and love and holiness, with modesty" (2:15). In the public forum and in the household, the ideal is exemplary behavior as understood in the context of the good order of the household in the Greco-Roman world.

Third, the offices of bishop and deacon are essential elements in the vision of the Church promoted in the Pastorals. From the start of the Jesus movement, the faith of Jesus and in Jesus was incarnated in human beings and social institutions rather than in books. As the local churches set their roots more deeply into the soil of the Mediterranean world, there was increasing need for leaders who were capable of guiding their communities and of impressing outsiders by their exemplary lives. This need may well explain why it is said in 1 Timothy 3:1 that those who aspire to the office of bishop desire a "noble task."

The lists of qualifications for bishop (see 1 Timothy 3:1–7) and deacon (see 3:8–13) emphasize their exemplary moral lives ("temperate, sensible, respectable, hospitable, an apt teacher") and their proven ability to manage their own household ("for if someone does not know how to manage his own household, how can he take care of God's church?" 3:5). There is also a warning about making a recent convert into a bishop (see 3:6), a warning perhaps based on some sad experiences. The note about "women" in 3:11 refers more likely to women deacons than to the wives of deacons.

Fourth, the Church is said to be "the household of God" as well as "the pillar and bulwark of truth" (1 Timothy 3:15). The emphasis on "household" management among the qualifications for bishop and deacon (see 3:4–5, 12) leads into the description of "the church of the living God" in terms of a house or household (oikos). This image evokes first of all the idea of the people who make up the household: father, mother, children, and grandparents, as well as servants and other retainers. As with the idea of the new "family" of Jesus in the gospel tradition, the notion of the Church as the "household of God" relativizes the importance of every human household while promoting a kind of "fictive kinship" among Christians.

The image of the Church as the oikos of God also evokes the architectural aspect of the word for house. In this perspective, "the church of the living God" is a "pillar" or column that holds up the truth as well as a "bulwark" or firm foundation for the truth. What that truth is, is specified by the christological confession quoted in 1 Timothy 3:16: "He was revealed in flesh, vindicated in spirit, seen by angels, proclaimed among Gentiles, believed in throughout the world, taken up in glory."

Fifth, the Pastorals make a close link between charism and official ministry. When encouraging Timothy to be a good "minister" (*diakonos*) in 4:6–13, the writer urges him to train himself in "godliness" (*eusebeia*), to set a good example for other believers, and to exercise his ministry in the public reading of Scripture (the Old Testament in this context) and in exhorting and teaching. Then in 4:14, he appeals to Timothy not to neglect "the gift that is in you, which was given to you through prophecy with the laying on of hands by the council of elders." Here Timothy's "gift" (*charisma*) is linked to the imposition of hands by the elders (or presbyterate). The description envisions a public ratification of Timothy's charism "through prophecy," the laying on of hands as both calling down God's blessing upon him and handing on spiritual power to him, and the presence of the board of "elders" (senior either in age or in Christian faith). A similar statement appears in 2 Timothy 1:6, where "Paul" instructs Timothy "to rekindle the gift of God that is within you through the laying on of my hands." Here Paul functions as the "elder" *par excellence*.

In the light of 1 Timothy 4:14 and 2 Timothy 1:6, the Pauline teaching about the charisms is being narrowed and institutionalized. Now charism is associated with public ratification and the imposition of hands. This is what comes to be known as ordination. The charism equips Timothy to carry out his responsibilities as a minister of the word. Charism is regarded as something that is within Timothy and something that he possesses. Charism is on the way toward becoming the power of office. And Timothy's major task is safeguarding sound doctrine (the "deposit of faith") through his ministry of the word.

Possibilities and Problems

The New Testament writings treated in this chapter—Ephesians, Acts, and the Pastorals—are all related to the apostle Paul but are generally regarded as written by disciples or admirers of Paul. Each represents the legacy of Paul in a different form: the essay, the narrative, and practical advice. All of them are assigned dates in the latter part of the first century A.D. Each in its own way illustrates the ability of first-century Christians to remain faithful to their traditions while adapting to new circumstances and challenges. Just as Paul adapted traditions from Jesus and about Jesus, so these members of the Pauline school adapted what they had received from Paul and other early Christians. In doing so they provide examples of "inculturating" the gospel in new times and places while trying to preserve the gospel as the core of Christian faith.

The topics that these New Testament writings treat have exercised enormous influence on the history of the Christian Church. For each writing we have focused on five issues. In Ephesians, for example, we looked at the Church as the place of Christ's power, the Church as the Body of Christ and the People of God, the apostles as the foundation of the Church, the place of the charisms in the Church, and the relationship between Christ and the Church. Luke's narrative about the early church in Acts has supplied the themes of mission, the Holy Spirit, Christian preaching, community life, and the "council" of the apostles at Jerusalem. And the Pastorals provided the following themes: the distinction between true and false teachings, the Church and the world, bishops and deacons, the Church as the household of God as well as the pillar and bulwark of truth, and charism and ministry. These themes have served historically as the basic elements or "building blocks" for the "great" or "catholic" Church of the second and third centuries A.D.

In some scholarly circles it has become customary to refer to Ephesians, Acts, and the Pastorals as representatives of "early catholicism" in the New Testament. That label is useful in calling attention to the presence within the New Testament of those elements that coalesced into the later "catholic" Church. And it is also helpful in highlighting the fact that these writings constitute a development beyond what appears in the undisputed Pauline letters from the fifties of the first century.

One problem that these "early catholic" writings raise is the significance of historical development within the New Testament. Do they represent progress, regress, or simply adaptation to changed historical circumstances? Those who regard them as progress contend that they represent the gradual unfolding of revelation within the New Testament, and thus they are normative for the Church in all ages. In other words, after a period of trial and error, the later New Testament writers under the guidance of the Holy Spirit finally got it right. Those who regard these works as regress view them as perhaps a natural development of Paul's theological legacy but not necessarily a good one. What is normative for the Church in all ages, according to this second view, is not the appurtenances found these books but rather the pure gospel proclaimed by Paul in his letters to the Galatians and the Romans. And those who regard them as simply adaptations to changed historical circumstances tend to take the disengaged "observer" viewpoints of the historian and sociologist, and leave the task of theological evaluation to others.

The "early catholic" writings in the New Testament raise other questions that are basic to Christian theology. Is the history of the early church a continuous development toward the most perfect form of Church, or does it represent a falling away from the pristine purity of the gospel? Is the Church a witness to and a sign of the kingdom of God, or is God's kingdom present within the Church and even the same as the Church? Should the Church keep its distance from the "world" (as an apocalyptic sect might do), or should it adopt whatever is good and true in secular culture and encourage its members to be "good citizens" in the present world order? Is ministry in the Church best understood in terms of activities and functions, or in terms of church offices and ordination? And granted that there are different and divergent voices within the New Testament canon and even within the Pauline tradition, which voices deserve the most attentive hearing and why?

Finally, the label "early catholic" itself is problematic on theological and historical grounds. Ever since the Protestant Reformation in the sixteenth century, it has often been used pejoratively to suggest that Protestantism is in continuity with earliest Christianity (Paul's gospel) and that Roman Catholicism is a deformation or falling away (*Abfall* in German) from the pure gospel. In recent times, some Catholic theologians have used the term apologetically to point to the presence of "catholicism" in the New Testament canon. But this term may bring too much theological baggage with it to be helpful today.

Moreover, it is probably a mistake to view Ephesians, Acts, and the Pastorals as coming from one school or group within early Christianity. While they all take Paul as their hero and inspiration, they use different literary forms and focus on and develop different aspects of his theological legacy. They provide the "elements" or "building blocks" that emerged in a new combination in the "catholic" Church of the second and third centuries. As such, they are best seen as representatives in a wider phenomenon as the Church settled into life within the Roman Empire and the Greco-Roman world.

For Reflection and Discussion

1. Do the New Testament writings treated in this chapter represent progress, regress, or simply historical adaptation? Why?

2. Which elements in these writings have been especially influential in your church's tradition?

3. From these writings can you draw some principles about the inculturation of the gospel today?

chapter eight

THE CHURCHES BEHIND
THE SYNOPTIC GOSPELS

The Gospels tell the story of Jesus, especially during his public ministry and his passion and death. As such, they provide us with some solid information about the historical Jesus, as we saw in the first two chapters. At the same time, the Synoptic Gospels were not put into their present form until at least forty years after Jesus' death. And so they also provide us with information about life in the early churches in the interim, and about the churches that the Evangelists addressed directly in their Gospels.

The need for reading the Gospels at three levels—Jesus, the early church, and the Evangelists—was explicitly recognized in the following statement from the Second Vatican Council's Dogmatic Constitution on Divine Revelation:

> The sacred authors, in writing the four Gospels, selected certain of the many elements which had been handed on, either orally or already in written form, others they synthesized or explained with an eye to the situation of the churches, the while sustaining the form of preaching, but always in such a fashion that they have told us the honest truth about Jesus (*Dei verbum* 19).

FROM JESUS TO THE SYNOPTIC GOSPELS:
WINDOWS ONTO CHURCH LIFE

Christianity is not a religion of the book. Rather, it is the religion of a person—Jesus of Nazareth, the Word of God who became flesh and dwelt among us (see John 1:14). Jesus did not write books. Rather, he communicated his message about God's kingdom by word and deed. The first Christians followed Jesus' example not only in proclaiming God's kingdom as he did (in word and deed) but also in celebrating what they believed God had done in and through Jesus' death and resurrection. Paul, the earliest New Testament writer, summarized the tradition that he received and that he in turn handed on to those whom he brought to Christian faith: "For I handed on to you as of first importance what I in turn had received:

that Christ died for our sins in accordance with the Scriptures, and that he was buried, and that he was raised on the third day in accordance with the Scriptures, and that he appeared to Cephas, then to the Twelve" (1 Corinthians 15:3–5).

The word *gospel* (*euangelion* in Greek) referred originally not to a book about Jesus but rather to the "good news" about what God did through Jesus—to what became the content of the books about Jesus. While early Christians like Paul focused on Jesus' death and resurrection, those who accepted the "good news" naturally began to inquire about what Jesus said and did during his public ministry and even about his birth and childhood. The answers to their questions were found in the small traditions that circulated in connection with Jesus in early Christian circles.

Form criticism is the process of describing both the literary forms in which the Jesus tradition was preserved and circulated, and the historical settings in which these traditions would have been most meaningful. So it is both a literary and a historical enterprise. Developed in the early part of the twentieth century, form criticism sought to illumine those pivotal forty years in which the Jesus tradition was formed and eventually coalesced into the canonical Gospels. The premise of form criticism is that much of the material about Jesus' teaching and activity took shape in the course of early Christian preaching.

Form criticism has been successful in isolating the basic discourse and narrative forms in which the Jesus tradition was expressed. One major discourse form was the apophthegm—a short narrative that culminates in a clever or decisive saying. These are sometimes controversies with opponents (see Mark 11:27–33), anecdotes about Jesus (see 10:13–16), or disputations about Scripture (see 12:28–37). There are also beatitudes (see Matthew 5:3–12), "I" sayings (see 5:17–20), antitheses (see 5:21–48), admonitions (see 6:1–18), wisdom sayings (see 6:19–34), similitudes and parables (see 13:1–52), and community rules (see 18:1–20).

The major narrative forms in the gospel tradition are exorcisms (see Mark 1:21–28) and healings (see 1:29–34, 40–45). They usually follow a pattern in which there is mention of the sufferer's condition (leprosy or paralysis), a display of faith on the part of the afflicted person (or friends), an intervention by Jesus in the form of a healing word (or touch in some cases), an immediate and complete cure, and some acknowledgment by witnesses that Jesus had indeed brought about the healing. There are also nature miracles, such as the stilling of the storm (see Mark 4:35–41) and Jesus' walking on the waters (see 6:45–52), as well as accounts about miraculous feedings (see 6:30–44; 8:1–10) and the divine interventions at Jesus' baptism (see Mark 1:9–11) and transfiguration (see 9:2–8).

These discourse and narrative traditions helped to fill out the picture of Jesus during his public activity in Palestine around the year A.D. 30. But they also spoke to the concerns and needs of Christians during the period from A.D. 30 to 70. For example, Mark 2:1–3:6 contains a block of five controversy stories in which Jesus enters into debate over such issues as the forgiveness of sins (see 2:1–12), eating with "sinners" (see 2:13–17), fasting (see 2:18–22), work on the Sabbath (see 2:23–28), and doing "good" on the Sabbath (see 3:1–6). The effect of these five controversies is to give the positions of Jesus (and of the early churches) on issues that would have been controversial among Jews and Jewish Christians, most likely in Palestine.

Likewise, the allegorical interpretation of the parable of the seeds in Mark 4:3–9 that appears in Mark 4:13–20 looks like a sermon outline directed at early Christians who were becoming discouraged by lack of success in preaching the gospel and by defections and apostasies among themselves. The failures are variously attributed to Satan, persecutions, and to "the cares of the world and the lure of wealth and the desire for other things" (Mark 4:19). The interpretation, however, points to the superior power of the seeds sown on the good soil who "hear the word and accept it and bear fruit, thirty and sixty and a hundred fold" (4:20). The language of the interpretation reflects the experiences of early churches in various parts of the Roman Empire, most dramatically Mark's community at Rome itself (see the next section).

Form criticism has been more successful as a literary tool (in identifying the literary forms) than as a historical tool (in writing the history of primitive Christianity). But at least the project of form criticism has managed to shine some light on how early Christians tried to bring the teachings and actions of Jesus to bear on the issues that greatly affected them: what they should say and do, where they stood with regard to Jewish laws and traditions, and what constituted success and failure for them.

MARK: A CHURCH UNDER PRESSURE

Both early Christian traditions and the results of modern scholarship generally support the position that Mark's Gospel was written for Christians who faced persecution in Rome after the emperor Nero tried to blame Christians for the great fire of A.D. 64. The Roman historian Tacitus reports that professed Christians were arrested and, on their testimony, still others were arrested and sentenced to death. Tacitus goes on to describe the horrible punishments that were inflicted on them: "they were covered with beasts' skins and torn to death by dogs; or they were fastened on crosses; and when daylight failed were burned to serve as lamps by night" (*Annales* 15.56).

The Christians at Rome had to face a double crisis in that some had suffered a cruel martyrdom and others had betrayed their brothers and sisters in Christ. Their situation was made even more complicated by the Jewish revolt in Palestine in A.D. 66 that culminated in the destruction of Jerusalem and its Temple in A.D. 70. They had to explain why their hero, Jesus of Nazareth, had been executed under the Roman prefect Pontius Pilate as "King of the Jews"—another way of saying "Jewish political revolutionary" among the Romans.

In his portrait of Jesus, Mark used many small traditions that had circulated in oral and written forms in the early churches. He also took over many titles applied to Jesus—Messiah, Son of God, Son of Man, Son of David, and so on—by the early Christians. And, of course, Mark sought to be faithful to what he knew about the scope of Jesus' public ministry: teaching and healing activity in Galilee, the climactic journey up to Jerusalem, and a brief ministry in Jerusalem and the passion and death. Nevertheless, even though Mark told his story of Jesus in the framework of tradition and history, he also produced a narrative that would have spoken eloquently to Christians who had suffered persecution and were facing the prospect of even more suffering.

The first major focus of Mark's Gospel is Jesus the suffering Messiah. Mark entitled his story of Jesus "the good news (*euangelion*) of Jesus Christ, the Son of God" (1:1). Thus he transformed the "good news" about what God had done through Jesus' death and resurrection (see 1 Corinthians 15:3–5) into the literary genre about Jesus that we know as the Gospel. After being proclaimed by the voice from heaven as "my Son, the Beloved" at his baptism (1:11), Jesus bursts onto the scene by proclaiming: "The time is fulfilled, and the kingdom of God has come near; repent, and believe in the good news" (1:15). But even after displaying his powers as a teacher and a healer, Jesus attracts opposition and hostility in the form of a plot to kill him on the part of the Pharisees and Herodians (see 3:6). Likewise, after his many parables about God's kingdom in 4:1–34, and his acts of power over the storm, demons, chronic sickness, and death in 4:35–5:43, the people of his own hometown refuse to believe in him (see 6:1–6). And even after his own disciples witness the miraculous feedings (see 6:30–44; 8:1–10) and other displays of power as a miracle worker and skill as a teacher, their hearts remain hardened (see 8:14–21). On all fronts, Jesus meets misunderstandings, unbelief, and active opposition.

On the way to Jerusalem (see Mark 8:22–10:52), Jesus presents three predictions about his passion, death, and resurrection (see 8:31; 9:31; 10:33–34). And at each point, his disciples show by their inappropriate reactions that they do not grasp (or refuse to do so) what Jesus is saying.

They show the most resistance in facing up to the mystery of the cross. When Peter refuses to accept the prophecy about the cross, Jesus rebukes him as "Satan" (8:33). After the second passion prediction, the disciples argue about who is the greatest among them (see 9:34). And at the third passion prediction, James and John show more interest in their prominent places in the kingdom of God (see 10:37).

When Jesus arrives in Jerusalem, his chief Jewish opponents are the high priests, scribes, and elders of the people. When Jesus criticizes their oversight of the Temple (see Mark 11:15–19), they are restrained from killing him only by their fear of the crowds who still regarded Jesus positively (see 11:18; 12:12, 37; 14:2). Their opportunity to arrest Jesus and to have him killed came with the offer by one of Jesus' own disciples (Judas) to betray him (see 14:10–11).

Throughout Mark's Gospel, Jesus is identified as the Messiah, Son of God, and Son of Man. But only at the trial before the Jewish authorities, when the shadow of the cross envelops everything, does Jesus accept these titles ("I am," 14:62), precisely because they are now qualified by the mystery of the cross. And at the moment of Jesus' death on the cross, the Roman centurion speaks for Mark's community when he says: "Truly this man was God's Son" (15:39). Mark's portrait of Jesus places the mystery of the cross at its center. His emphasis on the cross helped the Markan community around A.D. 70 to make connections with the person of Jesus around A.D. 30.

A second major focus in Mark's Gospel is the theme of *discipleship*. Each major subsection in Mark's account of Jesus' ministry in Galilee (see 1:14–8:21) features an early episode about the disciples: the call of the first disciples (see 1:16–20), the appointment of the Twelve (see 3:13–19), and the mission of the Twelve (see 6:7–13). The first disciples—Simon Peter and Andrew, James and John—respond to Jesus' call "Follow me" (1:17) immediately and generously, leaving their businesses and families to join with Jesus in proclaiming God's kingdom. The Twelve are appointed by Jesus "to be with him, and to be sent out to proclaim the message" (3:14). And they are eventually sent forth to share in Jesus' ministry of healing and preaching with orders to subordinate their material concerns to that mission (see 6:8–11). At the start at least, the disciples appear to be positive models whose generosity and dedication represent an ideal to be imitated.

However, as Jesus' ministry progresses, even his own disciples become part of the general response of misunderstanding regarding Jesus. At the end of the Galilean ministry (see 8:14–21), for example, Jesus indicts them for their failure to recognize who he is and what he is doing: "Do you still not perceive or understand? Are your hearts hardened?" (8:17). Their obtuseness is underscored during the journey narrative, where at each passion prediction they seem to miss the point. And during the passion narrative, they all flee at the time of Jesus' arrest (see 14:50), and Peter denies Jesus three times (see 14:66–72). And yet Jesus remains faithful to his disciples and promises to be with them again after his Resurrection (see 14:28; 16:7). In the second half of Mark's Gospel, the disciples become negative examples whose infidelity contrasts sharply with the fidelity displayed by Jesus.

Mark's positive ideal of discipleship in Christian community is expressed in the passage about the true family of Jesus in 3:31–35. When informed that he was being summoned by his mother and brothers, Jesus takes the occasion to redefine his family: "Whoever does the will of God is my brother and sister and mother" (3:35). In a culture in which blood family ties were very important, this was a challenging and revolutionary statement. Rather, commitment to doing the will of God is the major characteristic of those who wish to belong to the new family of Jesus.

Another important qualification for membership in the family of Jesus is a willingness to share in Jesus' suffering: "If any want to become my followers, let them deny themselves and take up their cross and follow me" (8:34). This challenge is what the Twelve seem to find so difficult to understand and accept. And yet in a Gospel where the shadow of the cross seems to be everywhere, a willingness to embrace the cross is an important condition for following Jesus.

Membership in the family of Jesus is open to all kinds of people, provided they commit themselves to do God's will and face up to the mystery of the cross. This point is made most obviously by Mark's insistence on Jesus' ministry to outcasts within Jewish society (lepers, paralyzed persons, the possessed, and so on), and even to those whose lifestyles and professions made them into "sinners": "I have come to call not the righteous but sinners" (2:17). And with Jesus' sojourns into Gentile territory in Mark 5–8 and especially in his feeding of the four thousand in 8:1–10, it appears that the family of Jesus has room for those outside of Israel. On the other hand, the thrust of Jesus' criticism of the chief priests and scribes regarding their oversight of the Temple (see Mark 11:17) is that they have made what should be "a house of prayer for all the nations" (Isaiah 56:7) into "a den of robbers" (Jeremiah 7:11). And it is a Gentile—a Roman centurion no less!—who correctly identifies Jesus at the hour of his death on the cross: "Truly this man was God's Son!" (15:39).

MATTHEW: THE CHURCH AND JUDAISM

Matthew's Gospel (and Luke's Gospel, too) can be described as a revised and expanded version of Mark's Gospel. One good reason that led to the revision is that the Evangelist whom we call *Matthew* wanted to expand substantially the content of Jesus' teaching. To do so, he included sayings of Jesus that he (and Luke independently) found in the source known as Q as well as other special traditions known as M, to which he had access. And so Matthew constructed out of his traditions from Mark, Q, and M five great speeches of Jesus: the Sermon on the Mount (see chapters 5–7), the Missionary Discourse (see chapter 10), the Parables (see 13:1–52), the Advice to a Divided Community (see chapter 18), and the Eschatological Discourse (see chapters 24–25).

Besides supplementing Mark, especially in the area of Jesus' teaching, Matthew also sought to respond to an event that had become a crisis for many in the early church and for all Jews: the destruction of the Jerusalem Temple in A.D. 70 by the Romans. With the loss of the Temple as the center of Jewish life, and the lessening of Jewish political power to almost the point of nonexistence, all Jews after A.D. 70 had to face the question: How do we continue the Jewish tradition without the Temple and without the land? For Jewish Christians, especially those who saw no incompatibility between Judaism and Christianity and even regarded Christianity as a kind of Judaism, this was a very important question.

The question about reconstituting Judaism after A.D. 70 evoked different answers from different groups within Judaism. Formative or early rabbinic Judaism focused on the one great pillar of Judaism that remained (the Torah) and on collecting and codifying the traditions surrounding the Torah in the Mishnah, the Tosefta, and the Talmuds. Jews with an apocalyptic orientation (as represented in *4 Ezra* and *2 Baruch*) held fast to the promises of God and looked forward to a definitive intervention by God on their behalf. Jewish revolutionaries kept up the Zealot movement and regrouped to prepare for a second (unsuccessful) revolt under Simeon Bar Kokhba in A.D. 132–135. And Jewish Christians like Matthew insisted that authentic Judaism is best carried on by those who gather around Jesus as Lord and as the authoritative interpreter of the Jewish tradition.

Matthew appears to have written his Gospel for a mainly Jewish Christian community in a city with a large Jewish population that was predominantly Greek speaking. Antioch in Syria is the best candidate, although Damascus and Caesarea Maritima are also possible. Several passages (see Matthew 21:41; 22:7; 27:25) suggest that the Jerusalem Temple had already been destroyed—suggesting a date around A.D. 85 or 90 as the most likely. In this context, the Evangelist sought to show that God's promises to Israel are best fulfilled in Jesus of Nazareth, and that the traditions of Judaism are best carried on in the Church. In making these claims, Matthew was entering into a great debate within Judaism in the late first century A.D.

That debate sometimes became heated. And so it is important always to bear in mind that this was a debate within Judaism, a kind of "family quarrel." Taken out of that context, Matthew's Gospel runs the risk of encouraging anti-Judaism.

Not all Jews, however, saw things as Matthew and his fellow Jewish Christians did. Thus, in many parables (see 13:1–52; 21:28–22:14; 24:45–25:30), the major theme is acceptance or rejection of Jesus and his proclamation of God's kingdom. Matthew 23, for example, is a bitter denunciation of the scribes and Pharisees for their religious hypocrisy. This speech was surely read in Matthew's community as an attack on "their synagogues" (see 4:23; 9:35; 10:17; 12:9). And the self-curse that the people in Jerusalem take upon themselves in 27:25 ("His blood be on us and on our children!") very likely reflects the early Christian idea (shared to some extent by Josephus) that the Jews of Jerusalem brought upon themselves the destruction of their city in A.D. 70.

Less obvious but also important for the theme of the Church and Judaism are those passages in which Matthew rewrote Mark on matters that were debated within Jewish circles in the late first century A.D. The effect of Matthew's editorial work is to place Jesus more squarely within the Jewish debates and at the same time to differentiate his views from those of other Jewish teachers.

For example, on the matter of Sabbath observance (12:1–8), Matthew adds the example of work that is allowed in the Temple (see 12:5–7) and omits the potentially radical saying in Mark 2:27 ("The Sabbath was made for humankind, and not humankind for the Sabbath"). And in 12:9–14, Matthew places the healing of a man with a withered hand in the context of the current Jewish discussions about what constitutes "work" by inserting the case of rescuing an animal that had fallen into a pit (see 12:11–12).

Likewise on the issue of ritual purity and food laws, Matthew omits the radical parenthetical comment in Mark 7:19 ("Thus he declared all foods clean") and makes the incident into a lesson about the primacy of moral "purity." And on the matter of marriage and divorce (see 19:3–12), Matthew turns the Markan episode (see Mark 10:2–12) into a Jewish debate about the grounds for divorce ("Is it lawful for a man to divorce his wife *for any cause*?"). He also introduces an apparent exception ("except for unchastity") into Jesus' absolute prohibition of divorce (see also Matthew 5:32). The precise nature of this exception (unchastity on the woman's part, marriage within forbidden degrees of kinship, etc.) has long been debated. But its inclusion serves to bring Jesus back into the late first-century Jewish debate and to align his views with those of the "conservative" Shammai against those of the more "liberal" Hillel.

Many features in Matthew's portrayal of Jesus point to his basic conviction that in Jesus the Jewish tradition reaches a certain fullness. The genealogy in Matthew 1:1–17, for example, places Jesus in line with Abraham, David, and the exile generation. The formula quotations from the Old Testament ("All this took place to fulfill what had been spoken by the Lord through the prophet ...") in the Matthean infancy narratives and in the body of the Gospel make explicit and concrete the theme of Jesus as the fulfillment of Israel's hopes. The christological titles that Matthew favors have rich Old Testament and Jewish backgrounds: Emmanuel, Son of David, Servant, Son of God, Messiah, Son of Man, Lord, and Wisdom.

Following the Jewish practice of avoiding too facile use of the divine name, Matthew generally refers to the "kingdom of heaven." He presents John the Baptist and Jesus as saying the same things in 3:2 and 4:17: "Repent, for the kingdom of heaven has come near." He extends Mark's eschatological discourse with a series of parables (see 24:37–25:30) that emphasize the attitude of constant watchfulness in the face of the coming kingdom of God.

The five great speeches provide abundant content for appropriate ethical conduct in light of the coming kingdom. In them Jesus functions as the authoritative interpreter of the Torah ("You have heard that it was said.... But I say to you ..."). However, all these interpretations are placed under the heading presented in Matthew 5:17: "Do not think that I have come to abolish the law or the prophets; I have not come to abolish but to fulfill." And there is also the typical Jewish emphasis on the practical nature of wisdom: "You will know them by their fruits" (7:16). For the Matthean community Jesus is the only teacher: "you have one instructor, the Messiah" (23:10).

Of the four Evangelists, Matthew is the only one who uses the word *church* (*ekklesia*; see 16:18; 18:17). The general absence of the term is not surprising, since the Gospels purport to tell the story of Jesus' life and ministry up to his passion and death, leaving "church" something of a literary anachronism in this context. Nevertheless, Matthew's Gospel is very important as a source for understanding the development of the Church in earliest times and throughout history.

At the announcement of his conception, Jesus is called "Emmanuel" (Matthew 1:23 = Isaiah 7:14), which means "God with us." As the Risen Jesus departs after Easter, he promises his enduring presence to the eleven disciples (the Twelve minus Judas) and through them to the Church: "I am with you always, to the end of the age" (28:20). It is the presence of God and the Risen Christ through the Holy Spirit that is to guide and animate the Church throughout history.

As in Mark, the disciples are paradigmatic figures who start well but fall away into misunderstanding and betrayal. But Matthew takes pains to upgrade the disciples' image somewhat by referring to them as persons of "little faith" (*oligopistoi*; see 8:26; 14:31; 16:8). The best example of "little faith" is Peter who, in 14:28–31, starts to walk on the waters only to falter and need rescue from Jesus. Peter is treated more positively in 16:16b–19, when Jesus, in response to Peter's confession of faith, declares him to be blessed as the recipient of a divine revelation and grants him the power to bind and loose (see pp. 168–170 for a full discussion of Peter). Matthew's interest in Peter some thirty years after his death indicates the prominence of this apostle in early Christian circles.

That the Matthean community also had its own internal problems is indicated by the discourse in Matthew 18. There the Evangelist uses traditional materials to address community problems associated with excessive pride, scandal, and members who strayed and sinned. This discourse is noteworthy for its three-step process for reproving and reconciling sinners in 18:15–17 (individual confrontation, meeting with one or two other members, meeting with the whole community) and for attributing the power to bind and loose to the whole community in 18:18 (compare Matthew 16:19). It concludes with the parable of the unforgiving servant in 18:21–35—a story that illustrates God's boundless mercy toward sinners and the link between God's willingness to forgive his "debtors" and their willingness to forgive those who are "debtors" to them (see Matthew 6:12, 14–15). Peter, whose question prompts the parable, is of course the best example of the forgiven sinner who becomes a great church leader.

Matthew's version of the parable of the vineyard in 21:33–46 (see Mark 12:1–12) serves as an apt conclusion for this section. The parable takes as its starting point the "song of the vineyard" in Isaiah 5:1–7 in which the vineyard is clearly a symbol for Israel: "For the vineyard of the Lord of hosts is the house of Israel" (5:7). In the New Testament parable, however, what is destroyed is not the vineyard (Israel, as in Isaiah 5) but rather the tenant farmers (the leaders of Israel) for their mistreatment of God's servants (the prophets) and Son (Jesus). Matthew's version seems to reflect of the events of A.D. 70: "He will put those wretches to a miserable death, and lease the vineyard to other tenants" (21:41). Then Jesus addresses the chief priests and Pharisees, and warns them: "the kingdom of God will be taken away from you and given to a people that produces the fruits of the kingdom" (21:43). In Matthew's perspective, Israel as God's people is put under new leadership. But Israel is not destroyed or rejected outright. The vineyard remains. What changes is the identity and manner of those who care for it.

LUKE: THE CHURCH IN HISTORY AND IN THE WORLD

Luke's Gospel has (deservedly) been called "the most beautiful book ever written." After his prologue (see 1:1–4), Luke presents by way of preparation the infancy narratives (see 1:5–2:52), the ministry of John the Baptist (see 3:1–20), and three passages in 3:21–4:13 (baptism, genealogy, and testing) that show us what kind of Son of God Jesus is. Then he describes the public ministry of Jesus in three large geographical segments: Galilee (see 4:14–9:50), the journey from Galilee to Jerusalem (see 9:51–19:44), and Jerusalem (see 19:45–21:38). The Gospel concludes with the passion, death, and resurrection accounts (see 22:1–24:53).

This Gospel was most likely composed around A.D. 85 to 90 on the basis of Mark's Gospel, the Sayings Source Q, and special Lukan traditions (L). Whether or not its author was Paul's co-worker is much debated. At any rate, the Evangelist whom we call Luke does have a distinctive theological vision that gives special attention to Jesus' place in salvation history, the role of the Holy Spirit in guiding and directing God's people, and the offer of salvation to all kinds of people. While it is hard to know exactly where the Gospel was written, its original audience probably included many non-Jews who nonetheless were expected to know a lot about Judaism (perhaps from frequenting synagogues as "God-fearers").

Luke is a consummate literary artist. With great skill he presents short narratives that are beautifully expressed and with interesting and memorable characters. At the same time, he develops a number of themes that run throughout his Gospel and into his Acts of the Apostles. Those who wish to appreciate his Gospel as it deserves need to be sensitive to both the details in his carefully etched literary portraits and to the larger surface on which he is presenting his tapestry of the life of Jesus and the story of the early church. In reading Luke's Gospel, it is very important to be aware of some of the Gospel's overarching themes and concerns. In particular, attention to these themes can be very helpful for understanding how Luke presents the place of the Church in history and in the world.

Holy Spirit: In the infancy narrative, Jesus is conceived through the Holy Spirit (see 1:35), and Zechariah and Simeon prophesy under the inspiration of the Holy Spirit. The Spirit descends upon Jesus at his baptism (see 3:21–22), and his public ministry is defined in terms of the coming of the Spirit upon him (see 4:18–19). Throughout his ministry of teaching and healing, Jesus is the bearer of the Holy Spirit, and he promises to send the Spirit upon his disciples after his Ascension (see 24:49). In Acts, the Spirit is the great principle of continuity between the time of Jesus and the time of the Church.

Salvation History: Luke's dominant concern is the integration of the story of Jesus in God's plan of redemptive history. That history is divided into three great periods: the Old Testament preparation up to and including John the Baptist (see 3:15–20; 16:16), the presence of salvation in Jesus ("today," "now"), and the age of the Church under the guidance of the Holy Spirit (Acts). Jesus inaugurates a movement that is an outgrowth of Judaism (see Luke 2:21–40), included Gentiles (see 4:16–30), and posed no political threat to the Roman Empire (see 23:1–16, 25–26).

Jesus the Prophet: The theme of Jesus the prophet is one of Luke's most important christological contributions. At the beginning of his public ministry (see 4:16–30), Jesus is presented as a prophet. He not only acts as a prophet (see 7:16) but he also dies as a prophet (see 13:33; 24:25–27). At Pentecost (see Acts 2) the Holy Spirit passes on to Jesus' followers in a kind of prophetic succession.

The Twelve Apostles: More than any other Evangelist, Luke is most responsible for bringing together the terms *twelve* and *apostles*. The key sentence is Luke 6:13: "he called his disciples and chose twelve of them, whom he also named apostles." Whereas in 9:1–2 Jesus sends out the Twelve (see 9:10), those who return are called *apostles*. These texts (see also Luke 11:49; 17:5; 22:14; 24:10) suggest an identity between the Twelve and the apostles. They also prepare for the many reference to the Twelve Apostles in Acts (see 1:2, 26; 2:37, 42, 43; 4:33, 35, 36; 5:2, 12, 18, 29, 34, 40, etc.). In Luke-Acts the Twelve Apostles also function as a principle of continuity between the time of Jesus and the time of the Church. From this Lukan theme, we get our concept of "apostolic succession."

Prayer: Luke is sometimes called the Gospel of prayer because in it Jesus is portrayed as praying at the decisive moments in his life: his baptism (see 3:21), the healing of the leper (see 5:16), the choice of the Twelve (see 6:12), Peter's confession of faith (see 9:18), the transfiguration (see 9:28–29), his arrest (see 22:40–46), and his death (see 23:34, 46). It also contains two large instructions about prayer: its content (the Lord's Prayer) and the value of persistence (see 11:1–13), and the need for persistence and humility in prayer (see 18:1–14).

Rich and Poor: Among the several passages that concern relations between rich and poor, the most important are the blessings and woes (see 6:20–26), the parable of the rich fool (see 12:13–21), planning the guest list for the banquet (see 14:12–14), the rich man and Lazarus (see 16:19–31), and the story of Zacchaeus (see 19:1–10). These texts suggest that Luke's community included both rich and poor members, and that one of his purposes in writing the Gospel was to warn the wealthy members about relying too much on riches.

Banquet: The Old Testament attaches special significance to meals in various contexts: covenant, sacrifices, wisdom, and eschatology. One of the most certain and controversial matters in Jesus' ministry was his custom of sharing meals with tax collectors and sinners. Luke gives great prominence to banquet scenes: the sinful woman with the ointment (see 7:36–50), the discourse against the Pharisees (see 11:37–52), the teachings about etiquette and the kingdom of God (see 14:1–24), the Last Supper (see 22:1–38), and the appearances of the Risen Lord (see 24:13–49). These banquets are occasions for Jesus' teachings and for fellowship with him, and point toward the banquet that will constitute the kingdom of God.

Women: In the infancy narratives Elizabeth, Mary, and Anna represent the best of Israel's traditions. The episode of the sinful woman in 7:36–50 illustrates the close relationship between love and forgiveness. Women accompany Jesus during his public ministry (see 8:1–3), and Mary and Martha provide hospitality to him along the way (see 10:38–42). Women feature in the parables of the lost coin (see 15:8–10) and the persistent widow (see 18:1–8). There are women at the cross (see 23:49) and at Jesus' tomb (see 24:10–11). Whether Luke promotes the cause of women or "keeps them in their place" is a matter of dispute among scholars today.

Jerusalem: Luke's story of Jesus begins in the Jerusalem Temple (see 1:5–25), and as a boy he displays his wisdom there (see 2:41–52). His journey ends with his taking possession of the Temple area and exercising a ministry there (see 19:45–21:38). After his Resurrection, Jesus appears to his disciples in Judea (on the road to Emmaus) and in Jerusalem (see 24:13–49), and the gospel is to go forth from Jerusalem (see 24:47).

Eschatology: The future coming of the Son of Man is certain in fact but indefinite in time. The proper attitude in the present is watchfulness (see 12:35–48). Even though the kingdom of God is "among us" (17:20–21), its future fullness will be so sudden and obvious that the search for signs is futile (see 17:22–37). The events surrounding the coming of the glorious Son of Man (see 21:5–36) call for patient endurance (see 21:19) but are ultimately an occasion for rejoicing since "your redemption is drawing near" (21:28).

Parallel Lives: In keeping with his emphasis on Jesus as an example for others, Luke draws many parallels between Jesus in his Gospel and Paul in Acts: the prophecy about suffering (see Luke 2:29–35; Acts 9:15–16), the preface to the ministry (see Luke 4:16–30; Acts 13:14–52), the way to Jerusalem (see Luke 9:51; Acts 19:21), the passion predictions (see Luke 9:22, 44–45; Acts 20:22–24; 21:10–12), the farewell speech (see Luke 22:21–38); Acts 20:18–35), heroism in the face of death (see Luke 22:39–46; Acts 20:36–38), and the trial narratives (see Luke 22:47–23:25; Acts 21:27–26:32).

This list of Lukan motifs could easily be expanded to include such themes as Jesus the Son of God, the great reversal (see 1:46–55; 6:20–26), attitudes toward Jews and Judaism, joy, mission, and other themes. The point is that familiarity with the recurrent Lukan themes enables the reader to make connections and to see where particular passages fit within the rich tapestry that is Luke–Acts.

Possibilities and Problems

Reading the Synoptic Gospels with an eye toward the churches behind them can illuminate the spirit and shape of Christian life in the late first century A.D. And besides their value as witnesses to early church history, the Gospels also open up perspectives on church life today. As a response to suffering and persecution, Mark provides guidance and encouragement to the many churches under pressure all around the world. As the Church of the twenty-first century tries to develop a new and constructive relationship with the Jewish people, Matthew can serve as a guide to understanding the Jewish roots of the Christian movement and to recognizing the possibilities and perils(!) involved in defining itself vis-à-vis Judaism. And Luke can help a Church that is now a world religion and a global phenomenon in locating itself in history and in the world and by providing the spiritual resources for remaining faithful to the Jesus tradition and for adapting to new conditions and new challenges.

This kind of analysis also shows the diversity of situations in which the early Christians found themselves and the diversity of responses they developed. While some (Mark's community) faced persecution from the Roman authorities, others (Matthew's community) felt the need to define themselves with respect to their Jewish roots and rivals; still others (Luke's community) sought to find their place in salvation history and in the world of the Roman Empire. And the responses that each Gospel provided are different, especially in the distinctive portraits of Jesus: the suffering Messiah (Mark), the authoritative teacher (Matthew), and the prophet and example (Luke).

Despite their diversity in situations and in responses, the three Synoptic Gospels converge in going to the person of Jesus for their solutions. Thus they illustrate the process that has inspired and enlivened the Church from its beginnings. The basis of the Church is the inexhaustibly rich character of Jesus. When faced with problems or challenges, the Church goes instinctively to the person of Jesus—and what it finds in Jesus then shapes and moves it onward. What formed the Gospels and the churches behind them is the process that is sometimes called the "hermeneutical circle" constituted by the person of Jesus, traditions and texts about Jesus, and Christian experience. In fact, the image of the "spiral" is preferable to that of the "circle" in capturing the forward and upward progress of this dynamic (rather than going around in circles).

Nevertheless, there are problems connected with reading the Synoptic Gospels as witnesses to the churches behind them. This approach is often called *mirror reading*, and the idea is that the Gospels (and other New Testament books) mirror early Christian experience. But when we look in a mirror, what we see is ourselves! This fact raises the methodological problem that in mirror reading we may be only finding ourselves, not early Christian experience. In fact, a better image for this kind of reading is the "window," in which the Gospels are regarded as windows onto the life of the communities behind them.

Along the same lines, there is the problem of making the Jesus of the Gospels into the projection of early Christian needs and hopes: a suffering community needs a suffering Messiah (Mark); a Jewish community needs a Jewish teacher (Matthew); and a cosmopolitan community needs a figure in world history (Luke). But this kind of reductionism is foreign to what the early Christians thought that they were doing in bringing the person of Jesus to bear on their distinctive situations.

And finally there is the problem of (ir)relevance. While it is illuminating to consider the experience of the communities behind the Gospels and how it affected their portraits of Jesus, it is also true that their problems and issues are never exactly the same as ours. We cannot expect the Evangelists to provide an exact blueprint for the churches of the twenty-first century. Looking at history can help us to see new possibilities and to avoid the mistakes of the past. But history never repeats itself.

For Reflection and Discussion

1. How might Mark's Gospel provide guidance and encouragement for suffering Christians in the twenty-first century?

2. Is Matthew's Gospel a help or a hindrance toward better relations between Christians and Jews?

3. How might Luke's Gospel serve as a resource for developing a solid Christian spirituality?

chapter nine

THE JOHANNINE COMMUNITIES

" That they may all be one." That quotation from John 17:21 expresses the hope of all who are concerned with church unity. Indeed, it has become the biblical motto for the ecumenical movement. But however much Christians may pray and work for church unity as a goal, they are also painfully aware of how divided the churches are now and how distant real unity seems.

A look at the churches represented by the Johannine corpus in the New Testament—the Gospel of John, the three Johannine letters, and Revelation—can teach Christians today about the theological foundations for church unity and the painful realities that often attend church life in the world. Jesus' farewell discourses in John 13–17 provide an ideal picture of what the community of Jesus should and could look like. However, in John's Gospel there are also reminders of fierce struggles with "the Jews" about who best represents and preserves Israel's heritage as God's people. The letters of John, with their beautiful rhetoric about love and unity, also bear witness to a painful schism over the doctrine of the Incarnation: "They went out from us, but they did not belong to us" (1 John 2:19). And the Book of Revelation addresses suffering Christian churches trying to maintain patient endurance and to keep hope alive amid internal community problems and threats from local Jewish communities and Roman officials. Thus the Johannine writings present a collection of snapshots of first-century churches at their best and at their worst.

JOHN'S BOOK OF SIGNS: JESUS AND "THE JEWS"

Since the late second century A.D. it has been customary to refer to John's Gospel as the *spiritual Gospel*. That epithet is appropriate because the text promotes the superiority of the "spirit" over the "flesh," because it emphasizes the role of the Holy Spirit/Paraclete in guiding and defending the Church, and because it has been a major source for Christian spirituality.

In John's Gospel, Jesus is both the revealer and the revelation of God. By his actions, speeches, and dialogues, Jesus as the Word of God reveals what God wants to say to humankind. At the same time, Jesus is the revelation of God in that to look at him is to look at his heavenly Father. Modern scholars often divide John's Gospel into two parts: the Book of Signs and the Book of Glory. In the "Book of Signs" (see chapters 1–12) Jesus exercises a public ministry in which he reveals both his Father and himself as the revelation of the Father. In the "Book of Glory" (see chapters 13–21) Jesus instructs his closest followers at the Last Supper (see chapters 13–17) and enters into the decisive "hour" of his passion, death, and resurrection (see chapters 18–21)—which, despite all appearances, is his hour of glory.

John's Gospel was the product of a movement in early Christianity that was associated with a figure called, somewhat mysteriously, the *beloved disciple*. This figure may have been John the son of Zebedee, one of the first disciples called by Jesus (see Mark 1:16–20), although other candidates have been proposed (including Lazarus, someone else named John, and the community as symbolized by this personal figure). And yet the Gospel that traditionally bears the name of John is not simply an eyewitness memoir (despite 21:24–25). Rather, it seems to have been the product of a "school" or "circle" in which traditions from and about Jesus have been handed on, adapted, and embellished.

In some cases, John's Gospel provides sound historical information: Jesus' three-year public ministry, his several trips to Jerusalem, his Last Supper as a pre-Passover meal, various geographical references, etc. The discovery of the Dead Sea Scrolls has showed that much of the theological vocabulary in John's Gospel was at home in first-century Palestine. Thus, scholarly opinion about its origin has shifted from assigning it to a "Greek" milieu to placing it in a more Semitic setting (Palestine, Syria, or Transjordan). The material contained in this Gospel suggests a fairly long process of reflection and articulation, with the final text being composed in the late first century.

John's Gospel is an extraordinarily rich theological document. Its focus is Jesus as the revealer and the revelation of God. It contributes to our understanding of the Church in two important areas. First, it shows how a predominantly Jewish-Christian community tried to define Jesus and itself with respect to Judaism, in the midst of a conflict with other Jews. Second, especially in the Farewell or Last Supper discourses in John 13–17, it conveys Jesus' instructions on Christian life without the bodily presence of Jesus and on how the Johannine community gathered in Jesus' name might carry on the work of Jesus after his death.

The central part of the Book of Signs (see chapters 5–10) is structured around important festivals in the Jewish calendar. In each episode the full meaning of an important Jewish festival is found in the person and activity of Jesus. On the Sabbath, for example, (see John 5:9) Jesus heals a crippled man by the pool and so performs works on the Sabbath that only God can do. At Passover (6:4) Jesus multiplies the loaves and feeds God's people as God did previously with the manna in the wilderness in Moses' time. At

Tabernacles or Booths (7:2) Jesus reveals himself as the "living water" (7:38) and the "light of the world" (8:12), thus alluding to the water and light ceremonies that were featured at Tabernacles. And at Hanukkah or Dedication (see 10:22), Jesus is "consecrated" as Messiah and Son of God, thus recalling the rededication of the altar in the Jerusalem Temple by Judas Maccabeus in 164 B.C.

The theological principle underlying these incidents is that, from the Johannine Christian perspective, Jesus is now the decisive point of reference in defining the identity of God's people. The true children of Abraham are those who listen to the words of Jesus as the one sent from God (see John 8:31–47). The fact that all these incidents take place in Jerusalem in the environs of the Temple suggests that the calendar of Jewish feasts, especially since the Temple had been destroyed in A.D. 70, is now best carried on with reference to Jesus and in the community of Jesus.

One of the great insights about John's Gospel (which is true also for the other Gospels) is that it should be read on three levels: as texts about Jesus in his own time (around A.D. 30), as texts about the early church, and as texts about the community in and for which this Gospel was written (around A.D. 90). A good example is the narrative about the healing of the man born blind in John 9:1–41. After the account of the man's miraculous healing (a "sign" in John's vocabulary) by Jesus in 9:1–7, there is a series of dialogues: the man born blind with his neighbors (see 9:8–12) and the Pharisees (see 9:13–17); the Pharisees or "the Jews" with the man's parents (see 9:18–23) and the man himself (see 9:24–34); and Jesus with the man (see 9:35–38) and the Pharisees (see 9:39–41). These dialogues trace the progress of the man from his state of physical blindness to his spiritual insight about Jesus as the Son of Man, while showing that "the Jews" remain spiritually blind even though they think they see correctly.

At the end of the dialogue between "the Jews" and the man's parents in 9:18-23, the Johannine narrator explains why the parents were so noncommittal about how their blind son came to see: "they were afraid of the Jews; for the Jews had already agreed that anyone who confessed Jesus to be the Messiah would be put out of the synagogue" (9:22). Many interpreters today take this comment as reflecting a decision made in the late first century, at least in some locales, that those who confessed Jesus as the Messiah should be regarded as "heretics" and excluded from the Jewish synagogue (aposynagogos). For confirmation, they point to the Jews' statement to the man in 9:28: "You are his disciple, but we are disciples of Moses." They find in John 9 not only a story about Jesus the healer but also a story about the Jewish Christian Johannine community and its exclusion from fellowship with other Jews in the late first century A.D.

The term aposynagogos found in John 9:22 appears elsewhere in the

New Testament only twice, both times in John's Gospel. In John 12:42 we are told that many people who believed in Jesus did not confess him in public "for fear that they would be put out of the synagogue." And in 16:2, in his farewell discourse, Jesus warns his disciples that "they will put you out of the synagogues." The threat (or even the reality) of expulsion from the synagogue seems to have been an important feature in the life of the Johannine community addressed in the late first century.

Associated with the issue of Johannine Christians being excluded from the synagogue is the frequent use of the term "the Jews" (*hoi Ioudaioi*) in a negative and even hostile sense in John's Gospel. Although there are positive references (see John 4:22; 8:31–32; 11:31, 33, 26, 45; 12:11) and neutral references (see 2:6; 3:22), "the Jews" appear, for the most part, in negative contexts as a way of talking about the chief opponents of Jesus. Besides engaging Jesus in hostile debates, the Jews are said to have persecuted Jesus because he healed on the Sabbath (see 5:16), and to have sought to kill Jesus (see 11:8). The motif of "fear of the Jews" runs through Jesus' public ministry (see 9:22), his passion and death (see 19:38), and his resurrection appearances (see 20:19). And John's passion narrative suggests that without the pressure applied on Pontius Pilate by "the Jews," Jesus would not have been crucified. In fact, John 19:16 even gives the impression that the Jews executed Jesus: "Then he [Pilate] handed him [Jesus] over to them [the Jews] to be crucified."

The negative portrayal of "the Jews" in John's Gospel can be explained on several levels. From the perspective of sociology, the Gospel's portrayal of "the Jews" represents part of an attempt by Johannine Christians to define themselves over against other Jewish groups in the late first century, when the Jerusalem Temple had been destroyed since A.D. 70 and there was little or no Jewish sovereignty over the land of Israel. From the perspective of history, the Johannine Christians had to explain how their hero, Jesus of Nazareth, had been crucified as the "King of the Jews." They did so by claiming that the Roman prefect only acceded to pressure from "the Jews." And from the perspective of theology, John's negative characterization of "the Jews" fits well with his other dualisms (light versus darkness, heaven versus "this world," etc.) and with the early Christian effort at showing that Jesus (and not the Torah or the synagogue) represented the fullness of Judaism.

The Evangelist whom we call *John* seems to have been a Jew writing for a largely Jewish Christian community. Moreover, he was writing at a time (the late first century A.D.) when Jewish Christians were being excluded from the synagogue (see 9:22; 12:42; 16:2) and the Church was becoming an institution distinct from the synagogue. In this context, "the Jews" seem to represent those who control the synagogues and stand in opposition to the Johannine Christians. As with Matthew's Gospel, we seem to be witnesses to a Jewish "family quarrel." The problem comes when John's Gospel is taken out of its original setting in Jewish history, and its references to "the Jews" are taken to mean those Jews who attend the local synagogues. When that happens, John's Gospel can (and has) become a vehicle for anti-Semitism. Recognition of the historical context of John's references to "the Jews" is fundamental for future progress in dialogues between Christians and Jews.

JOHN'S BOOK OF GLORY: THE COMMUNITY OF THE BELOVED DISCIPLE

The first half of John's Book of Glory (see chapters 13–17) is devoted to Jesus' farewell discourse. In fact, there are several farewell discourses. After the foot washing (see 13:1–20), the five major sections concern prophecies of betrayal and the new commandment (see 13:21–38), assurances and promises (see 14:1–31), love and hate (see 15:1–16:4), Jesus' departure and return (see 16:5–33), and the prayer of God's Son (see 17:1–26). These discourses, which probably were developed over time within the Johannine community, are set at Jesus' Last Supper on the night before he died. Their primary theme is how Jesus' disciples are to carry on after his exaltation to the Father, when he is no longer present among them as he was during his public ministry.

In this framework, Jesus' farewell discourses provide advice to the Church in all ages, since without the earthly Jesus the Church is in the same situation as Jesus' first disciples would soon be after his death. The advice that Jesus gives in John 13–17 is expressed more in terms of spirituality than in structures and offices. Eight themes contribute especially to our understanding of the ideal Church.

First, the saving significance of Jesus' life, death, and resurrection must be appreciated and accepted by his disciples. The foot washing (see 13:1–20) that precedes the farewell discourses first of all symbolizes the service that Jesus will perform through his death on the cross. Peter's reluctance to accept that service is a negative example, and so Jesus admonishes him: "Unless I wash you, you have no share with me" (13:8). There may be an allusion to baptism here. Once having washed his disciples' feet, Jesus goes on to point to himself ("your Lord and teacher") as a positive example of the humble service of others. The Church of Jesus Christ must accept Jesus' saving work and imitate his example of the humble service of others.

Second, love is the spirit that is to prevail in the community of Jesus. The farewells begin with what Jesus calls a "new commandment": "that you love one another" (13:34). This love is based on the love that Jesus has shown to his followers: "Just as I have loved you, you also should love one another." And the love that his disciples show to one another is a sign by which outsiders will come to recognize the disciples of Jesus (see 13:35). Later, in 15:12–17, Jesus repeats the love commandment and challenges his followers to take love to its ultimate measure (as he will soon do): "No one has greater love than this, to lay down one's life for one's friends" (15:13). The Church of Jesus Christ must be a community of love.

Third, faith is essential to the community of Jesus. The object of faith is Jesus and his revelation of the Father: "Do you believe that I am in the Father and the Father is in me?" (14:11). Throughout the Fourth Gospel, Jesus is both the revealer and the revelation of God, but he does not function as a separate or subordinate entity. Rather, he and the Father are one. The Church of Jesus Christ is based on the conviction that Jesus and the Father are one, and that Jesus is the way by which people can come to God: "I am the way, and the truth, and the life. No one comes to the Father except through me" (14:6).

Fourth, the Holy Spirit/Paraclete will guide and direct the movement begun by Jesus. The farewell discourses are punctuated by Jesus' promises about sending a figure called the *Paraclete*. The Greek word *parakletos* may be translated variously as "helper," "consoler," "advocate," and "counselor." It also can refer to a defense attorney who pleads the case of someone who is on trial. In John 14:15–17 Jesus states that "I will ask the Father, and he will give you another Advocate, to be with you forever." To call the Holy Spirit "another Advocate" means that, in a sense, the Spirit will take the place of the earthly Jesus and will carry on the work of Jesus within the community of believers: "he abides with you, and he will be in you." According to 14:26, the Spirit/Paraclete will teach the community and remind them of what Jesus taught. In 15:26 the Spirit of truth will bear witness or testify on behalf of Jesus. According to 16:7–15, the Spirit will convict "the world" in the sense of bringing to light its failure to accept Jesus as the revealer and the revelation of God and its condemning Jesus to death. Thus the Holy Spirit/Paraclete takes Jesus' place as the abiding presence of God in the community, teaches and keeps alive the wisdom of Jesus, bears witness to Jesus, and convicts the world of sin. The Church of Jesus Christ is sustained and directed by the Spirit/Paraclete.

Fifth, the followers of Jesus continue to exist in a relationship of vitality and dependence. In 15:5 Jesus proclaims: "I am the vine, you are the branches." As the vine, Jesus is the source of life for all the "branches" who exist in and from him. At the same time, there is no abiding in Jesus without bearing fruit (in good deeds), nor is there any bearing fruit without abiding in him (in faith and love). What animates the true vine (whose vinedresser is the Father) and its branches is love: "As the Father has loved me, so I have loved you; abide in my love" (15:9). The imagery here is analogous to that of the Body of Christ in Ephesians, where Christ is the head and the Church is his body. Both patterns identify Christ as the directing and animating source of life for those who are "in Christ." The Church of Jesus Christ receives its life from Christ the vine.

Sixth, Jesus' disciples are urged to be people of hope—even in the midst of sorrow and persecution. They are sorrowful because Jesus has told them about his imminent departure: "A little while, and you will no longer see me" (16:16a). But they can be hopeful because Jesus promises: "and again a little while, and you will see me" (16:16b). Thus they are assured of the Second Coming, or Parousia, of Jesus, and so their sorrow will be only temporary. Likewise, the disciples may be frightened because of the perse- cution they will meet from outsiders: "In the world you will face persecution" (16:33b). Here "the world" refers to those forces—human and superhuman—that are opposed to God and to God's Son. But they can be peaceful because "I have conquered the world" (16:33c). By way of anticipation, Jesus prepares them for understanding his passion, death, and resurrection not as a defeat but as a victory over Sin, Death, and the Evil One. The Church of Jesus Christ is a place of hope and peace.

Seventh, the community of Jesus has a mission. In John 17 Jesus prays as God's Son on behalf of himself (see 17:1–5), his disciples (see 17:6–19), and those who become disciples through them (see 17:20–26). In praying for his disciples, Jesus asks his Father to protect them from the dangers to which they are exposed from "the world." And Jesus promises to send his disciples on a mission into the world. As with so many other themes, Jesus traces the motif of mission back to his relationship with God the Father: "As you have sent me into the world, so I have sent them into the world" (17:18). The Church of Jesus Christ has a mission in the world.

Eighth, Jesus prays for unity within his community: "that they may all be one" (17:21a). The basis for their unity is the unity that exists between Jesus and his heavenly Father: "As you, Father, are in me, and I am in you, may they also be in us" (17:21b). As was the case with love, so unity will serve as a sign by which outsiders may recognize the community of Jesus (see 17:21c). Jesus prays again that "they may be completely one" (17:23), and speaks of their unity as a reflection of his own unity with the Father ("I in them and you in me") and as a proof to the world that the Father has loved Jesus and sent him forth. The Church of Jesus Christ is to be one, and its unity is rooted in the unity between Father and Son.

The second half of John's Book of Glory (see chapters 18–21) tells the story of Jesus' passion, death, resurrection, and exaltation. The one who is "lifted up" on the cross is also the one who is lifted up to his heavenly

Father. What appears on the surface to be a shameful defeat is, to the eyes of faith, a glorious victory. When Pilate asks cynically "What is truth?" (18:38), Truth Incarnate is standing before him in the person of Jesus the Word of God. When Pilate condemns Jesus sarcastically as the "King of the Jews" in 18:28–19:16, it really is the King of the Jews who is on trial. And when "the Jews" assert that "we have no king but the emperor" (19:15), they ironically turn their backs on their True King.

The community of the Beloved Disciple emerges at the foot of the cross (see 19:25–27). This community consists of three women (the Mother of Jesus, Mary the wife of Clopas, and Mary Magdalene) and "the disciple whom he loved." From the cross Jesus commends the Beloved Disciple to his mother ("Woman, here is your son") and his mother to the Beloved Disciple ("Here is your mother"), and together they form a circle of compassionate love.

Later, the Beloved Disciple outraces Peter to the tomb of Jesus (see 20:1–10), and he seems to grasp why the tomb is empty: "Then the other disciple, who reached the tomb first, also went in, and he saw and believed" (20:8). When he saw the tidy tomb (see 20:6–7), he perceived that Jesus had been raised from the dead. On Easter evening (the Johannine Pentecost), the disciples receive the gift of the Holy Spirit from the Risen Jesus: "he breathed on them and said to them, 'Receive the Holy Spirit'" (20:22).

Although John 21 may not have been part of the original form of John's Gospel, it certainly comes from the Johannine school and now stands as a fitting conclusion, especially with its episodes about the catch of 153 fish ("fishers of men") in 21:1–14 and the commissioning of Peter by the Risen Jesus for pastoral ministry ("feed my lambs") in 21:15–19. The Fourth Gospel closes in 21:20–23 with the Risen Jesus' comment about the death of the Beloved Disciple in relation to his own parousia: "If it is my will that he remain until I come, what is that to you?" Finally, John 21:24–25 identifies the Beloved Disciple as the one on whose testimony this Gospel has been based. In that sense, the Church that the Fourth Gospel describes is the community of the Beloved Disciple.

THE JOHANNINE LETTERS: THE STORY CONTINUES

John's Gospel and the three Johannine letters are witnesses to a movement in early Christianity described by modern scholars as the Johannine "school" or "circle" and as the community of the Beloved Disciple. This movement developed its own theological traditions and vocabulary, and had a distinctive history independent of the Synoptic and Pauline traditions. From a sociological perspective, it looked like a sect or a *conventicle* at the margins of Judaism. While open to the world in its hope that "they may all be one" (John 17:21), at the same time it was closed in on itself in the sense that it very likely understood the love commandment as referring primarily, if not exclusively, to the members of its own Christian community.

The Johannine community had its beginnings with the Beloved Disciple, most likely a historical figure (rather than a symbol) who once had been a follower of John the Baptist and then became a disciple of Jesus. He may have been John the son of Zebedee. This Johannine group consisted mainly of Christian Jews who were part of the Jewish synagogue and not alienated from their Jewish heritage. Their traditions about Jesus took the form of miracle stories (the basis for the Book of Signs), discourses (the basis for the long speeches in the Book of Signs and in the farewell discourses), and a narrative about Jesus' passion, death, and resurrection.

The destruction of the Jerusalem Temple in A.D. 70 presented all Jews, including the Johannine Christians, with a crisis about Jewish identity and survival. Various groups came forward: military revolutionaries like the Zealots, apocalyptists like the authors of *4 Ezra* and *2 Baruch*, Torah-observant teachers like the early rabbis, and Christians Jews like the Johannine (and Matthean) Christians. As the different groups put forward their rival claims before other Jews, there developed an increasing hostility between the synagogue and the Church. This, in turn, issued in the forcible expulsion of Christian Jews from the synagogue and the labeling of them as *apostates*. At the same time, Christians Jews began to define themselves in opposition to the synagogue, which helps explain John's expression "the Jews" (and Matthew's phrase "their synagogues").

Near the end of the first century A.D. a member of the Johannine school put the Gospel into something similar to what has come down to us. It was in part an attempt by Christian Jews who had been expelled from the synagogue to define themselves over against members of the Jewish synagogue and even those Christian Jews who tried to "straddle the fence" and remain in the synagogue (see 9:22). There were also internal problems that the Gospel tried to address: the disappearance of the original disciples of the earthly Jesus (see 21:23), and doctrinal disputes about the humanity of Jesus (see 1:14).

The three Johannine letters—1, 2, and 3 John—help us to see what problems the Johannine Christians encountered in the course of the community's history and how they dealt with them. Although none of these letters bears the name "John" (two are from the "elder," see 2 John v. 1 and 3 John v. 1), their vocabulary and content mark them as coming from the Johannine school. Written around A.D. 100 (after the Gospel), they are documents of a living community with real problems.

The First Letter of John is an exhortation about Christian life in the light of Jesus' life, death, and resurrection. Its language and style, for the most part, match those of John's Gospel. A careful reading shows that there had been a traumatic split within the Johannine community: "They went out from us, but they did not belong to us; for if they had belonged to us, they would have remained with us" (1 John 2:19). The occasion for this exodus from the Johannine community seems to have been a dispute about the human nature of Christ: "every spirit that confesses that Jesus Christ has come in the flesh is from God, and every spirit that does not confess Jesus is not from God" (4:2–3). It seems that those who had departed refused to accept the affirmation that "the Word became flesh" (John 1:14).

The Second Letter of John is from "the elder to the elect lady and her children" (v. 1). The final comment about "the children of your elect sister" (v. 13) indicates that it was a matter of the elder (John) writing from one church to another. The principal problem glimpsed in 2 John is the schism that occurred over the Incarnation (see John 1:14; 1 John 4:2–3). In one of the saddest verses in the New Testament, the elder writes: "Many deceivers have gone out into the world, those who do not confess that Jesus Christ has come in the flesh; any such person is a deceiver and the antichrist" (v. 7).

In the Third Letter of John, the elder addresses Gaius, and goes on to praise him and his community and to commend Demetrius. In between, however, he strongly criticizes a man named Diotrephes (see vv. 9–10). He accuses Diotrephes of not acknowledging the authority of the elder, spreading false charges against the elder, refusing to welcome his emissaries, preventing those who were willing to offer them hospitality from doing so, and expelling such persons from the church. Here we have a Johannine community in which a leader called Diotrephes is challenging the authority of John the elder and treating badly those associated with him. Thus, besides the doctrinal dispute about the Incarnation, there also were personal conflicts in the Johannine community.

REVELATION: HOPE FOR SUFFERING CHRISTIANS

The Book of Revelation has traditionally been placed in the Johannine corpus along with the Gospel of John and the letters of John. Most scholars today, however, prefer to treat it separately because of its very different language, content, and theological perspectives. Whatever the connections, they are not very compelling. The most obvious link is the attribution to "John." But John was a common name among first-century Jews and Christians, and so the author may simply be just another man named John.

There is a value, however, in including the Book of Revelation here in a treatment of the Johannine churches. This work provides further insights into the problems that arose in early Christian communities and how and why early Christians hoped to be delivered from their various tribulations. Because it offers hope for suffering Christians, marginal and oppressed peoples throughout the centuries have understood it best.

Revelation is an apocalypse that is a prophecy in letter form. As an apocalypse, it provides visions about the heavenly realm and about the future. In it, the Risen Christ instructs John to write about "what you have seen, what is, and what is to take place after this" (1:19). Written in the late first century A.D., Revelation first presents a vision of the Risen Christ (see chapter 1) and addresses problems that had arisen in seven churches located in western Asia Minor (see chapters 2–3). Then in the main part (see chapters 4–22), there is a series of eschatological scenarios arranged usually in sevens that purport to reveal what will happen in the "last days." The whole book is presented as a vision granted to John in exile on the island of Patmos, off the coast of Asia Minor (Turkey).

The problems that had arisen in the seven churches of Asia Minor are listed in the seven "letters" from the Risen Christ to the "angel" of each church. The letters contain five basic elements: the address, the identification of the Risen Christ as the speaker, the reasons for praise and blame, a call to hear, and a promise to those who remain faithful and so "conquer."

The sections devoted to praise and blame are most important for our purposes. The church at Ephesus (see Revelation 2:1–7) is praised for its patient endurance and its discernment regarding false teachers, but is criticized for abandoning "the love you had at first." The church at Smyrna (see 2:8–11) is encouraged to remain faithful in the face of opposition from the "synagogue of Satan," a disparaging reference to the local Jewish community. The church at Pergamum (see 2:12–17) is praised for their martyr Antipas, but warned against eating food sacrificed to pagan gods and practicing "fornication" (that is, idolatry). The church at Thyatira (see 2:18–29) is criticized for tolerating a false teacher here given the name "Jezebel." The church at Sardis (see 3:1–6) is judged to be spiritually dead. The church at Philadelphia (see 3:7–13) is praised for its patient endurance in the face of suffering instigated by "the synagogue of Satan." And the church at Laodicea (see 3:14–21) is described as "lukewarm" in its piety and as proud for the wrong reasons.

The great virtue displayed by some of these churches is patient endurance in the face of suffering. The great internal problems are spiritual tepidity and toleration of "false teachers" who allowed eating food sacrificed to pagan gods and participating in the worship of the Roman emperor as a god and the goddess Roma as a personification of the empire. This cult seems to have been promoted by a local political and/or religious official in western Asia Minor (see Revelation 13:1–18). Some Christian teachers like "Jezebel" apparently found no obstacle to Christian participation, but the Book of Revelation condemns it as "fornication" (idolatry) and strongly prohibits any such participation. And there is also a tense relationship with the local Jewish communities ("the synagogue of Satan"), probably about who the "real Jews" are.

Revelation addresses Christian communities living under pressures coming from various directions. The main part of the book (see chapters 4–22) explains why these suffering Christians should practice patient endurance and maintain their hope for their future vindication. The ground of Christian hope is the Risen Christ—the slain Lamb and the firstborn from the dead—who alone in the heavenly court (see chapters 4–5) is found worthy to open the seven seals on the book that will disclose and put in motion the series of events that will issue in the fullness of God's kingdom.

The central part of Revelation features three series of seven events: the opening of the seven seals (see 6:1–8:1), the blowing of the seven trumpets (see 8:2–9:21), and the pouring out of the seven bowls (see 15:1–16:21). Each one of these scenarios affirms the sovereignty of God and of the Lamb, the defeat of evil forces, and the ultimate vindication of the righteous. Their message is that God and the Lamb are in charge and are guiding the course of history toward fullness of life in God's kingdom for those who have remained faithful.

These sequences of sevens are punctuated by scenes that anticipate the final victory: the sealing or protecting of the 144,000 representing God's people (see 7:1–17); the victory of God and the Lamb over the "unholy trinity" consisting of Satan, the beast from the sea (the emperor), and the beast from the land (the local official promoting the cult of the emperor and the goddess Roma) in 12:1–14:20; and the fall of Babylon/Rome in 17:1–19:10. The last and most decisive series of seven eschatological events (19:11–21:8) culminates in the vision of the new heaven and the new earth. What remains is the New Jerusalem (see 21:9–22:5), where God and the Lamb reign forever over the righteous: "the throne of God and of the Lamb will be in it, and his servants will worship him" (22:3). These various eschatological scenarios served to keep alive the hope of suffering Christians and made possible their patient endurance during their tribulations.

Possibilities and Problems

The Johannine corpus can and should play an important role in current conversations between Christians and Jews. The dominant approach to John's Gospel today views it as the product of a largely Jewish Christian community defining itself over against other Jewish communities. As such, it provides a window onto a "family quarrel" in the late first century A.D. that had as its focus claims about Jesus. In the Book of Revelation the churches and the local Jewish communities were fighting over which group best represented the Jewish tradition. These conflicts sometimes descended to polemics ("the Jews") and even nastiness ("the synagogue of Satan"). Today, the Johannine corpus provides challenges to both Christians and Jews as they study a decisive point in their history and try to reconceive and renew their relationship in the twenty-first century.

The farewell discourses in John 13–17 provide a checklist of ideal characteristics against which every Christian community might examine and evaluate itself. These characteristics are acceptance of Jesus' saving work and imitation of his example of the humble service of others, love, faith, openness to the Holy Spirit, a vital relationship with Jesus, hope, mission, and unity. The instruction by the Johannine Jesus to his disciples remains the best advice for Christian communities in the twenty-first century.

The Johannine writings also reveal problems that early Christians encountered from outside forces or brought upon themselves. In John's Gospel, for example, there is external opposition from "the Jews" and "the world." In the Johannine letters there is a doctrinal dispute about the Incarnation and a schism, as well as personal problems between Christian leaders and disputes about authority in the Church. In Revelation apathy and false teachers within the churches as well as opposition from Jews and Roman officials are the principal problems. A major issue seems to have been pressure to participate in what were perceived as pagan rituals. Recognition of the problems in the Johannine communities can guide and encourage Christians today.

One obvious problem presented by the Johannine texts is their potential for encouraging anti-Judaism. When taken out of their first-century "family quarrel" context, the Johannine passages about "the Jews" and "the synagogue of Satan" can be inflammatory and dangerous. Both Christians and Jews need to understand and respect the historical setting of these texts.

Another problem is that the ideal characteristics of a Christian community according to John 13–17 may be too "theological" and more appropriate for a small group or sect than for the larger "catholic" Church. Moreover, there is not much evidence for attention to community structures and church offices in the literature of the Johannine communities. Can such a community last, or does it necessarily dissolve quickly?

And while it is important to recognize that the Johannine Christians had serious problems and needed to learn from their experiences, as do Christians today, it is also true that history does not repeat itself. The challenges facing first-century Christians, while often illuminating today, are not exactly the same as those we may face in the twenty-first century.

For Reflection and Discussion

1. How would you explain the use of the term *the Jews* in John's Gospel to a group of Jewish friends? How do you think they might respond?

2. To what extent does your church fit the profile of the ideal Christian community set forth in John 13–17? What is present? What is lacking?

3. What are the problems facing your church? What can you learn from the Johannine Christians? What is different?

chapter ten

THE CHURCH IN THE WORLD

In his letter to the emperor Trajan (see *Epistles* 10.96), Pliny described the results of his investigation of the Christian movement in his province. He learned that they met on Sunday at dawn, sang a hymn to Christ, swore to observe what sounds like the Ten Commandments, and shared "food of an ordinary kind." Despite the paucity and innocence of these findings, Pliny was greatly alarmed by what he called a "depraved and excessive superstition," and felt obliged to "check and cure it" before it spread further in the cities, villages, and rural districts of the province. He apparently regarded Christians as a threat to the traditional Roman religions and to the social fabric of the empire.

The world in which the early church took shape was the Roman Empire. This chapter explores some dimensions of that reality and its significance for understanding how the first Christians made their way in that world. In particular, it considers how the early Christians related to the Roman imperial government, how they related to one another as men and women, where they derived their moral values, and why they attracted new members.

CHURCH AND STATE

The expression "church and state" is really not appropriate to describe first-century conditions. The *state* here was the Roman Empire, covering most of the Mediterranean world. While working with local leaders like the Herod family, the Romans could and did intervene quickly and brutally when the local situation seemed to be getting out of control (as in Judea in 63 B.C. and in A.D. 4, 66, and 132). Their system of roads and their campaigns against the pirates at sea made it possible to travel more easily and safely from place to place (but see 2 Corinthians 11:25–27). They also facilitated the transport of food, natural resources, and luxury goods to Rome as the imperial capital (see Revelation 18:1–20). With regard to the Roman Empire, the term *state* actually says too little.

Likewise, in the case of the early Christian movement, *church* says too much. In *The Rise of Christianity*, sociologist Rodney Stark estimates that by A.D. 40 there were 1,000 Christians in the world, by A.D. 50 there were 1,400, and by A.D. 100 there were 7,530 (which represents 0.0126% of the

Roman Empire). From such a tiny minority, one could hardly expect a social-political theory or political activism. Moreover, many Christians shared the belief that "this world" was passing away and would soon be replaced by the fullness of the kingdom of God (see Romans 13:11–12). Thus, the New Testament contains no developed doctrine of "church and state," nor could the early Christians have been expected to produce one. Instead, we find several different attitudes or perspectives that reflect, to a large extent, the particular situation in which Jesus or members of his movement found themselves.

That Jesus was executed as the "King of the Jews" (see Mark 15:26) has inspired suspicions that he was, in fact, a political revolutionary. These suspicions have been fueled by the fact that Galilee in the first century was the home of several Jewish revolutionary movements and by the presence of Simon the Cananaean (which can be interpreted as "Zealot party member") and Judas Iscariot (which can be understood as derived from the Latin *sicarius* or "dagger man") in Jesus' inner circle of the Twelve. But neither interpretation is certain. Furthermore, almost all of Jesus' teachings (e.g., "turn the other cheek") are against violence and cannot be taken as revolutionary in the political or military sense. Moreover, while Pontius Pilate probably did regard Jesus as another fanatical Jewish messiah figure ("King of the Jews"), he made no effort to arrest the followers of Jesus and so to squash his movement. Finally, there is no evidence that the Jewish Christians of Palestine joined in the revolt against Rome in A.D. 66–74. Indeed, the only report we have says that before the action began, the Jerusalem Christians escaped to Pella in the Decapolis, one of the "ten cities" in northern Jordan and southern Syria that had undergone Greek and Roman influences.

Nevertheless, while the evidence for the thesis that Jesus was a political-military revolutionary, or at least sympathetic to such movements, is weak, there was certainly a political dimension to Jesus' proclamation of the kingdom of God. If God is the real king, the Roman emperor is not. If enough people came to believe in the kingship of the God of Israel, they would eventually cease to respect and obey their local kings and even the Roman emperor.

Mark 12:13–17 is often taken as the classic text about "church and state" in the New Testament. Its ambiguity reflects the dangerous position in which Jesus and his first followers found themselves in first-century Palestine. In this controversy story, the Pharisees (whose political views wavered between active involvement and relative passivity, depending on who was in power) and the Herodians (by name, supporters of the Herod family) set out to trap Jesus. After trying to soften up Jesus by flattery ("we know that you are sincere," 12:14), they ask their carefully devised question: "Is it lawful to pay taxes to the emperor or not?" (12:14). If Jesus says "yes," he will lose favor with Jewish nationalists and activists. If he says "no," the Herodians will see to his arrest as a dangerous revolutionary.

Instead of answering the question directly, Jesus asks for a coin bearing the image and inscription of the Roman emperor. When he gets his questioners to acknowledge that the coin belongs to the Roman emperor, Jesus delivers a saying that amazes the onlookers by its cleverness: "Give to the emperor the things that are the emperor's, and to God the things that are God's" (12:17). Since his questioners were using the emperor's coins and so were part of the emperor's system already, they should pay the emperor's tax. However, by reminding his questioners that they have (even greater) obligations to God, Jesus is also calling attention to the ultimate sovereignty of God that extends even to the emperor and his system. Thus Jesus eludes the trap by an attitude that suggests both cautious cooperation with the empire and an affirmation of God's rule over everyone and everything.

In writing to the Christians at Rome, Paul encourages them to cooperate with their government officials: "Let every person be subject to the governing authorities" (Romans 13:1). He goes on to say that these authorities have been put in place by God, that those who are good and righteous have nothing to fear from them, and that Christians should pay their taxes to the state (see Romans 13:1–7). In short, Christians should be good citizens in the Roman Empire. Paul's positive attitude is echoed and developed in 1 Peter 2:13 ("For the Lord's sake accept the authority of every human institution, whether of the emperor as supreme . . . ") and in 1 Timothy 2:1–2 ("I urge that supplications, prayers, intercessions, and thanksgivings be made for everyone, for kings and all who are in high positions . . . ").

While on the surface the position taken by Paul and others in the Pauline school encourages acceptance of the Roman Empire and cooperation with its officials, some historical factors need to be taken into account. Jews and Jewish Christians had only recently been allowed to return to Rome after having been expelled under the emperor Claudius as troublemakers. There is then perhaps a pragmatic dimension ("Let's be on our best behavior") to Paul's teaching. Moreover, Paul and other early Christians probably did not expect the Roman Empire to last long ("the night is far gone, the day is near," Romans 13:12). And so Paul might have been counseling short-term acceptance rather than working out a definitive Christian position on church and state. Finally, Paul may well have been giving his advice against the assumption of ideal (and even) utopian conditions where government officials ruled wisely and justly, and so really could be understood as agents of God. But conditions in the Roman Empire were not always ideal.

From patristic times (with Irenaeus), the Book of Revelation has been assigned a date late in the reign of the emperor Domitian (A.D. 81–96). The occasion was the zealous promotion of the cults of the emperor and the goddess Roma by a local religious and/or political leader in western Asia Minor. It appears that Christians were being forced into participation as a civic duty. From the perspective of John the prophet, any involvement in these cults constituted "fornication," a biblical code word for idolatry. When the local official tried to get Christians to take part, some resisted to the point of martyrdom (see Revelation 2:13) and so were celebrated as the real victors (see 7:1–17). Those Christian teachers who counseled cooperation and participation were dismissed by John as false prophets and one even as "Jezebel" (see 2:20–23).

The central section of Revelation (see 12:1–14:20) describes the defeat of the Dragon/Satan in heaven and his subsequent efforts to persecute the Church on earth. In these efforts, Satan is abetted by two other members of the "unholy trinity": the beast from the sea (the emperor) and the beast from the earth (the local official who was promoting these cults). The result will be the vindication of the martyrs (the 144,000 who "have not defiled themselves with women" = those who have not committed idolatry) and the fall of "Babylon the great" (= Rome).

Revelation 17 depicts Roma as a "great whore who is seated on many waters" sitting on "a scarlet beast that was full of blasphemous names" (the emperor Domitian was called "my lord and my god" in some circles). In case there is any doubt about the object of this parody, the seven heads of the beast are equated in 17:9 with "seven mountains" (the seven hills of Rome) and the woman is identified as "the great city that rules over the kings of the earth" (17:18).

So there are several attitudes displayed toward the Roman Empire in various New Testament texts: the cautious ambiguity manifested by Jesus, the apparent acceptance of and cooperation with the empire promoted by Paul and his followers, and the nonviolent resistance proposed by John the prophet. Each of these teachings presupposes a different historical-political situation, and no one of them represents the definitive Christian position on "church and state."

MEN AND WOMEN

According to the famous baptismal slogan quoted by Paul in Galatians 3:28, there is "no longer male and female." In the Greco-Roman world of the first century, that was a radical (if not absurd) statement. One can wonder whether it was meant to be taken literally, or was it simply the assertion of a spiritual unity in Christ that transcends gender differences.

The Mediterranean society in which the Church came to be was very conscious of gender and class differences. At the top of the social and political pyramid were a few wealthy and powerful citizens, almost all men, under the patronage of the Roman emperor. At the base of the pyramid were large numbers of slaves and former slaves, farmers, and other laborers. In between, a relatively small group of "retainers" played a mediating role.

Within the household, the husband or father served as the head or *paterfamilias*. Women who were citizens married into a household and oversaw its smooth running, while fulfilling their primary function of bearing children. Slave women were regarded as property and were subject to sexual abuse. Women from the lower classes served as vendors, and some, like Lydia ("a dealer in purple cloth," Acts 16:14), came to manage their own businesses. Most women married young and bore children at an early age, and many died by forty, mainly due to complications associated with childbirth.

There were some pagan religious movements in which women served as priestesses, and there were some festivals primarily for women. In private religious associations, women could and did function as leaders. The life of Jewish women in the New Testament era, however, fit the general pattern that was dominant throughout the Roman Empire, with the added responsibility to observe the ritual purity rules laid down in the Torah or deduced from it. Moreover, they could not act as priests or Levites. All these women lived in a hierarchical society that was very conscious of gender, class, and social status.

In this historical context, the prominence given to women in the early Jesus movement is striking. According to Luke 8:1–3, Jesus and the Twelve were accompanied on their journeys by "Mary called Magdalene . . . and Joanna, the wife of Herod's steward Chuza, and Susanna, and many others who provided for them out of their resources." Jesus shows compassion toward sinful women (see Luke 7:36–50; John 7:53–8:11), accepts hospitality from women (see Luke 10:38–42; John 11:1–44), tells stories in which women are prominent characters (see Luke 15:8–10; 18:1–8), and heals women who are suffering physical ailments (see Mark 1:29–31; 5:21–43; Luke 13:10–17). In one case, a Gentile woman apparently teaches Jesus a lesson about the scope of his own mission beyond Israel (see Mark 7:24–31; Matthew 15:21–28).

At the cross, most of the disciples who remain faithful are women (see Mark 15:40–41; Matthew 27:55–56; Luke 23:49; John 19:25–27); those who first discover Jesus' tomb empty on Easter morning are women (see Mark 16:1–8; Matthew 28:1–8; Luke 24:1–12; John 20:1); and some of those women then receive an appearance of the Risen Jesus (see Matthew 28:9–10; John 20:11–18). In the Lukan infancy narratives, two women, Elizabeth and Mary, are major characters who represent all that is good in their Jewish tradition, with Mary emerging as the model disciple in Luke-Acts (see Luke 1:26–56; 2:51; 8:21; 11:27–28; Acts 1:14).

In this historical setting, Jesus' absolute prohibition of divorce had particular significance as a protection for women. On the basis of Deuteronomy 24:1–4, a husband could divorce his wife by writing "a bill of divorce" and sending her away. In Jesus' time there was a debate among Jewish teachers, not about the legality of divorce but about the grounds on which a husband could divorce a wife. The ambiguous phrase "something objectionable" in Deuteronomy 24:1 was interpreted strictly by Shammai to mean sexual misconduct on the wife's part and more liberally by Hillel and Aqiba to cover whatever the husband wished. Jesus cut through this debate and forbade divorce entirely (see Luke 16:18; Matthew 5:31–32; 19:3–12; Mark 10:2–12; 1 Corinthians 7:10–11). Whatever other consequences this teaching has had, it did give married women some degree of security (assuming that it was observed) from being thrown out of the house on the husband's whim. (For some modifications of this absolute teaching, however, see Matthew 5:32; 19:9; 1 Corinthians 7:12–16.)

The prominence of women in the Pauline mission is nicely illustrated by the personal greetings in Roman 16:1–16. There are many female names on this list: Phoebe, Prisca, Mary, Junias, Tryphaena, Tryphosa, Persis, Julia, and Olympas. In 16:1–2 Phoebe is described as a "deacon" (*diakonos*) of the church at Cenchreae and Paul's *prostatis* ("patroness") while in 16:7. Junia is said to be "prominent among the apostles" and so an "apostle" herself according to most interpreters today. In 1 Corinthians 11:2–16, Paul assumes that women pray and prophesy in the assembly (see 11:5), but insists that women should look like women in their hairstyles (or head coverings), perhaps because Galatians 3:28 ("no longer male and female") was being taken too literally. The view that women should be silent in the assembly (see 1 Corinthians 14:33b–35) is best taken not as Paul's own command (compare 11:5) but as a position promoted by some Corinthians and rejected by Paul in 14:36.

The Deuteropauline letters display a reversion to more generally accepted cultural norms regarding the place of women in society. The "household codes" direct wives to be subject to their husbands (see Colossians 4:18; Ephesians 5:22; 1 Peter 3:1), while noting that both are subject to the Lord and have mutual responsibilities toward each other. Likewise, women are exhorted to dress modestly and be distinguished for their good works (see 1 Timothy 2:9–10; 1 Peter 3:2–6). There is a prohibition against a woman publicly teaching and having authority over her husband (see 1 Timothy 2:12), a rule traced back to Adam and Eve (see Genesis 2:7, 21–22; 3:1–6). The expectation, according to 1 Timothy 2:15, is that women "will be saved through childbearing, provided they continue in faith and love and holiness, with modesty." Nevertheless, the same letter lays out detailed regulations for the care of "widows who are really widows" (5:3–16). All these Deuteropauline texts manifest tendencies toward seeking order within the household and external respectability for the church in the broader society.

Several Pauline texts refer to homosexuality in negative ways. While homosexual behavior was acceptable in some circles in the Greco-Roman world, Jews took a more negative attitude on the basis of Leviticus 18:22 (as well as 20:13): "You shall not lie with a male as with a woman; it is an abomination." Among those excluded from the kingdom of God, according to 1 Corinthians 6:9 (see also 1 Timothy 1:10), are *malakoi* ("effeminates") and *arsenokoitai* ("those who sleep with males"). In his meditation on the power of sin over the Gentile world (see Romans 1:18–32), Paul includes a section on homosexual behavior as unnatural and enslaving (see 1:26–27). Today, however, scholars debate the precise meaning of the terms as well as the validity of the assumptions held by Paul and his contemporaries about nature and power in sex and about homosexuality itself (orientation or behavior?).

The New Testament does speak directly about abortion. However, the Greek text of Exodus 21:22–23 ("if it be perfectly formed, he shall give life for life, eye for eye") and *Didache* 2:2 ("do not kill a fetus by abortion") forbid it explicitly. Philo of Alexandria argued against it lest the human race die out. No Jewish or early Christian writer defends it, and the silence about it probably means that it went beyond their sensibilities (which was not the case among their pagan contemporaries).

EARLY CHRISTIAN VALUES

There is much continuity between the core values of the Jesus movement and those of the early churches. Indeed, we know about the former values mainly because they were transmitted orally and in written form by early Christians. Those core values included closeness to God, the primacy of love, concern for marginal persons, radical ethical stances, and forgiveness—and they remain foundational for the Church in any age.

The early Christians regarded the Old Testament as an authoritative source of theological and moral teachings. Even though Paul insisted that Gentiles who became Christians did not have to observe those parts of the Torah that especially distinguished Jews from other people (circumcision, purity and food law, Sabbath observance), he nonetheless appealed frequently to Old Testament texts as a source and confirmation of his own teachings. While Mark deduced that Jesus "declared all foods clean" (7:19), he begins his Gospel by quoting Old Testament texts (Malachi 3:1 and Isaiah 40:3) to show that God willed for John the Baptist to prepare the way for Jesus.

Early Christians also freely borrowed social and oral values from the pagan society around them. One example is the use of the household codes found in Colossians 3:18–4:1 and Ephesians 5:21–6:9, which reflect not only the structures of the household in Greco-Roman society but also the fondness for hierarchy, order, and male dominance. The various lists of vices and virtues (see Romans 1:29–31; 1 Corinthians 5:10–11; 6:9–10; Galatians 5:16–24; etc.) contain many items that would have been affirmed by pagan moralists of the day. The natural virtues required of bishops and deacons, according to 1 Timothy 3:1–13, demand that these church officers be good examples according to the moral standards of the wider pagan society.

What teachings the early Christians took from Jesus, the Old Testament, and Greco-Roman society are now found embedded in the context of the twenty-seven books of the New Testament. These books are not simply anthologies of wise teachings excerpted from various sources. Rather, the teachings are presented in the context of narratives about Jesus (Gospels) and the apostles (Acts), as well as instructions from great church leaders to their communities (Epistles and Revelation). Moreover, these teachings appear in a theological framework according to which God our Father in heaven loves us all (see Matthew 5:45), the death and resurrection of his Son Jesus has made possible right relationship with God for all (justification), and all will be judged according to their deeds and rewarded or punished accordingly. The core values of the early Christians flow from and are part of a story and a theological vision.

A sample of the core values of Jesus and the early Christians can be found in the Sermon on the Mount in Matthew 5–7. This epitome of religious and moral teachings was put together by the Evangelist mainly from the Sayings Source Q and special traditions. (A shorter epitome of Jesus' teachings appears as the Sermon on the Plain in Luke 6:20–49.)

The Sermon the Mount takes the form of a wisdom instruction from Jesus as the authoritative interpreter of the Torah and the great teacher of wisdom. It provides the ideals and basic convictions of Jesus that are to be lived out by those who seek to follow his way. It appears in the context of the early phase of Jesus' public ministry and expresses what he stands for.

The Beatitudes (see Matthew 5:3–12) sketch the virtues that should characterize Jesus' followers (poverty of spirit, compassion, meekness, seeking justice or righteousness, mercy, integrity, peacemaking, fidelity), and promise eternal rewards for those who practice them. As salt of the earth, light of the world, and the city built on a hill (see 5:13–16), those who follow Jesus' teachings are said to have a significance that goes far beyond their own small community. In 5:17–20 Jesus challenges his followers to observe the values of the Torah as interpreted by him while surpassing the scribes and Pharisees in their quest for righteousness.

The six antitheses in Matthew 5:21–48 juxtapose quotations from the Torah ("You have heard . . .") and teachings from Jesus ("But I say . . .") on anger, lust, divorce, oaths, retaliation, and love of enemies. Rather than abolishing the Old Testament laws (see 5:17), Jesus goes to the root of each topic and shows his followers how to be "radical" in the most basic sense of that word.

In treating the acts of piety that were most prominent in Judaism (almsgiving, prayer, and fasting), Jesus asks his followers to carry these out in such a way as to please God without concern for seeking a reputation for holiness among the general public (see Matthew 6:1–18). In 6:19–7:12 Jesus gives wise teachings on a wide array of topics, from what constitutes "treasure" for humans to the "golden rule" ("do to others as you would have them do to you").

The concluding admonitions (see Matthew 7:13–27) remind us about the significance and challenge of practicing the teachings of Jesus. They represent a firm foundation on which to build, and emphasize the narrow gate and rough way to the kingdom of heaven. They are to be practiced and not simply repeated or admired. Conversely, their practice ("fruits") will reveal those who have truly understood and embraced the wisdom of Jesus.

In their beliefs about Jesus and in practicing the values of Jesus, the early Christians found an exalted identity as well as a source of alienation. First Peter is a good illustration of both points. On the one hand, early Christians experienced "a new birth into a living hope through the resurrection of Jesus from the dead" (1 Peter 1:3). Moreover, even though many of them were not Jews by birth (see 1:18), they could now be addressed as "a chosen race, a royal priesthood, a holy nation, God's own people" (2:9). And they had as their mission to proclaim what God had done on their behalf in leading them "out of darkness into his marvelous light" (2:9).

On the other hand, their new identity in Christ made them "aliens and exiles" (1 Peter 2:11) with regard to many of the people around them, because they now refused to give into the "desires of the flesh." Their new faith and new moral standards meant that they no longer did "what the Gentiles like to do, living in licentiousness, passions, drunkenness, revels, carousing, and lawless idolatry" (1 Peter 4:3). Rather, their new code of conduct marked them as different and annoyed their contemporaries:"They are surprised that you no longer join them in the same excesses of dissipation, and so they blaspheme" (4:4).

One of the purposes of 1 Peter was to encourage new Christians to remain faithful despite their social alienation and ostracism. It does so by reminding them of how Christ suffered even though he did no wrong (see 2:18–25; 3:8–22) and of the Last Judgment, when everyone will have to "give an accounting to him who stands ready to judge the living and the dead" (4:5).

One interpreter of 1 Peter (John H. Elliott) has described the basic theme of this letter as the Church being "a home for the homeless." This phrase suggests that various kinds of people—Jews and Gentiles, slaves and free, and men and women—found a home in the early Christian communities. In their new home they also found a new way of looking at the world around them and a new personal and communal identity and code of conduct that made it possible for them to overcome whatever alienation and hostility they endured from their families and neighbors. This process was greatly facilitated by the emphasis among early Christians on hospitality and compassion/mercy.

HOSPITALITY AND COMPASSION

Two values that help explain the attractiveness and success of the early Christian movement are hospitality and compassion. When men and women became Christians, they found in the church a home and a new family (see Mark 3:31–35). At the end of his long and elaborate sermon, the author of Hebrews exhorts his readers:"Do not neglect to show hospitality to strangers, for by doing that some have entertained angels without knowing it" (Hebrews 13:2; see Genesis 18:18; 19:1–3). And in his Sermon on the Plain, Jesus teaches:"Be merciful, just as your Father is merciful" (Luke 6:36). These two values, or virtues, seem to have been pivotal in the development of Christian community and in attracting outsiders to become part of the group.

Hospitality can be defined as the friendly reception and treatment of strangers or guests. In the Old Testament and in the ancient world in general, hospitality was a positive ideal. For example, the promise made to Abraham that he and Sarah would have a son (Isaac) was a consequence of his willingness to show hospitality to the three mysterious strangers by the oaks of Mamre (see Genesis 18:1–15). The Holiness Code commands that God's people Israel should "love the alien as yourself, for you were aliens in the land of Egypt" (Leviticus 19:34). In Proverbs 9, Lady Wisdom invites the "simple" to her banquet:"Come, eat of my bread and drink of the wine I have mixed" (9:5). In contrast, two of the most terrifying narratives in the Old Testament concern egregious failures in hospitality: the attempted rape of the two angels who were Lot's guests in Sodom (see Genesis 19:1–29), and the rape and dismemberment of the Levite's concubine at Gibeah (see Judges 19:1–30).

With these positive and negative precedents as a background, the major New Testament writers present distinctive perspectives on hospitality. In the Synoptic tradition, for example, those who follow Jesus and seek to do the will of God constitute the new family of Jesus (see Mark 3:31–35). In turn, they are promised "houses, brothers and sisters, mothers and children, and fields" (Mark 10:30). In their itinerant ministries, Jesus and his first followers had to rely upon the kindness of strangers (see Mark 6:10–11) or of friends among the local populace (see Luke 10:38–42). Matthew's Gospel stresses that those who show hospitality to Jesus' followers in fact welcome Jesus and his Father in heaven (see Matthew 10:40 and 25:35). The Last Supper (see Mark 14:22–25) is the climax in a series of meals at which Jesus presides in a kind of enacted parable about the kingdom of God (see Luke 14:7–24). And the appearances of the Risen Jesus often occur in the context of a meal shared by his disciples (see Luke 24:13–35, 36–49; John 21:1–14).

Paul and other apostles necessarily enjoyed the hospitality of other Christians by continuing the itinerant ministry of Jesus and his first followers, although mainly in the major cities of the Roman Empire rather than in rural Palestine. While Paul made it a principle to support himself by working at his trade (see 1 Thessalonians 2:9) and disciplined himself to "be content with whatever I have" (Philippians 4:11), one of the reasons he wrote to the Romans was to ask for their hospitality on his way to begin a mission in Spain (see Romans 1:8–15; 15:22–29) after having taken the proceeds of the collection to Jerusalem. And the reason for one of Paul's harshest criticisms of the Corinthians was due to the failure by wealthy Christians there to extend their hospitality to the less fortunate within their community (see 1 Corinthians 11:17–34). Their failure in hospitality leads Paul to assert: "When you come together, it is not really to eat the Lord's Supper" (11:20).

The element of hospitality is also evident in the farewell discourses in John 13–17, which take place in the context of a meal at which Jesus presides. He begins the meal by taking on the role of a servant or slave in washing the feet of his guests (see John 13:1–20). Then, in his discourses, he addresses his disciples as "friends." The friends of Jesus are those who have been taught by him and seek to keep his commandments to believe and to love: "I have called you friends, because I have made known to you everything that I have heard from my Father" (15:15). In Revelation 3:20, the Risen Christ is cast in the role of the mysterious stranger (see also Genesis 18 and Luke 24:13–35): "I am standing at the door, knocking; if you hear my voice and open the door, I will come into you and eat with you, and you with me." On the contrary, in 3 John the elder complains that Diotrephes fails to provide the appropriate hospitality in that he "refuses to welcome the brothers, and even prevents those who want to do so and expels them from the church" (v. 10).

As a value, or virtue, with deep roots in human existence and in the Old Testament, hospitality in the New Testament is linked to the meals of the earthly Jesus (including his Last Supper) and of the Risen Jesus. It was the exercise of hospitality that greatly facilitated the Christian mission and made Christian communities attractive to those in search of acceptance and love in Christ.

If hospitality is a value deeply rooted in human life, compassion or mercy is a deeply rooted divine value, or virtue. *Compassion* means literally "suffering with," and may be defined as the capacity to be moved by the sufferings of others and to enter into them. *Mercy* involves responding positively to the sufferings of others. The New Testament teaching about compassion/mercy is neatly stated in Luke 6:36: "Be merciful, just as your father is merciful."

In the Old Testament compassion/mercy is primarily an attribute of God. The Hebrew term for it is *rehem*, which refers also to a woman's womb, and the use of this root in connection with God as the "merciful one" (*rahum*) conveys the emotional quality of the concept. Among the attributes of God listed in Exodus 34:6, mercy comes first: "The Lord, the Lord, a God merciful and gracious, slow to anger. . . ." The mercy of God is made manifest in various contexts: covenant renewal (see Exodus 33: 18–23), repentance (see Proverbs 28:13), the wrath of God (see Hosea 1:6–9; 2:23), and national restoration (see Ezekiel 39:25).

As Luke 6:36 indicates, the New Testament emphasizes that although compassion/mercy is a divine quality, it is to be imitated by humans. The pertinent Greek words are *eleos* ("mercy") and *oiktirmon* ("compassion-ate") as well as *splanchna* (literally "innards or "guts"). Having experienced God's mercy in Christ, Christians are then urged to imitate God's attitude in dealing with others.

In Luke's infancy narrative, the coming of Jesus as the Messiah is cel-ebrated as the great manifestation of God's mercy according to the hymns known as the *Magnificat* (see Luke 1:50, 54) and the *Benedictus* (1:72, 78). Jesus displays his own compassion or mercy toward others in healing a leper (see Mark 1:41) and in feeding a crowd of five thousand (see Mark 6:34). His teaching about compassion/mercy is presented most memorably in the parable of the Good Samaritan (see Luke 10:25–37), especially with its concluding challenge: "Go and do likewise" (10:37).

When Paul reflects on how Gentiles could become part of God's people, he attributes it to the mercy of God (see Romans 9:15). In Ephesians 2:4, God is described as "rich in mercy." When addressing what was perhaps his favorite Christian community, Paul listed "compassion and sympathy" as being among its essential characteristics (see Philippians 2:1). And in introducing his meditation on Christ the great high priest, the author of Hebrews evokes his ability to "sympathize with our weaknesses . . . who in every respect has been tested as we are, yet without sin" (Hebrews 4:15).

According to the New Testament, the Christian community is constituted by those who have received the mercy of God through Jesus Christ and so are willing to show compassion toward others in response. The coming of Jesus among us was the climactic manifestation of God's mercy to his people. The proper human response to Jesus the merciful high priest is to show compassion toward others. Along with hospitality, compassion/mercy clearly was an important factor in attracting and retaining new members who were seeking a home and a family in the early church.

Possibilities and Problems

The context in which the early church took shape—the Roman Empire—both facilitated the spread of Christianity and presented it with an overwhelming social reality within which and against which it had to define itself. The classic "church and state" texts in the New Testament remind us that there is no one Christian position on the topic: Jesus urges caution and points to God as the ultimate king (see Mark 12:13–17); Paul exhorts the Roman Christians to cooperate with the Roman authorities as instruments of God (see Romans 13:1–7); and John, in Revelation, counsels nonviolent resistance in the face of governmental claims that encroach upon the essentials of Christian faith. This variety of perspectives allows Christians in the different situations in which they find themselves today to be good citizens and to resist injustice without being tied to any one political ideology.

The recovery of the prominent roles that women played in the Jesus movement and in the early churches has been one of the great contributions of modern biblical scholarship. One can, of course, explain this phenomenon to some extent by the sociological principle that new religious movements generally break through social divisions and conventions, including traditional gender roles. But the theological vision that in Christ "there are no longer male and female" (Galatians 3:28) also seems to have had an impact. The Church of the twenty-first century, however, will have to develop a more inclusive vision to keep up with that of the New

Testament and to honor and encourage greater participation and leadership by women if it is to be true to its biblical heritage.

Attention to the religious and moral teachings found in the New Testament can help Christians today to better grasp what it felt like to be an early Christian. In the context of the Roman Empire, these people represented a tiny minority—but they had a very high opinion of their importance "in Christ" and an ethos that both attracted new members and set them apart from most of their contemporaries. The values of hospitality and compassion contributed greatly to the success of their movement.

One serious problem posed by the New Testament "church and state" texts is their potential for misuse—a potential that has frequently been realized throughout church history. For example, Mark 12:13–17 has sometimes been used to found a doctrine of "two kingdoms" and to focus on the heavenly kingdom to the neglect of the earthly kingdom. Romans 13:1–7 also has been manipulated by totalitarian governments in the twentieth century to keep sincere Christians under political control and to prevent them from struggling against injustice. And the Book of Revelation has sometimes been a source of sectarian hostility toward governments and of neglect of civic responsibilities by Christians. While the abuses do not nullify the value of these biblical passages, they do show the importance of analyzing carefully the political situation and discerning the proper Christian response to it.

Besides highlighting the place of women in early Christianity, modern biblical scholarship has also established the tendency in the later New Testament writings to revert to the general cultural norms regarding the place of women in the household and in the Christian community. Here again the issue of theological evaluation arises: Is this progress or regress? Does the later perception represent the authoritative Christian position, or was it simply the appropriate historical response to a situation that has long since disappeared? Moreover, Christian interpreters need to be aware of and sensitive to the possibility of their claims about the freedom granted to women in the early Jesus movement being used to denigrate Judaism by invidious comparisons.

Finally, the "minority" status of the earliest Christians deserves to be taken very seriously as both a challenge and an opportunity for Christians in the twenty-first century. In places where Christians are a minority (China, India, Japan, etc.), Christians may paradoxically find it easier to connect with the experiences of the churches glimpsed in the New Testament. For those in lands where Christianity is at least the nominal religion of the majority and even the established religion, it may ironically be more difficult to build bridges between the first and the twenty-first centuries and to recapture the spirit that early Christians displayed.

For Reflection and Discussion

1. What contributions might we expect (and not expect) from the New Testament in developing a Christian social ethics?

2. How do you evaluate theologically the totality of the New Testament evidence about the place of women in the Jesus movement and in the early church?

3. In your time and place, what does it feel like to be a Christian? What can you learn by way of consolation and challenge from the New Testament on this matter?

chapter eleven

MINISTRY

As the early Christians gathered in communities, they understandably faced various problems and developed various self-understandings. For example, where humans gather, there is always a division of labor—and where there is a division of labor, there are leaders and followers. This fact of human existence brings us into the area of leadership and ministry in the early church.

In the Christian tradition the many ways of responding to divine grace on behalf of others are called *services* or *ministries*. They could be called many other things, but the fact remains that what Christians do for others within the context of the Church is generally called *ministry*. Thus, the Christian leader, in whatever area, is challenged to act as the servant of others.

Because there have been poor leaders throughout Christian history, it is easy to be suspicious about the idea of leadership as service of others. Many scoundrels have justified unscrupulous and oppressive behavior as providing a "service." Yet, the misuse of a good idea by some is no excuse for avoiding the challenge of the New Testament.

According to the New Testament, leadership is service, and service is leadership. This paradox summarizes what is essential about Christian leadership according to the New Testament—and this idea is deeply rooted in the life and person of Jesus.

After considering Jesus as the servant leader, this chapter will look at other terms and patterns of leadership that were available to early Christians. Then it will discuss what the Gospels say about the first followers of Jesus (the "disciples") and the significance of that material for understanding ministry in the Church. Finally, with Paul as a guide, it will reflect on the ministry of the word as a fundamental way of handing on the gospel.

JESUS AS THE SERVANT LEADER

To most people, the word *ministry* refers to the profession of those who work for and in the Church: "the clergy." But the term *ministry* more basically means "service." Thus, its use in describing religious professionals suggests that those who work for and in the Church are in the business of serving others.

According to Paul, each Christian is a gifted or graced person. Individual Christians must respond to the Holy Spirit according to the gifts that have been given to them for the common good and for the benefit of others. As Romans 12:6–8 indicates, there are different gifts and different ways of actualizing those charisms: prophecy, "ministry," teaching, exhortation, giving generously, administration, and compassion and cheerfulness. These all are ways of responding to God's grace on behalf of others and so can be called *ministry* or *service*.

The basis for Christian action as ministry or service is the teaching and example of Jesus. Near the end of the pivotal journey narrative, according to Mark 10:35–45, Jesus expresses his teaching about leadership in his community: "Whoever wishes to become great among you must be your servant, and whoever wishes to be first among you must be the slave of all" (10:43–44).

The great structural principle of Mark's journey narrative (see 8: 22–10:52) is that there are three passion predictions (see 8:31; 9:31; 10:33–34) followed by misunderstandings on the part of the disciples and positive teaching by Jesus about who he is and what it means to follow him. Jesus' definition of leadership appears in the instruction following the third passion prediction. In this most detailed of the three passion predictions (see 10:33–34), Jesus describes the fate that awaits him at the end of the journey: "See, we are going up to Jerusalem, and the Son of Man will be handed over to the chief priests and the scribes, and they will condemn him to death; then they will hand him over to the Gentiles; they will mock him, and spit upon him, and flog him, and kill him; and after three days he will rise again." Every detail appears again in Mark 14–16. So detailed is this account that most interpreters view it as having been rewritten in the light of the Markan passion narrative.

And yet James and John—two sons of Zebedee, and among the very first disciples called by Jesus—pass over all the references to Jesus' suffering and death, and attend only to the glorious reign of Jesus and their place in it. Their failure to understand is expressed by the selfishness of their request: "Grant us to sit, one at your right hand and one at your left, in your glory" (Mark 10:37). Their foolishness, however, provides Jesus with the occasion to confront them with the challenge of suffering entailed in following him: "The cup that I drink, you will drink; with the baptism with which I am baptized, you will be baptized" (10:39). The images here refer to the cup of suffering and to baptism as a kind of drowning or dying.

The annoyance and anger shown by the other disciples against James and John provides the occasion for Jesus to contrast his ideal of greatness as the service of others with patterns of leadership that prevailed in the Greco-Roman world (and in the world today). There greatness is understood as having power over others, and leadership means making one's power felt: "You know that among the Gentiles those whom they recognize as their rulers lord it over them, and their great ones are tyrants over them" (10:42). By way of contrast, greatness in the community of Jesus is to be measured in terms of the service of others and the leader is to be the "slave of all" (10:44).

Jesus' teaching on leadership as service is not simply wise teaching in general. Rather, it expresses his way of understanding greatness and leadership with reference to his own death and resurrection. As the climax of all his teachings in the journey narrative, Jesus states: "For the Son of Man came not to be served but to serve, and to give his life as a ransom for many" (10:45). Here Jesus uses the title "Son of Man" to refer to himself as both a representative human being (see Ezekiel) and a glorious heavenly figure (see Daniel 7:13–14) in the context of his passion. He interprets his suffering as the service of others and as the means of atonement and redemption ("ransom") for others. The saying fits well with the early Chrisian interpretation of Jesus' death as a sacrifice "for us" and "for our sins." Thus, Mark 10:35–45 plays off the disciples' misunderstanding of greatness and power over against Jesus' ideal of and example of leadership as the service of others.

The servant-leadership of Jesus, manifested especially in his death and resurrection, is celebrated in the early Christian hymn preserved in Paul's Letter to the Philippians (see 2:6–11). This witness to early Christian faith interprets the Incarnation as Jesus' self-emptying: "taking the form of a slave, being born in human likeness" (2:7). It goes on to describe Jesus' death on the cross as the extreme point in Jesus' service of others: "he humbled himself and became obedient to the point of death—even death on a cross" (2:8). According to the second part of the hymn (see 2:9–11), Jesus' humble service of others resulted in his resurrection and exaltation, as well as the confession by all creation that "Jesus Christ is Lord" (2:11). Here the Christ event (Jesus' life, death, and resurrection) is portrayed in terms of his servant leadership.

The theme of Jesus' death as the service of others is woven into the Gospel passion accounts. For example, at the Last Supper, according to Mark 14:24, Jesus says these words over the cup: "This is my blood of the covenant, which is poured out for many." Matthew 26:28 adds to this saying the phrase "for the forgiveness of sins." Luke places Jesus' instruction about servant-leadership in the context of a farewell discourse at the Last Supper (see Luke 22:24–38). And in his farewell discourse according to John, Jesus gives as the ultimate manifestation of love a willingness to die for others: "No one has greater love than this, to lay down one's life for one's friends" (John 15:13).

Because Jesus' loving service of others sets the pattern for greatness and leadership in the Christian community, it is primarily in the light of his teaching and example that it is meaningful and appropriate to speak about "ministry" in the Church. At its root, ministry is not simply a profession or a church office. Rather, it is a way of responding to the gift of the Holy Spirit and of living a Christian life for others. As such, ministry involves a vital awareness of the lordship of Christ and the grace of God, as well as concern for others and, indeed, for the whole Church. It demands a recognition that one's abilities and resources come through the Holy Spirit, along with a willingness to work with others and even suffer for others as Jesus himself did. The example of Jesus the Servant of God (see Isaiah 40–55 for Old Testament precedents) remains as both the ideal and the goal of Christian ministry, and the standard by which every Christian ministry is to be measured.

OTHER TERMS AND PATTERNS

The most important term for describing Christian servant-leadership in the New Testament is *diakonia* ("service, ministry"). Its basic meaning is the humble service of others, exemplified by those who wait at tables (see Acts 6:1–6). It was not the usual Greek word for describing the service of God (rather, *leitourgia* or *latreia* were more common), and it did not carry the religious overtones of those terms. But in the New Testament it came to be used with reference to ministering to the material needs of others as well as performing services in the church.

The New Testament writers generally avoid "power" language when talking about relationships between Christians—an avoidance that seems to have been a consequence of the confession "Jesus is Lord." Just as the lordship of Christ prevented the church from using "power" terms internally, so the servanthood of Christ provided the pattern for the alternative vocabulary of ministry.

The avoidance of power language does not mean its total absence, however. But it does mean that power terms appear in other contexts and have a meaning that is shaped to fit Christian faith and its concept of ministry. For example, words with the Greek roots *archein* ("rule") and *kyrieuein* ("lord over") are seldom used with reference to relationships between Christians (see Mark 10:42; see the striking exception in 1 Timothy 5:17–20). They do occur with reference to Christ as ruler and lord. While the apostle Paul may give some "commands" in defending the gospel and condemning behavior that he regarded as contrary to the gospel, in his ethical instructions addressed to fellow believers he generally preferred the language of exhortation and encouragement. And while *honor* (*time*) was widely used in the Mediterranean world to refer to the personal dignity, social status, and exalted office of a person, in the New Testament *honor* occurs primarily in the context of mutual honor among human persons ("honor one another") or where it is clear that God is the source and horizon of all real *honor*. In early Christian faith, God in Christ Jesus is ruler and lord, gives commands, and is honored above all.

With respect to patterns of leadership, there were many social structures and models available to Jesus and the early Christians. While they did take some elements and terms from contemporary social institutions, the Church emerged from the New Testament period as a distinctive and indeed unique entity.

Ancient Israel was ruled by kings, and in the Roman Empire all power resided in the emperor. But while Jesus proclaimed the coming kingdom of God and was called by the royal titles "Messiah" and "King of the Jews," the early church did not take over the pattern of monarchy or the office of king in carrying out its everyday affairs. Indeed, in claiming that Jesus is king, the early Christians relativized all human claims to kingship.

In both Judaism and the Greco-Roman world of the time, the family and the household (including wives, children, and servants) constituted a major social reality. Again, while the earliest Christian communities met in private households and so were naturally influenced by the authority structures of the household (especially by the role of "patriarch" and the prominence of women), there was also a movement to redefine and expand the notion of the Christian household (see "the household of God" in 1 Timothy 3:15). Thus, with time, the church gradually outgrew the structures of the household.

The word *ekklesia* is rooted in Greek democracy. Although Athenian democracy involved the assembly (*ekklesia*) of all free residents, only landowners could be elected to office in the polis. In some places power was in the hands of a small group of citizens, whereas in other cases, citizenship was based on heredity or property. When early Christians took over the word *ekklesia* and its concept of constituting a body of persons, however, they did not set out to establish a political democracy. In fact, they were far more inclusive (see Galatians 3:28) than were the classical Greek democracies.

Voluntary associations were a major feature in the world of the New Testament. These groups or clubs ranged along the spectrum from labor guilds to burial societies and religious communities. To outsiders in the Greco-Roman world, the early churches looked very much like these voluntary associations. Indeed, the terms bishop (*episkopos*) and deacon (*diakonos*) most likely originated in this context.

Various Jewish religious movements such as the Pharisees, Saduccees, and Essenes would have been regarded as voluntary associations in the wider context of the Greco-Roman world. These groups developed their own unique identities, had their own rules, met regularly, and could decide on admitting and expelling members—just as the early churches did. What set the early churches apart from them was primarily their focus on the person of Jesus and on the values that he taught and exemplified.

The word *synagogue* derives from a Greek term that means "gathering or assembly." For Jews, the synagogue became the center of Jewish culture, education, social activity, and religion, especially outside the land of Israel. The government of a synagogue was entrusted to a board of elders (*presbyteroi*) who were responsible for financial matters and who exercised general oversight. According to the Acts of the Apostles and other New Testament books, many of the early Christians—whether they were Jews by birth or Gentiles who were attracted to Judaism—had come to the church through the synagogue. The early church's office of elder or presbyter was very likely based on the administrative structure of the Jewish synagogue.

These are but a few samples of social institutions and patterns of leadership contemporary with the early Christian movement. While the early churches accepted some elements from all of them, they accepted none of them fully. In a sense, the Church is *sui generis*, or unique. One distinctive feature of early Christianity, in fact, was its insistence on leadership as service after the example of Jesus the servant. His servant-leadership should set the theological pattern for bishops and deacons, presbyters, and all others who exercise Christian leadership and ministry.

DISCIPLES OF JESUS

In the Synoptic Gospels, the first disciples called by Jesus have an exemplary significance, both positive and negative. The first four are fishermen—Simon and Andrew, and James and John (see Mark 1:16–20; Matthew 4:18–22; Luke 5:1–11). As fishermen by the Sea of Galilee, these men would have enjoyed a relatively stable existence in the present, and would have had decent prospects for the future, since commercial fishing in the Sea of Galilee was (and is) a fairly prosperous business enterprise. There is no indication that they had met Jesus previously or knew anything about him. This serves to highlight the extraordinary power of Jesus' call and the attractiveness of his person. Moreover, the usual Jewish pattern by which students became associated with a master teacher was by their seeking out the teacher. However, by the power of his word alone ("Follow me, and I will make you fish for people," Mark 1:17), Jesus chooses and gathers to himself the disciples who will be with him throughout his public ministry.

The essence of discipleship is to be with Jesus and to share his mission (see Mark 3:14). The simple lifestyle recommended in the various missionary discourses (see Mark 6:7–13; Matthew 10:1–42; Luke 9:1–6; 10:1–12) is in the service of sharing in Jesus' proclamation of God's kingdom and healing those in need.

The absolute and radical claims involved in following Jesus may demand separation from one's natural family and becoming part of the "new family" of Jesus (see Mark 3:31–35). At the very beginning of Luke's journey narrative, for example, Jesus refuses the requests of prospective disciples to bury a father or to say farewell to those at home (see Luke 9:59–62). In a culture in which family ties and obligations were enormously important, this was powerful teaching. Indeed, Jesus promises division within the household (see Luke 12:51–53), and even envisions situations in which prospective disciples might actually "hate" their family members (see Luke 14:26).

These family tensions are illustrated by the case of Jesus himself. According to Mark 3:21, members of his own family try to restrain him on the grounds that people were saying, "He has gone out of his mind," thus bringing shame upon the entire family. In response, Jesus redefines his true family as "whoever does the will of God" (Mark 3:35). His disciples— those dedicated to his ideals and mission—now constitute the family of Jesus.

Luke 9:1–6 describes the mission of the Twelve Apostles as the extension of Jesus' own mission of teaching and healing. A similar passage appears in Luke 10:1–12 in which a group of seventy (or seventy-two) disciples is appointed to prepare the way for Jesus as he and his followers make their way to Jerusalem in the journey narrative (see 9:51–19:44). The fact that the two instructions are so much alike suggests that they were intended for a larger circle than that constituted by the Twelve Apostles.

The "mission of the Twelve" consists of a narrative framework (see Luke 9:1–2, 6) and an instruction (see 9:3–5). In the first part of the narrative (9:1–2) Jesus determines to share his powers as a teacher and healer, and in the concluding section (see 9:6) the Twelve set out on their mission. In Luke's two-volume narrative (the Gospel According to Luke and the Acts of the Apostles), the Twelve Apostles serve as an important principle of continuity between the ministry of the earthly Jesus and the early days of the church in Jerusalem after Jesus' Resurrection and Ascension (see Acts 1–9). Here they are called to do what Jesus does in his ministry and to share actively in his mission from God.

The instruction (see Luke 9:3–5) assumes that the Twelve Apostles will be on the move as they carry forward Jesus' mission. According to 9:3, they are to avoid all unnecessary baggage ("neither walking stick, nor sack nor food, nor money . . . "), and to place their trust totally in God to provide for their needs. On the practical level (see 9:4), they are to rely on the hospitality and generosity of those whom they encounter and who accept them into their households. Rather than spending time and energy on seeking better accommodations, the Twelve Apostles are told to be satisfied with what is first given them by their hosts. If and when they meet opposition and rejection (see 9:5), the proper response is for them to move on peacefully, with only a symbolic gesture of leave-taking: "Shake the dust from your feet in testimony against them."

These instructions fit the context of first-century Palestine and of the Greco-Roman world in general. There philosophies were spread by traveling missionaries who either begged for food and support, or relied more subtly on help and hospitality from others along the way. What is distinctive about Luke 9:1–6 and other such texts in the Synoptic Gospels is the specific religious context—sharing in Jesus' mission of teaching and healing—in which the instructions are set. The truly important tasks are proclaiming the kingdom of God and healing, as a sign of the presence of that kingdom. The simple lifestyle is entirely in the service of the mission, subordinate to and useful only as a help toward preaching God's kingdom in word and deed.

The disciples, especially the Twelve Apostles but also presumably the wider circle, are promised rewards not only in the future but also "in the age to come" (Mark 10:28–31). During Jesus' public ministry they have the benefit of receiving Jesus' wisdom and even his foreknowledge of the suffering that awaits him—and them. Nevertheless, in all the Synoptic Gospels they are more or less obtuse, and instead of growing in spiritual insight they regress on the way from Galilee to Jerusalem. Ultimately, when Jesus is arrested in Jerusalem, they scatter, and Peter denies Jesus three times. By contrast, the women followers emerge as the faithful ones, when they witness Jesus' death and burial and go to his tomb on Easter Sunday.

The major problem posed by these Synoptic Gospel texts is the applicability or transfer to Christians beyond the first century. Or to the put the same point in another way, can we use Jesus' instructions to his disciples in envisioning Christian ministry in the twenty-first century?

In the Christian tradition there has been a long-standing debate on this issue. Some contend that the discipleship teachings are incumbent on all Christians. Others make a distinction between a Christian elite and ordinary Christians. From the perspective of biblical studies, the question is usually posed and treated in a historical framework. Some would argue that the extreme teachings about discipleship—especially the simple lifestyle and the separation from family—pertain only to the mission of the historical Jesus in first-century rural Palestine. Others argue that the teachings about lack of family, possessions, and stable abode best fit the rural conditions of the earliest days of the post-Easter Christian mission. In both periods, those who proclaimed the kingdom of God went from place to place, dependent upon the hospitality and generosity of the local population.

The link between the very concrete instructions most at home in first-century Palestine and the generalizing tendency in the Christian theological tradition is best found in the editorial work of the Synoptic Evangelists. Each gospel writer used traditional materials in a new urban context outside the land of Israel: Mark in Rome around A.D. 70, Matthew in Antioch around A.D. 85–90, and Luke perhaps in Greece around A.D. 85–90. They all faced the challenge of translation or transfer, and each of them gave distinctive emphases to the discipleship tradition: success and failure along the way (Mark), learning from Jesus the teacher (Matthew), and carrying the message and work of Jesus (Luke). It seems that the very process of interpretation and development as illustrated by the Evangelists provides the bridge between discipleship in Jesus' time and in other times and places.

It is neither possible nor useful to imitate the lifestyle of Jesus and his first followers in all its details, or to try to put into practice all the concrete instructions that he gave to his first disciples. But we can and should discern some core values in the discipleship passages in the Synoptic Gospels that can give shape to Christian discipleship in any age and place: absolute dedication to God's kingdom, a desire to share in Jesus' mission, a simple lifestyle in the service of that mission, the willingness to subordinate or forgo human ties and physical comforts, and the assurance of opposition and suffering for the sake of the gospel. These core values can serve as the starting points for reflecting on the use of Jesus' discipleship teachings in ministry today. (Material in this section has been adapted from my book *Why do we suffer? A scriptural approach to the human condition,* Sheed & Ward, 2000, pp. 95–100.)

THE MINISTRY OF THE WORD

In the various lists of charisms in the New Testament, there is great emphasis on ministries of the word; that is, the ways in which the gospel and related wisdom might be communicated. These ministries of the word are recognized as being essential to serving the community and building up the Body of Christ.

In 1 Corinthians 12, for example, there are two lists of spiritual gifts.

The first list (see 1 Corinthians 12:8–10) includes the utterance of wisdom and knowledge, prophecy, and interpretation of tongues. The second list (see 12:28) begins with apostles, prophets, and teachers—all ministers of the word. Even the list in Romans 12:6–8, where there is no discernible effort at arranging the gifts in a hierarchy of importance, mentions prophecy, teaching, and exhortation. The list in (the Deuteropauline) Ephesians 4:11 consists entirely of ministers of the word: "apostles, some prophets, some evangelists, some pastors and teachers."

It is clear from these lists that one very important way of carrying on the mission of Jesus is through the various ministries of the word. Surprisingly little attention is given in the New Testament to who administers baptism (apart from 1 Corinthians 1:10–17, where Paul's point is that the identity of the minister is not important) or to who presides at the Eucharist. But much is said, however, about preaching the gospel and about the content of the gospel.

Paul the apostle is the minister of the word *par excellence* in the New Testament epistles, proudly bearing the title "apostle" (which means "one who is sent"). In Judaism, an "apostle" was an emissary sent from one community to another. This practice seems to have had some influence in the early churches. For example, according to Acts 13:1–3, the church at Antioch sends Saul/Paul and Barnabas on a mission to other places. And in 2 Corinthians 8:23, Titus and other co-workers of Paul are called "apostles of the churches."

Paul, however, regarded his apostleship as coming directly from his encounter with the Risen Jesus: "sent neither by human commission nor from human authorities, but through Jesus Christ and God the Father who raised him from the dead" (Galatians 1:1). Paul viewed himself as having been especially commissioned by the Risen Lord to preach the gospel to non-Jews, taking as his task the founding of Christian communities in places where the gospel had not yet been preached (see Romans 15:14–21).

Paul's First Letter to the Thessalonians (A.D. 51–52) is generally regarded as the earliest complete document in the New Testament. After he founded the church in Thessalonica and had moved on to other places, Paul wrote letters to stay in contact and to give pastoral advice about certain problems that had arisen since his departure. One of the issues seems to have involved an attack on Paul's apostleship. And so Paul's defense of his apostleship in 1 Thessalonians is the earliest (and most eloquent) reflection on the ministry of the word in the New Testament.

As a minister of the word, Paul regards himself as an instrument of God's power. He had been entrusted with the gospel (see 1 Thessalonians 2:4), and his only goal to is please God. His love for those to whom he brought the gospel is such that he also shares his very self with them (see 2:8). He uses the images of a gentle nurse caring for her charges (see 2:7) and a father exhorting his children (see 2:11–12) to describe his own work. All this is in the service of the gospel: "what it really is, God's word, which is also at work in you believers" (2:13). The word of God is a dynamic entity, and Paul the apostle is its bearer.

Paul also insists that he did not undertake the ministry of the word for personal gain or comfort. Nor does he seek praise from others, and he even refuses the financial support that as an apostle he had the right to expect (see 1 Thessalonians 2:6–7). On the contrary, so as not to burden anyone, Paul worked at some kind of manual labor (probably leather working) to pay his own way (see 2:9). And he is confident that both God and the Thessalonians will testify "how pure, upright, and blameless our conduct was toward you believers" (2:10).

Nevertheless, Paul's ministry of the word aroused opposition. He was accused of being a deceiver (see 1 Thessalonians 2:3) and was called a flatterer and a greedy person (see 2:5). He had already been "shamefully mistreated at Philippi" (2:2) and expelled from Judea by fellow Jews (see 2:15). And yet he looked upon his sufferings as part of being a follower of Jesus and an apostle.

What Paul was preaching was the "good news" about Jesus' life, death, and resurrection, referring to it in 1 Thessalonians as "the gospel of God" (2:2, 8, 9), "the gospel" (2:4), and "the word of God" (2:13). As such, it was the extension of Jesus' own proclamation of God's kingdom, for in Jesus' own ministry the kingdom of God was inaugurated. What Paul preached as the gospel can be found by one account in 1 Corinthians 15:3a: "For I handed on to you as of first importance what I in turn had received." That early Christian confession focused on the saving significance of Jesus' death and resurrection.

The context in which Paul quoted that confession is a good example of Paul's ministry of the word. In citing the confession, Paul appeals to the common body of beliefs that he can presume are shared by all Christians in Corinth: the death of Jesus the Messiah (the Christ) was an expiatory sacrifice; he was restored to life; his death and resurrection were in accord with the Old Testament; and he appeared alive to many followers. In appealing to Christ's work as the agent of justification and salvation, Paul shows himself faithful to the objective core of Christian faith. But in the rest of 1 Corinthians 15, Paul addresses specific problems that had arisen among the Corinthian Christians regarding the implications of Christ's Resurrection for them. While remaining faithful to the core of Christian faith, Paul serves as creative teacher by expressing the significance of Jesus' Resurrection in dealing with the problems that his people faced in the present. In this sense, Paul was a pastoral theologian.

These perspectives on the ministry of the word are not unique to Paul in the New Testament. For example, in the missionary discourse addressed to the Twelve (see Matthew 10), the same profile of the minister of the word appears: an instrument of God's power in Christ, no concern for personal gain or comfort, opposition and persecution, and total commitment to proclaiming the "good news." Likewise, when the confession in 1 Corinthians 15:3b–5 is compared with the speeches in Acts, the same core beliefs emerge: Jesus as the Messiah, his fulfilling the Scriptures, his death and resurrection as bringing about deliverance from sin and making possible right relationship with God, and his exaltation to God's right hand.

Because the New Testament gives a certain primacy to the ministry of the word, it is only fitting that the prologues to John's Gospel (see 1:1–18) and 1 John (see 1:1–4) should celebrate Jesus as the Word of God. The idea is that God who had spoken his word in creation ("in the beginning") and in the history of Israel as God's people, now has spoken his definitive word in the person of Jesus. The Word who became flesh (see John 1:14) is both the revealer and the revelation of God. He offers a revelation superior to that of Moses (see 1:17), and he alone has made the Father known (see 1:18). All ministries of the word flow from Jesus the Word of God, and ministers of the word share in and continue his ministry. The dynamism behind all ministries of the word is Jesus the Word of God.

Possibilities and Problems

The model of servant-leadership not only aptly characterizes Jesus but also provides a pattern for all those try to follow Jesus. This model captures what the Gospels say about Jesus' public ministry and expresses the significance of his passion, death, and resurrection (as Philippians 2:6–11 shows). It also relates Jesus to the figure of God's Servant found prominently in Isaiah 40–55. It also challenges everyone who is any kind of leader in the Church to take seriously the duty of serving others and contributing to the common good. The measure of Christian life and leadership must be the service of others.

The model of discipleship in the Synoptic Gospels can and does apply to all Christians; it is not for an elite group only. This model conveys the core values of Christian life: absolute dedication to God's kingdom, sharing in Jesus' mission, a simple lifestyle, a willingness to subordinate or forgo human ties and physical comforts, and the assurance of opposition and suffering for the sake of the gospel. For all who seek to "minister" in the Church (and this should include every Christian), the positive picture of

Jesus' first followers offers a way of life and a challenge to walk upon that way. The call to follow Jesus involves the service of the gospel and the service of others.

The prominence given to the ministry of the word in the New Testament is a reminder that the most precious thing that Christians have to share is the gospel; that is, the revelation of God's way of looking at human existence and the world through Jesus, and the values and ideals that Jesus taught and practiced. There is no better summary of that gospel than "Christ has died; Christ is risen; Christ will come again." When a church loses focus and makes other ideals or projects more important than proclaiming the gospel, it loses its identity and its reason for existing.

One problem is that the example of Jesus the servant-leader may seem to be too lofty a model. The Evangelists wrote their Gospels from the perspective of Easter; they knew how the story of Jesus' life came out, and that his passion and death were not the end of the story. They believed that in the Resurrection everything that Jesus said and did took on new significance. As a result, they provided what to some extent is an idealized portrait of Jesus that perhaps may seem to be impossible to fulfill and so serves as a source of spiritual discouragement.

A second problem is the perception that the positive model of discipleship put forward in the Gospels can be appropriated by only a spiritual elite. This has often been the case throughout the Church's history. For example, in Catholic circles the "evangelical counsels" have been taken as applying mainly (if not exclusively) to members of religious orders or to the clergy; such analogous distinctions have arisen among other Christian denominations as well. Here it may be helpful to look again at the Gospels' emphasis on the inadequacies and failures of Jesus' first followers. They fail to understand; they ask foolish questions and make inappropriate comments; they abandon Jesus in the hour of his passion and death. Yet, their failings are forgiven, and they become fearless ministers of the word. Clearly, fear of failing to have a "perfect record" should not dissuade Christians from embracing and practicing the core values of Christian discipleship.

Finally the term *word* can be conceived too narrowly. The ministry of the word is not simply the formal preaching of the gospel. Rather, it embraces activities as varied as prophecy, exhortation, and interpretation. Moreover, since the Word became flesh (and not a book!), it is possible to proclaim the gospel in being who we are and in doing what we do. The early Christians recognized that the most effective missionary strategy is the good example shown by believers. People became Christians in the first century largely because they were favorably impressed by what they saw in those who were already Christians. Clearly, the gospel can be preached without words; what was true in the first century is also true in the twenty-first century. The ministry of the word is wider than formal preaching.

For Reflection and Discussion

1. Does the New Testament's picture of Jesus as a servant leader encourage you? Have you ever encountered such a leader?

2. Is the Gospels' positive model of discipleship intended for all Christians or for only a few? Does the theory fit the practice? Why or why not?

3. What might be some effective ways of exercising the ministry of the word in the twenty-first century?

chapter twelve

Ministers

Ministry in the sense of the service of others should be part of every Christian's life. But members of every social institution very quickly recognize the need to develop stable structures and ongoing offices of some sort. Someone has to call the group together, set the agenda, lay down procedures, and so forth. Otherwise, chaos reigns.

The early church was no exception to the rules of sociology. And the early church developed structures and offices that have stood the test of almost two thousand years. This chapter will first examine the offices of bishop, presbyter, and deacon, and will explore how these three positions came to fit together in one church order. Then it will discuss the various forms of priesthood: the priesthood of Christ, the priesthood of Christians, and the ministerial priesthood. Finally, with reference to the figure of Peter in the New Testament, it will consider the Petrine ministry and Petrine office. Because these are all sensitive areas in church life throughout history and today, they deserve close attention and an openness to what the New Testament says and does not say about them.

Church Offices

The term *office* in business, politics, education, and church life refers to a position having tenure, duration, specific duties, and rewards of some kind. In the context of first-century Palestinian Judaism, however, Jesus did not hold an office. There is no indication that he was trained under a rabbi (although John the Baptist may well have been a mentor) or that he held the office of "rabbi" (although in the Gospels he is sometimes called "rabbi" in the honorific sense of "my great one"). In fact, it appears that the office of rabbi and the concept of rabbinic ordination emerged only after Jesus' time, probably in the late first century A.D. (see Matthew 23:7–8). Instead, Jesus acted as a teacher and healer without any official human authorization. He was a charismatic prophet whose authority came directly from God.

One of the things that Jesus the charismatic prophet did was to gather disciples who accompanied him and shared in his mission. The group of Twelve was a prominent feature in Jesus' ministry and makes most lists of what can be said with great confidence about the historical Jesus. The number, of course, recalled the twelve tribes of Israel and made a symbolic statement about Jesus' program for the renewal of Israel as God's people. The Twelve (*hoi dodeka*) and the other disciples (*hoi mathetai*) were formed by Jesus and were sent out as "apostles" to spread Jesus' gospel of God's kingdom. While the Twelve and the other disciples had "positions" in the Jesus movement, from the perspective of first-century Jewish society they held no recognized office. Whatever authority they had came from Jesus the charismatic prophet.

The emergence of church offices as fixed positions was a gradual development in early Christianity. It is probably best understood in terms of the "routinization of charisma" by which Jesus the prophet's charism was given permanence. In this process, the earliest disciples of Jesus (Peter, James, John, etc.) played important roles, as did comparative latecomers like James the Lord's brother and Paul the apostle. The concept of discipleship as it developed in the gospel traditions also made significant contributions. It provided guidelines and inspiration as early Christians responded to historical and sociological necessities and came to depend on more fixed and defined forms of ministry.

In their accounts about Jesus' public ministry, the Evangelists give much attention to the "disciples" and the "Twelve" (although the "twelve apostles" is rare). They provide few clues about the church structures of their own time, however, which is understandable since they are writing about Jesus around A.D. 30. Luke uses the concept of the "twelve apostles" as a way of emphasizing the continuity between the time of Jesus and the time of the Holy Spirit or the Church (see Acts 1:12–26). In his account of the Jerusalem council in Acts 15 (see 15:2, 4, 6, 22), Luke places a group called "elders" (*presbyteroi*) beside the "apostles." He also refers to "elders" as church officials (see Acts 11:30; 14:23; 20:17, 28; 21:18) who seem to function as a board of directors according to the pattern set by Jewish synagogues. And in Acts 6, Luke narrates the appointment (by the apostles) of Stephen and his companions to care for the "Hellenist" widows as initiated by the Twelve and in terms ("wait on tables") that suggest a (probably anachronistic) connection with the office of "deacon."

The earliest New Testament reference to "bishops and deacons" appears in Paul's Letter to the Philippians (around A.D. 56). In the salutation (see Philippians 1:1–2), Paul and Timothy greet "all the saints in Christ Jesus who are in Philippi, with the bishops and deacons." Note that there is no mention of the office of "elder" here or elsewhere in Paul's undisputed letters. Nor is there any indication of what these "bishops" (note the plural!) and "deacons" did elsewhere in Paul's undisputed letters.

The fullest New Testament evidence about bishops, deacons, and presbyters/elders appears in the Pastoral Epistles (see 1 Timothy 3:1–13;

5:17–20; Titus 1:5–9). As we saw in the treatment of the Pauline heritage (see pp. 93–96), the Pastorals place a heavy emphasis on church officers as guardians of the deposit of faith and as guarantors of the Church's good order and respectability in society.

First Timothy 3:1–13 lists the kinds of natural virtues that the bishop (*episkopos*) and deacon (*diakonos*) should possess. The office of bishop is described at the outset as "a noble task" to which one can aspire (3:1), and those who aspire to this office should have the appropriate natural virtues ("temperate, sensible, respectable, hospitable"), prove themselves able to manage their own families and households, and "be well thought of by outsiders." These qualifications suggest that the *episkopos* exercised "oversight" (the meaning of the Greek verb *episkopein*) with regard to the life and financial affairs of the local Christian community.

Although the deacons seem to be subordinate to the bishops, their qualifications and functions seem to be much the same. From 1 Timothy 3:11 it appears that women ("Women likewise must be serious . . .") were admitted to the office of deacon; see the case of Phoebe the "deacon" (*diakonos*) in Romans 16:1. These lists of personal qualities bear witness to the effort in the Pastorals to promote local and stable forms of official ministries. The terminology and functions seem to have been taken over largely from the organizational patterns found in clubs and other voluntary associations in the Greco-Roman world.

First Timothy 5:17–20 describes procedures connected with the office of "presbyter/elder," with its primary task being to "rule well," presumably in the sense of overseeing the affairs of the community. This office is analogous to the board of "elders" who oversaw the life of local Jewish communities (see the "elders" in Acts). Some elders, however, also "labor in preaching and teaching," and so are worthy of "double honor." This second task, while not essential to being an elder, is regarded as praiseworthy. Moreover, there are provisions for removing an elder from office or at least rebuking in public an elder who has strayed. The accusation must be based on the evidence of two or three witnesses (see Deuteronomy 19:15; Matthew 18:16). The "elders" were older men either in age or in church membership who directed the local community.

In Titus 1:5–9 the two church orders—bishops and deacons, and presbyters/elders—come together, although in a very awkward way. In 1:5–6 Titus is first told by "Paul" to "appoint elders in every town" and is given a list of personal qualities ("blameless, married only once . . .") much like those in 1 Timothy 3:1–13. Then immediately and awkwardly, 1:7–9 provides a list of personal qualities "for a bishop" (which is noteworthy for its emphasis on the teaching responsibilities of the bishop in 1:9). The juxtaposition suggests an equivalency between "elders" and "bishops."

How did the three offices—bishop, deacon, and presbyter/elder—fit together? Eventually they came to exist side by side in the same community. In this arrangement, the bishops and deacons are active church officers who are responsible to the board of elders (some of whom may also perform pastoral tasks).

At the time of the Pastorals in the late first century or even early second century A.D., however, it appears that two distinct church orders had been in operation and were in the process of fusion. The *presbyteral* model found in Acts and 1 Timothy 5:17–20 (see also James 5:14; 1 Peter 5:5; 2 John 1; 3 John 1) was based on the organizational model of the Jewish synagogue. The "bishop and deacon" pattern as it is mentioned in Philippians 1:1 and 1 Timothy 3:1–13 was founded more on the structures of voluntary associations in the Greco-Roman world. It appears that in the Pastorals, as in Titus 1:5–9, these two models were in the process of being put together. That the process was still at an early stage is confirmed by the obvious use of traditional short pieces ("patches") about personal qualities and about procedures, and the awkwardness with which they fit together. At the same time, the process of their fusion illustrates the effort at strengthening local church life and creating a structure that embraced both Jewish and Gentile patterns while creating a new and unique pattern of church order.

IGNATIUS OF ANTIOCH

How the three offices of bishop, presbyter, and deacon came to fit together in church life is best illustrated by the letters of Ignatius of Antioch, the second bishop of Antioch in Syria, after Evodius. Ignatius had been condemned to death and sent to Rome to be executed by wild beasts in the amphitheater there. On the way he passed through various cities and had contact with local bishops and church members. At two places he wrote letters to five churches in Asia Minor (Ephesus, Magnesia, Smyrna, Philadelphia, and Tralles) and to the church at Rome. His martyrdom is generally placed in A.D. 108, in the reign of the emperor Trajan.

The immediate purpose of Ignatius's letters to the churches in Asia Minor was to thank the recipients for their kindnesses to him as he passed through their cities. In writing to the Roman Christians, however, Ignatius sought to dissuade them from intervening on his behalf and so robbing him of the "crown" of martyrdom. Through his letters Ignatius also hoped to gain support for the church at Antioch and to warn against two kinds of "heretics" within the churches: those who claimed that the sufferings of Christ were apparent rather than real (Docetists), and those who wished to retain and/or introduce Jewish practices into church life (Judaizers).

Because Ignatius was concerned, above all, with church order, he sought to strengthen respect for the local bishop and for a structure that included the bishop with the deacons and the presbytery. Although there is some dispute among scholars about the authenticity and original text of the letters, the usual approach to them is that they were written by Ignatius before his death in A.D. 108 and so provide important information about the churches in the early second century A.D.

According to Ignatius, the bishop is the pivotal figure in the local church. In writing to the Ephesians, for example, Ignatius warns: "Let us then be careful not to oppose the bishop, that we may be subject to God" (*Ephesians* 5:3). He describes the bishop as the representative of God and God as "the bishop of all," and says that those who try to deceive the bishop are really "dealing wrongly with him who is invisible" (*Magnesians* 3:1–2). And he insists that whatever is done in the churches should be done with the knowledge and approval of the bishop, and observes that whoever "does anything without the knowledge of the bishop is serving the devil" (*Smyrnaeans* 9:1).

In the local church as envisioned by Ignatius, there is only one bishop (compare "bishops and deacons" in Philippians 1:1). The technical term for this arrangement is *monepiscopate,* that is, one bishop in any given place who is given almost absolute authority over the local church and is said to be God's own representative. The technical term is *monarchical episcopate*; that is, the bishop is the one and ultimate authority. Ignatius perceived that if the churches were to avoid the errors of the Docetists and Judaizers, there was need to have strong and stable local church leaders as bishops.

Ignatius supported and promoted a church order consisting of "one bishop with the presbytery and the deacons" (*Philadelphians* 4:1). He envisioned a harmonious relationship among them, and even compared the presbytery as "attuned to the bishop as the strings to a harp" (*Ephesians* 4:1). Again, in writing to the Trallians, he encourages them to be subject to the bishop "as to Jesus Christ" and to the presbytery "as to the Apostles of Jesus Christ," and urges that "deacons of the mysteries of Jesus Christ" be pleasing to all (*Trallians* 2:1–3). These comments suggest that the presbyters form a group or collective, like the board of directors in the synagogue, and that the deacons were taking a liturgical role and not just waiting at table.

Ignatius makes more than one comparison to describe the threefold church order. In *Trallians* 3:1 he urges that all respect "the deacons as Jesus Christ, even as the bishop is also a type of the Father, and the presbyters as the council of God and the college of Apostles." Thus he imputes the highest (divine) authority to these church officials. He goes on to say that "without these the name of 'church' is not given." According to Ignatius, the threefold ministry of bishop, presbytery, and deacons is essential to church life. When addressing the Smyrnaeans, Ignatius tells them that all should "follow the bishop as Jesus Christ follows the Father, and the presbytery as if it were the Apostles, and reverence the deacons as the command of God" (8:1).

With regard to the celebration of the sacraments, Ignatius attributes jurisdiction to the bishop: "It is not lawful either to baptize or to hold an 'agape' without the bishop" (*Smyrnaeans* 8:2). A valid Eucharist is one that is "celebrated by the bishop or by one whom he appoints" (*Smyrnaeans* 8:1). He describes the ministry (*diakonia*) of the bishop as one that "makes for the common good" (*Philadelphians* 1:1), and says that nothing should be done "without the bishop and presbytery" (*Magnesians* 7:1). Those who do otherwise "do not hold valid meetings" (*Magnesians* 4:1). And whoever does anything "apart from the bishop and the presbytery and the deacons is not pure in his conscience" (*Trallians* 7:2).

Ignatius sought to promote unity and order in the churches through church offices. His vision of the local church is summed up in his letter to the *Philadelphians* 4:1: "Be careful therefore to use one Eucharist (for there is one flesh of our Lord Jesus Christ, and one cup for union with his blood, one altar, as there is one bishop with the presbytery and the deacons, my fellow servants), in order that whatever you do you may do it according unto God." Unity and church order go together according to Ignatius.

Although the letters of Ignatius do not belong to the Church's canon of Holy Scripture, they are, nonetheless, very important as witnesses to church life in the early second century A.D. in a large number of cities between Antioch and Rome. There is, of course, a certain polemical character to what Ignatius wrote. In fact, so strenuous is Ignatius's insistence on one bishop and the harmonious working together of bishop, presbytery, and deacons that one gets the idea that he "protests too much" and that his ideas were not universally obvious or acceptable to everyone. Nevertheless, Ignatius and his fellow bishops apparently viewed the monepiscopate and the threefold structure of church offices as the sure means of defense against Docetists, Judaizers, and other "heretics."

Whatever the concrete historical circumstances may have contributed, the ecclesiastical structures that Ignatius promoted in his letters have been extraordinarily influential in church history. He helps us understand how the fragments that appear in the Pastorals and other New Testament writings came to together in real life and were put into practice in the churches. His letters show that at least in some church circles there emerged a church order in which the one bishop was the pivotal figure, there were three major church offices (bishop, presbytery, and deacons), the sacraments were under the bishop's jurisdiction, and union with the bishop was regarded as the best defense against heresy.

Priesthood

The English word *priest* derives from the Latin term *presbyter*, which is in turn the same as the Greek *presbyteros* meaning "elder." But if *priest* is defined as one who presides at religious rituals and offers sacrifices, the proper Latin word is *sacerdos* and the Greek term is *hiereus*.

In the Letter to the Hebrews (which is, in fact, a sermon to Jewish Christians), Jesus is called *hiereus* and even *archiereus* ("high priest"). This description is part of a long and sophisticated theological reflection on the saving significance of Jesus' life, death, and resurrection. Its starting point was the very early Christian idea that Jesus' death was the effective sacrifice for sins ("for us," "for our sins") that made possible a new relationship with God. Another element was the tradition that Jesus willingly went to his death "for us." Using the terminology and ideas surrounding sacrifices and sin offerings in the Old Testament, the author of Hebrews developed the idea that Christ was both the perfect sacrifice for sins and the one who offered the sacrifice (the high priest). While the Jewish high priests offered sacrifices every year on the Day of Atonement for the sins of the people, Jesus offered himself "once for all," and so brought about the atonement prefigured by the Old Testament sacrifices. By offering himself as the perfect sacrifice, he served as the great high priest.

According to the Old Testament Law, Jesus could not have been a priest. He did not belong to the right family or tribe (Levi): "For it is evident that our Lord was descended from Judah, and in connection with that tribe Moses said nothing about priests" (Hebrews 7:14). And so the author of Hebrews goes to great lengths to show that Jesus represents a priesthood older than and superior to the Levitical priesthood. This is the mysterious priesthood of Melchizedek based on Psalm 110:4: "You are a priest forever according to the order of Melchizedek."

The priesthood of Christ, according to Hebrews, is based on the "priestly" character of Jesus and on the perfect sacrifice that he offered. In Hebrews 5:1–4, the author lays out three qualifications for being a priest: The priest must be chosen from the people, able to sympathize with sinners, and called by God. Then, in 5:5–10, he shows in reverse order that Christ was called by God (on the basis of Palms 2:7 and 110:4), was able to sympathize with humans, and became the representative of God's people and the source of their salvation. And the sacrifice that Christ offered for sins (himself) was the one perfect sacrifice that did what no other sacrifice had done: he brought about right relationship with God. The essence of the priesthood of Christ is stated in Hebrews 7:27: "Unlike the other high priests, he has no need to offer sacrifices day after day, first for his own sins, and then for those of the people: this he did once for all when he offered himself."

Does the perfect sacrifice and the perfect priesthood of Christ leave room for any other priesthood? From the perspective of Hebrews, the Jewish Levitical priesthood was a shadow or prefiguration of the perfect priesthood of Christ, and has been rendered obsolete by Christ's new covenant (see Hebrews 8:13). There is no mention of Christian priests in Hebrews besides Christ the great high priest. Hebrews is primarily a biblical-theological interpretation of Jesus' death and resurrection. It is generally silent on the matter of church ministers (but see 13:7: "Remember your leaders"). And it has been read as both affirming and denying the Christian ministerial priesthood. The reason for the ambiguity is its silence. Some Protestant traditions have argued that Christ the priest has made all priesthoods obsolete, and that now Christian worship consists only of "a sacrifice of praise to God" (see 13:15). Other traditions (Catholic, Orthodox) have contended that Christ has founded a new priesthood, and that those who are called "priests" (*sacerdotes, hiereis*) share in the one perfect sacrifice of Christ.

Although there are several texts in the New Testament that do call Christians "priests," they speak more about the Christian community taken as a collective rather than about pastoral ministers. The inspiration for these New Testament "priesthood" texts comes from two Old Testament passages. In Exodus 19:6 Israel, gathered at Mount Sinai under Moses' leadership, is called to be "a priestly kingdom and a holy nation." Their "priestly" character resides in their closeness to God as a consequence of their having been set apart from other nations as God's own people. In Isaiah 61:6 the community that has returned from exile to Jerusalem is promised that "you shall be called priests of the Lord, you shall be named ministers of our God." Just as the Levites formed a holy and priestly tribe within the twelve tribes of Israel (see Deuteronomy 18:1–5), so the Jerusalem community will have a special status as "priests" and "ministers" for the whole world. In both passages, the priesthood of Israel is metaphorical and collective. In Exodus 19, the context is fidelity to the covenant, while in Isaiah 61, the context is future or even eschatological hope for Israel's special status among the nations of the world.

In 1 Peter 2:9 the community of the baptized is addressed as "a chosen race, a royal priesthood, a holy nation, God's own people." Here the prerogatives of ancient Israel at Sinai (see Exodus 19:6) are being transferred to the Christian community. By the image of a "royal priesthood," the community is challenged to devote itself to the worship and service of the

Father of Jesus as the only real king. As in the Old Testament, this priest-hood is metaphorical and collective.

In the Book of Revelation Christians are called "priests" (*hiereis*) three times. In 1:6 those who have been redeemed by the blood of Christ are described as "a kingdom, priests serving his God and Father." In 5:10 it is said that by his death and resurrection Christ has made us into a "kingdom and priests serving our God." Both texts show the influence of Exodus 19:6 and Isaiah 61:6, and both use the metaphor of "priests" to describe the holiness of God's people and its nearness to God. In 20:6 the martyrs who refused to participate in pagan worship and remained faithful even to the point of death are promised a share in the "first resurrection" and in the thousand-year reign of Christ: "they will be priests of God and of Christ, and they will reign with him a thousand years." Their priesthood is eschatological (see Isaiah 61:6), as well as metaphorical and collective. None of these texts refers directly or exclusively to church officers. Rather, they are ways of describing the Christian community's closeness to God and holiness.

Where, then, did the "ministerial priesthood" come from? It repre-sents the combination of biblical elements that came together by the late second century A.D. The Greek term *hiereus* (Latin *sacerdos*) is not used for church ministers in the New Testament. Rather, its introduction came with the Church's separation from Judaism (where priests had to be Levites) and with the interpretation of the Eucharist as a sacrifice (see Ignatius's reference to "one flesh . . . one cup . . . one altar" in *Philadelphians* 4:1).

The spirituality of Christian priests is rooted in the New Testament passages about Jesus' calling his first disciples and his instructions about discipleship. The work of the Christian priest is based in part on that of the Old Testament priests (teaching God's people and interceding with God on their behalf) and of the New Testament apostles (sent forth to proclaim the gospel and working with and for God's people). The office of the Christian priest (especially in presiding at the Eucharist) combines ele-ments from the New Testament offices of *episkopos* (more like a local pastor than a modern bishop) and *presbyteros* (an elder charged with directing and administering the community). And the theme of the priest's closeness to God echoes the biblical "priesthood" texts (see Exodus 19:6; Isaiah 61:6; 1 Peter 2:9; Revelation 1:6; 5:10; 20:6). Given this context, the ministerial priesthood is better viewed as the fruit of historical development than as having been established in definitive form in the New Testament.

PETER

According to all four Gospels (see Mark 1:16–18; Matthew 4:18–20; Luke 5:1–11; John 1:40–42), Simon was one of the first persons Jesus called to become a disciple. This Simon (a common Jewish name) came to be known also as "Cephas/Peter" (which means "rock" in Aramaic and Greek, respectively), a name Jesus gave him most likely on the basis of Peter's personal characteristics. The former fisherman by the Sea of Galilee became very prominent among Jesus' regular companions and subsequent followers. He often serves as their spokesman and is always named first in the lists of the Twelve Apostles. Although Simon very likely made a confession about Jesus' identity in terms of Jewish expectations about the Messiah, his confession reflected an inadequate understanding of Jesus' (suffering) messiahship—plus his denial that he even knew Jesus at the time of Jesus' trial before the Sanhedrin (see Mark 14:66–72). This is not the kind of story that early Christians would have invented.

The early Christian confession of faith preserved in 1 Corinthians 15:3b–5 states that the Risen Jesus appeared first to Cephas/Peter and then to the Twelve. According to the early chapters in Acts, Peter's experiences of the Risen Jesus and his empowerment by the Holy Spirit at Pentecost transformed him into a fearless preacher of the gospel, willing to undergo imprisonment and even death in order to proclaim the saving significance of Jesus' life, death, and resurrection. Simon Peter remained the most important among the Twelve, first in Jerusalem and then in Antioch of Syria (see Galatians 2:1–14). Peter seems also to have had a missionary career (see 1 Corinthians 9:5). In theology he represented a mediating position between Paul and James (see Galatians 2:1–14; James 2:14–26; 2 Peter 3:15–16). According to Christian tradition, he came to Rome (see 1 Peter) and served as that church's leader (bishop) until his martyrdom under the emperor Nero around A.D. 64.

Interest in Peter did not cease with his death, however. Rather, he became one of the major figures in the New Testament, where he is portrayed as the recipient of a divine revelation, a witness to the Risen Lord, the repentant sinner, the great fisherman (in a missionary sense), the pastor, the guardian of the faith, and a martyr. The widespread and continuing interest in Peter in the New Testament suggests that he was regarded as more than a figure in the past.

The most famous and significant passage about Peter appears in Matthew 16:17–19: "You are Peter, and on this rock I will build my church." This text is frequently quoted as the New Testament basis for the Petrine office, or papacy, according to which the Bishop of Rome as the successor of Peter carries on the Petrine ministry as first among the bishops in the Church.

The text appears in the context of Simon Peter's confession about the identity of Jesus. In this narrative, Matthew depends heavily on Mark 8:27–33 for his wording and outline. In his Markan source, Matthew found Jesus' initial question ("Who do people say that I am?") and some answers, Jesus' question to his disciples ("But who do you say that I am?") and Peter's confession ("You are the Messiah"), Jesus' command to silence, the first passion prediction, and Peter's refusal to accept a suffering Messiah and Jesus' rebuke of him ("Get behind me, Satan").

Within this Markan outline, Matthew has greatly expanded Peter's confession of Jesus' messiahship by adding both "the Son of the living God" to "the Messiah" (Matthew 16:16b) and Jesus' declaration about Peter as the "rock" on which his church is to be built (16:17–19). These additions have the effect of softening Jesus' rebuke of Peter and strengthening his position among the disciples and in the post-Easter church.

In Matthew 16:17 Jesus declares Peter "blessed" or "happy" on the grounds that in his confession ("You are the Messiah, the Son of the living God") he has been the recipient of a revelation from God: "For flesh and blood has not revealed this to you, but my Father in heaven." Then in 16:18 Jesus proclaims that "You are Peter, and on this rock I will build my church," a declaration that plays on the name "Cephas/Peter" meaning "rock." It promises that Peter is to be the rock on which the Christian community (*ekklesia*) will be built after Jesus' death and resurrection, and that no power in opposition to God ("the gates of Hades") will be able to destroy that community. Finally, in 16:19, Jesus offers to give to Peter "the keys of the kingdom of heaven" (the right to allow or refuse entrance, see Isaiah 22:22) and the power to "bind and loose" (which is given to the whole community in Matthew 18:18). Although the precise meaning of *binding* and *loosing* is disputed—it could refer to forgiving or not forgiving sins, imposing or lifting excommunications, laying down rules or giving exemptions, or even performing or not performing exorcisms—Peter is clearly being given great authority.

The very Semitic language of this passage ("Blessed are you, Simon bar Jonah ... flesh and blood ... my Father in heaven" and so on) indicates that it originated in an Aramaic or Semitic Greek milieu, and that it came to Matthew as a tradition. It reflects a special interest in Peter as the recipient of a divine revelation about Jesus, as the foundation stone ("rock") of the Church, and the bearer of great authority. It has been variously interpreted as a statement by the earthly Jesus, an account of the appearance of the Risen Jesus to Peter (see 1 Corinthians 15:5; Luke 24:34; John 21:15–17), or a tradition about Peter as the founding apostle of the church at Antioch.

In the context of Matthew's Gospel (most likely written at Antioch), the passage is part of the Evangelist's special interest in Peter displayed most prominently in chapter 14–18. In 14:28–31 (another Peter tradition unique to Matthew), Peter, in his failure to continue walking on the water, is the exemplar of "little faith." Elsewhere Peter serves as the spokesman for the other followers of Jesus regarding Jewish food regulations (see 15:15), paying the temple tax (see 17:24–27), and forgiveness within the community of Jesus (see 18:21–22). While flawed (see 14:28–31 and especially 26:69–75), Peter emerges from Matthew's Gospel as first among the apostles and as a great leader in the church.

Although the New Testament provides the biblical-theological foundations for the Petrine ministry (especially Matthew 16:17–19), it does not speak about it directly as a church office. Indeed, the Petrine office is best seen (like the ministerial priesthood) as the development of the data found in the New Testament. According to this development, jurisdiction as the supreme pastor was given to Peter, Peter's primacy has been handed on from generation to generation, and this primacy has been and is carried on by the bishops of Rome.

Possibilities and Problems

Study of church offices in light of the New Testament reveals the importance of historical development in understanding the early church. The Jesus movement grew rapidly from being a Jewish apocalyptic sect in Palestine to an urban-based religious phenomenon spread all over the Mediterranean world, with a membership that was no longer exclusively Jewish. In fact, its Gentile members very quickly came to dominate. This movement could no longer be contained within traditional Jewish social structures. In the matter of official ministries, the early Christians displayed a remarkable ability to adapt and to innovate. Their fusion of the Hellenistic bishop/deacon pattern with the board of "elders" from the Jewish synagogues into a new and distinctive structural pattern illustrates this point nicely.

Examination of the priesthood texts in the New Testament can help uncover certain rich theological themes. For reasons that are easily understandable, the ministerial priesthood gets a good deal of attention today. But few Christians give much thought to the priesthood of Christ or to the priesthood of Christians. However, as the Letter to the Hebrews shows, the idea of Christ as the great high priest willingly offering himself as the perfect sacrifice "once for all" is a powerful way of probing more deeply the meaning of the early Christian proclamation that Christ died "for us" and "for our sins." Likewise, the application of the terms *priesthood* and *priests* to the Christian community taken as a collectivity highlights the vocation of the whole Church to be holy and close to God.

Attention to the figure of Peter across the pages of the New Testament indicates that he continued to be a focus of great interest. The various facets of his character range from Peter as the exemplar of "little faith" and even cowardice to Peter as the fearless herald of Christ and the shepherd of God's people. His primacy among the Twelve cannot be doubted. And even after his death, the figure of Peter influenced and fascinated Christians.

One problem raised by recognition of the development of the official ministries in the early church is the matter of their ongoing significance. Does the emergence of the bishop-presbyter-deacon pattern represent the final form of ministerial structures? Or was it only a necessary but time-conditioned response to circumstances in the late-first-century Mediterranean world? Does it set the pattern for the Church in all times and all places? In fact, the churches have generally been quite successful in retaining the traditional offices in some form while adapting them to changing circumstances.

Another problem, at least for many, is the difficulty posed by not finding the fully developed offices of "priest" (in the senses of *sacerdos* and *hiereus*) and "pope" (in the sense of Peter's successors as the bishops of Rome) in the New Testament. Here we must recognize that the New Testament does not provide everything we need to know about the Church or Christian life. We do know that the Christian story did not stop with the end of the first century, and that the development of the ministerial priesthood and the papacy, while responding to new circumstances and new challenges, is firmly rooted in biblical traditions.

A third problem is the division surrounding the Petrine office. On the one hand, the papacy is a great sign and means toward the unity of the "catholic" (world wide) Church. As the "first among equals," the Bishop of Rome can and does represent Christians all over the world. On the other hand, as Pope John Paul II has recognized, the papacy (or at least its exercise) has been a source of division between the churches of the East and the West, and in the West, since the Reformation between Catholics and Protestants. The challenge facing the bishops of Rome in the future is to work toward making the Petrine office into an even greater force for unity—rather than a source of division—among Christians.

For Reflection and Discussion

1. How essential to the Church today are the offices of bishop, presbyter, and deacon? What value do you attach to the evidence about ministries from the letters of Ignatius of Antioch?

2. What do you understand by the texts in 1 Peter and Revelation that talk about the priesthood of Christians?

3. How might the New Testament passages about Peter contribute to making the Petrine office an even greater force for church unity today?

GLOSSARY

Abfall: a German word meaning "falling off, decay" that is sometimes used to suggest that later developments in early church life and organization represent the corruption of the pristine Pauline form of Christianity.

adoptionist Christology: the doctrine according to which the man Jesus became the Son of God only at his baptism or Resurrection.

Annales: The conventional title of the history of the early Roman Empire (preserved only up to Nero) by Cornelius Tacitus.

anthological style: a method of literary composition by Jews and early Christians in which biblical words and phrases were used in new combinations and new contexts.

aorist passive tense: a Greek verbal form used to locate an event at a particular point in the past and (sometimes) to suggest divine agency.

Apocalypse of Weeks: a Jewish apocalyptic vision of history from creation to the fullness of God's kingdom arranged in a framework of "ten weeks" and presented in *1 Enoch* 91 and 93.

apocalypse/apocalyptic: a revelation (often in a dream or a vision) of future events, especially those pertaining to the end of the present age and to the fullness of God's kingdom.

apophthegm: a saying set in a short narrative and serving as the climax of the story.

apostolic succsssion: the uninterrupted succession or descent of the Church and its officers from the first followers of Jesus, especially his Twelve Apostles.

Aqiba: a prominent Jewish teacher or rabbi in the land of Israel in the late first and early second century A.D.

Assumption **(or** *Testament***)** *of Moses:* a Jewish writing from the first century A.D. purporting to provide Moses' farewell discourse and climaxing in a vision of the coming kingdom of God.

Augustus: the first and greatest Roman emperor. He ruled from 37 B.C. to A.D. 14. He is also known as Octavian.

Baruch (2): a Jewish apocalypse from the late first or early second century A.D. that reflects on the destruction of Jerusalem and its Temple and on God's fidelity to his promises to Israel.

body politic: a city (*polis*) or other social unit conceived as a human body in which every member has an important role.

Book of Glory: a modern title for the Gospel of John 13–21, which consists of Jesus' farewell discourses and the passion-resurrection narrative conceived as the time of Jesus' glorification.

Book of Signs: a modern designation for the Gospel of John 1–12, in which Jesus performs miracles and gives speeches that point to his identity as the revealer and revelation of God.

canonical: belonging to the *canon* (measure, rule), and therefore normative or authoritative, applying especially to those books accepted by the Church as part of Holy Scripture.

charism: a spiritual gift bestowed by God and to be used for the common good of the Christian community.

charismata: the Greek plural form of the noun *charisma*, and so the spiritual gifts or charisms.

charismatic community: a Christian community made up of divinely gifted members exercising their gifts for the common good.

chiasmus: a literary figure in which there is an inversion in the order of words in two corresponding parallel phrases or clauses.

chief priests: members of the most prominent Jewish priestly families who had special concern for the Jerusalem Temple in Jesus' time.

Christology/christological: the study of how the person, titles, and significance of Jesus Christ have been and are understood.

cognitive dissonance: a sociological concept referring to how people make the best of a bad situation by ignoring its negative implications and finding new ways of carrying on.

corpus: a collection or "body" of writings united by their topic, literary style, or a person (such as Paul or John).

criticism (form): analysis of the discourse and narrative literary forms (and their history) in which traditions incorporated in the New Testament were transmitted in the early church.

criticism (source): analysis of the oral and written materials that the biblical writers used in composing their works.

Day of Atonement: the Jewish feast of Yom Kippur, which in Jesus' time featured temple sacrifices offered to wipe away or atone for the Jewish people's sins (see Leviticus 16).

deposit of faith: the essentials or core of Christian beliefs as handed on in the Church and guarded by the Church.

Deuteropauline: New Testament letters (Colossians, Ephesians, 2 Thessalonians, 1 and 2 Timothy, and Titus) ascribed to Paul but generally regarded as having been composed after Paul's death by students and admirers.

Diaspora: a collective term for Jews living outside the land of Israel and also later applied to Christians living in the world.

Didache: a late first- or early second-century Christian handbook on topics such as almsgiving, ethics, baptism, fasting, prayer, the Eucharist, and church offices.

Docetists: early Christians who believed that Jesus only *appeared* to be human or to have a body.

ecclesiastical: pertaining to the Church (*ekklesia*), especially to its organization, government, officers, and structures.

ecclesiology: the study of the Church (*ekklesia*) with regard to its historical and theological foundations, structures, and mission.

economy of salvation: the divine plan or design (*oikonomia*) by which humans might be brought to right relationship with God through Christ.

elders: leaders in the early churches who were chosen because of their human and religious maturity to guide the local communities, and who were known as *presbyteroi* ("elders" in Greek).

Enoch (1): a Jewish apocalyptic writing containing material originating from the third century B.C. to the first century A.D. that purports to narrate what Enoch (see Genesis 5:24) saw on his journeys to heaven.

Ephesians: the name given to letters addressed to early Christians at Ephesus (in Asia Minor/Turkey) in the name of Paul and by Ignatius of Antioch.

episkopos: the Greek word for "overseer" used in the early church for a local Christian official and usually translated as *bishop*.

Essenes: a Jewish religious movement active in the land of Israel from the second century B.C. to A.D. 70, which is generally regarded as the group behind the Qumran settlement where many of the Dead Sea Scrolls were found.

exegetes: those who explain and interpret biblical texts, with attention to their literary, historical, and theological significance.

Exile (the): the period in Jewish history (587–520 B.C.) when the political and religious leaders of Judah were deported to Babylonia.

Ezra (4): a Jewish apocalypse from the late first century A.D. that explores the theological implications of the destruction of Jerusalem and its Temple in A.D. 70.

Feast of Dedication: the Jewish feast of Hanukkah that commemorates the restoration of Jewish worship at the Jerusalem Temple in 164 B.C.

Feast of Weeks: the Jewish spring harvest festival (also known as Pentecost) celebrated fifty days after Passover.

form and content: the combination of how (form) and what (content) biblical texts communicate as the object of exegesis.

Gentile mission: the early Christian effort at bringing the message of Jesus (the gospel) to non-Jews.

glossolalia: speaking in tongues, which referred originally to deep sighs and groans (see 1 Corinthians 12–14) and later came to mean speaking foreign languages (see Acts 2).

gnostic: derived from the Greek word "know," and referring to persons in New Testament times who claimed to have esoteric knowledge about God, the cosmos, and the human condition.

Greco-Roman: those areas of the Mediterranean world (including the land of Israel) under the political, economic, linguistic, cultural, and religious influence of Hellenism from Alexander the Great (died 323 B.C.) to the end of the Roman Empire.

Hanukkah: the Hebrew name for the Feast of Dedication (see that entry).

Hebrew Bible: the collection of texts in Hebrew (with some Aramaic parts) that are regarded by Jews (and Protestants) as canonical Scripture.

Hellenistic Jews: ethnic Jews, whether in the Diaspora or Israel, whose language and culture were strongly influenced by Greek language and culture.

heresy/heretics: derived from the Greek word for "choice," originally referring to opinions held by a group, and later referring to beliefs and practices that deviated from what was regarded as orthodoxy.

hermeneutical circle: the process of textual interpretation as it moves from the reader's horizon, through encounter with the text, to the reader's changed or deepened understanding that may lead to action.

Herod Antipas: the son of Herod the Great who ruled as tetrarch in Galilee and Perea from 4 B.C. to A.D. 38 (and so during Jesus' entire lifetime).

Herod Archelaus: the son of Herod the Great who ruled as ethnarch over Judea, Samaria, and Idumea from 4 B.C. to A.D. 6, when he was deposed by the Romans.

Hillel: a Jewish teacher roughly contemporary with Jesus who generally held more liberal views than his colleague Shammai and became very influential in the Pharisaic movement.

Holiness Code: the corpus of Old Testament laws found in Leviticus 17–26, focusing mainly on religious and cultic matters.

hortatory context: those parts of New Testament writings, especially in the Epistles, in which the author chastises, warns, and encourages the readers.

Ignatius of Antioch: Bishop of Antioch in Syria, he was taken to Rome and martyred around A.D. 115. His letters are important witnesses to church life and organization in the early second century A.D.

incarnational religion: because Jesus as the Word of God became flesh (*carnis* in Latin), according to John 1:14, Christianity respects all that is good about the human body and the material world.

inculturation: the effort to express the fundamental beliefs and practices of Christianity in the language and traditional practices of cultures hitherto not exposed to Christianity.

Irenaeus: Bishop of Lyon in France in the second century, he provided descriptions and refutations of various heresies, especially those labeled as *gnosticism*.

Isis cult: originally an Egyptian religion, the cult of the goddess Isis became very popular in the Greco-Roman world and was a rival of early Christianity.

Jewish Christianity: movements in early Christianity that were led by ethnic Jews and took conservative stances toward traditional Jewish practices such as circumcision, Sabbath observance, and food and purity laws.

Josephus: a Jew from a priestly family who fought briefly in the Jewish revolt (A.D. 66–74) and then went over to the Roman side. His major writings include the *Jewish War*, the *Jewish Antiquities*, his *Life*, and *Against Apion*.

Judaizers: Jewish Christians who insisted that gentile converts to Christianity adopt the Jewish way of life, including circumcision, Sabbath observance, and food and purity laws.

L (source): the symbol used to designate traditions found only in Luke's Gospel.

Law (Mosaic): the 613 commandments preserved in the Pentateuch (Genesis through Deuteronomy), which is also known as the Torah.

Levi/Levites: tracing their ancestry back to Levi (a son of Jacob), Levites performed cultic functions in the Jerusalem Temple and formed a kind of Jewish priestly class.

Livy: a Roman historian (59 B.C.–A.D. 17) who wrote a history of Rome from its founding onward in 142 volumes, only 35 of which are extant.

Luke–Acts: the two-volume narrative about the life of Jesus (Luke's Gospel) and the spread of the early church from Jerusalem to Rome (the Acts of the Apostles).

M (source): the symbol used to designate traditions found only in Matthew's Gospel.

Maccabean revolt: the Jewish uprising led by members of a Jewish priestly family from 165 B.C. onward against Syrian control of Judea and the Jerusalem Temple.

Maccabees: derived from the Hebrew word for "hammer," the nickname given to Mattathias and his five sons (Judas, Jonathan, Simon, etc.) who eventually brought religious and political independence to Judea in the second century B.C.

Melchizedek: the king of ancient Salem (Jerusalem) and priest of the Most High God who blessed Abraham (see Genesis 14:18–20), was connected with the Israelite kingship and priesthood (see Psalm 110:4), and served as the type for the priesthood of Christ in Hebrews.

methodological: conforming to the rules developed by modern scholars for the critical study of biblical texts as literature, history, and theology.

Mishnah: the rabbinic collection of Jewish traditions generally pertaining to legal and cultic matters that was codified around A.D. 200 by Rabbi Judah the Prince.

Mithraism: a religious movement with roots in India and Persia that became very popular in the Roman Empire, especially in military circles.

parallelism: a practice in ancient Hebrew poetry whereby an idea is repeated in similar (synonymous) or opposed (antithetical) statements.

passive construction: the use of verbs in the passive voice, frequently with the implication that God is the real agent; sometimes called the divine or theological passive.

pastoral theologian: one like Paul who worked out his theological vision in response to pastoral problems that arose within Christian communities that he founded and/or with which he was in contact through letters.

Petrine circle: Christians at Rome and elsewhere who took the apostle Peter as their hero and produced writings in Peter's name or about him.

Pharisaic Judaism: the variety of Judaism promoted by the Pharisees, who at times had great influence over other Jews in Israel and are portrayed as the chief rivals of Jesus and the early church in the New Testament.

Pharisees: a lay Jewish religious movement active between the second century B.C. and the first century A.D. that was especially concerned with table fellowship, traditions surrounding the biblical laws, and belief in resurrection.

Philadelphians: the name given to the letter written by Ignatius of Antioch to the early Christian community in Philadelphia, a city in western Asia Minor (now Turkey).

Philo of Alexandria: a Jewish biblical interpreter and philosopher active in the first century A.D. and most famous for his allegorical commentaries on parts of the Pentateuch.

Pliny (the Younger): the Roman governor in Bithynia (northern Asia Minor) in the early second century A.D. who wrote a description of early Christian worship, teaching, and conduct, and their official repression (see *Epistles* 10.96).

pneumatology: the study of the person and activities of the Holy Spirit (*pneuma* in Greek).

polis: the Greek word for "city" and the basis for the word "political."

Pontius Pilate: the Roman governor or "prefect" of Judea between A.D. 26 and 36 who was legally responsible for the death of Jesus.

prefect (Pontius Pilate): the official Latin title (*praefectus*) for the office that Pontius Pilate held according to an ancient inscription found at Caesarea Maritima.

Psalms of Solomon (17): in the collection of eighteen Jewish poems or hymns composed in the first century B.C., Psalm 17 presents an extensive description of the hopes for a Messiah/Son of David who will act as warrior, judge, and ruler and so restore Israel's fortunes as a nation.

Q (Sayings Source): the (hypothetical) collection of Jesus' sayings used independently by Matthew and Luke in addition to Mark's Gospel.

rabbinic period: the period in Jewish history from the second to the seventh century A.D. when the corpus of rabbinic literature (Mishnah, Tosefta, Talmuds, Midrashim) took shape.

rabbinical academy: the center for rabbinic activity (teaching and writing) under famous Jewish scholars in various times and places during the rabbinic period.

reductionism: the tendency to explain divine or supernatural events in the Bible as due only to human or natural factors.

rhythm: the practice in ancient (and modern) poetry whereby the words unfold according to recurrent syllabic patterns.

routinization of charisma: the sociological concept according to which the spiritual and intellectual energy of a great figure is carried on and channeled by disciples and in various institutional structures.

Sadducees: a Jewish religious movement active between the second century B.C. and the first century A.D. that included the priestly aristocracy and took more conservative views than the Pharisees did on Scripture, tradition, and life after death.

Second Temple Judaism: the period in Jewish history after the Jerusalem Temple was rebuilt (515 B.C.) until its destruction in A.D. 70.

Septuagintal Greek: the language used in the Greek version (Septuagint) of the Hebrew Scriptures, which is heavily influenced by Semitic syntax and idioms.

scribes: persons not only able to read and write but also trained in Scripture and traditional wisdom (see Sirach 38:24–39:11), who are portrayed in the Gospels as generally hostile to Jesus.

Shammai: a Jewish teacher roughly contemporary with Jesus who generally took more conservative positions than Hillel did on disputed matters of Jewish law and tradition.

Smyrnaeans: the name given to the letter written by Ignatius of Antioch to the Christian community in Smyrna, a city in western Asia Minor (modern Turkey).

soteriology: the study of salvation (*soteria* in Greek), with special reference to the significance and effects of Jesus' death and resurrection for human beings.

Synoptic Gospels: a term used to refer to the Gospels of Matthew, Mark, and Luke, because they present a "common view" of Jesus (one that is different from John's Gospel).

Tabernacles or Booths: the Jewish fall harvest festival, also known as Sukkot, recalling how harvesters camped out in the fields in makeshift tents or booths.

Talmuds: collections of rabbinic commentaries on the Mishnah that are associated with Palestine/Jerusalem (fourth century) and Babylonia (fifth century).

theocracy: the political theory according to which God is the real ruler and God's law provides the legal framework.

Thucydides: the author of the (incomplete) history of the war between Athens and Sparta (431–404 B.C.) in eight books.

Torah: derived from the Hebrew verb "teach, instruct," the word *Torah* is generally translated as "the (Mosaic) Law," and can refer to the Old Testament in general, the Pentateuch (Genesis to Deuteronomy), the 613 commandments in the Pentateuch, and/or the traditions about them collected in the Mishnah and the Talmuds.

Tosefta: derived from the Hebrew word "add," this is the collection of "additional" traditions on legal and cultic matters beyond those gathered in the Mishnah.

Trallians: the name given to the letter written by Ignatius of Antioch to the Christian community in Tralles, a city in western Asia Minor (modern Turkey).

Yohanan ben Zakkai: a late first-century A.D. Jewish teacher who was especially prominent in the transition from Temple-centered Judaism to Torah-centered Judaism after A.D. 70.

Zealots: a Jewish political-religious-theocratic movement active in the first century A.D., especially during the early stages of Jewish revolt (A.D. 66–74), in guerilla operations against Roman and Herodian rule.

FOR FURTHER STUDY

Arlandson, James M. *Women, Class, and Society in Early Christianity. Models from Luke-Acts.* Peabody, MA: Hendrickson, 1997.

Ascough, Richard S. *What Are They Saying about the Formation of the Pauline Churches?* New York: Paulist, 1998.

Aune, David E. (ed.). *The Gospel of Matthew in Current Study.* Grand Rapids: Eerdmans, 2001.

Bauer, Walter. *Orthodoxy and Heresy in Earliest Christianity.* Philadelphia: Fortress, 1971.

Beard, Mary, and J. North and S. Price. *Religions of Rome.* Cambridge, NY: Cambridge University Press, 1998,

Bowersock, Glenn W. *Martyrdom and Rome.* Cambridge, NY: Cambridge University Press, 1995.

Bradshaw, P. F. *The Search for the Origins of Christian Worship.* New York: Oxford University Press, 1992.

Brown, Raymond E. *The Churches the Apostles Left Behind.* New York: Paulist, 1984.

———. *The Community of the Beloved Disciple.* New York: Paulist, 1979.

———. *Priest and Bishop: Biblical Reflections.* New York: Paulist, 1970.

_____ and John P. Meier. *Antioch and Rome: New Testament Cradles of Catholic Christianity.* New York: Paulist, 1983.

———.et al (eds.). *Peter in the New Testament.* Minneapolis: Augsburg, 1973.

Brox, Norbert. *A History of the Early Church.* London: SCM Press, 1994.

Burtchaell, James. *From Synagogue to Church.* Cambridge, NY: Cambridge University Press, 1992.

Cassidy, Richard J. *Christians and Roman Rule in the New Testament.* New York: Crossroad, 2001.

Clarke, Andrew D. *Serve the Community of the Church. Christians as Leaders and Ministers.* Grand Rapids: Eerdmans, 2000.

Crowe, Jerome. *From Jerusalem to Antioch.* Collegeville, MN: Liturgical Press, 1997.

Cullmann, Oscar. *Peter: Disciple, Apostle, Martyr.* Philadelphia: Westminster, 1962.

———. *The State in the New Testament.* New York: Scribner's, 1966.

———. *Unity Through Diversity.* Philadelphia: Fortress, 1988.

Cwiekowski, Frederick J. *The Beginnings of the Church.* New York: Paulist, 1988.

Donfried, Karl P. and Peter Richardson (eds.). *Judaism and Christianity in First-Century Rome.* Grand Rapids: Eerdmans, 1998.

Doran, Robert. *Birth of a Worldview: Early Christianity in Its Jewish and Pagan Context.* Boulder, CO: Westview Press, 1995.

Downing, Francis. G. *Cynics and Christian Origins.* Edinburgh: T & T Clark, 1992.

Dunn, James D. G. *Unity and Diversity in the New Testament: An Inquiry into the Character of Earliest Christianity.* Philadelphia: Westminster Press, 1977.

————. *The Partings of the Ways between Christianity and Judaism and Their Significance for the Character of Christianity.* Philadelphia: Trinity Press International, 1991.

Elliott, John H. *A Home for the Homeless. A Sociological Exegesis of 1 Peter, Its Situation and Strategy.* Philadelphia: Fortress, 1981.

Esler, Philip F. *Modelling Early Christianity.* London, New York: Routledge, 1995.

———— (ed.). *The Early Christian World.* London, New York: Routledge, 2000.

Fischer, Georg and Martin Hasitschka. *The Call of the Disciple: The Bible on Following Christ.* New York: Paulist, 1999.

Frend, W. H. C. *The Archeology of Early Christianity.* Minneapolis: Fortress, 1996.

————. *The Rise of Christianity.* Philadelphia: Fortress, 1984.

Gamble, Harry Y. *Books and Readers in the Early Church: A History of Early Christian Texts.* New Haven: Yale University Press, 1995.

Hanson, Paul D. *The People Called: The Growth of Community in the Bible.* Philadelphia: Fortress, 1980.

Harrington, Daniel J. *God's People in Christ: New Testament Perspectives on the Church and Judaism.* Philadelphia: Fortress, 1980.

————. *Light of All Nations: Essays on the Church in New Testament Research.* Wilmington, DE: Michael Glazier, 1982.

————. *Paul on the Mystery of Israel.* Collegeville, MN: Liturgical Press, 1992.

Hellerman, Joseph H. *The Ancient Church as Family.* Minneapolis: Fortress, 2001

Hengel, Martin. *Acts and the History of Early Christianity.* Philadelphia: Fortress Press, 1980.

————. *Between Jesus and Paul.* Philadelphia: Fortress Press, 1983.

————. *Christ and Power.* Philadelphia: Fortress, 1977.

————. *Property and Riches in the Early Church.* Philadelphia: Fortress, 1974.

————. *Victory over Violence. Jesus and the Revolutionists.* Philadelphia: Fortress, 1973.

———— and Maria Schwemer. *Paul between Damascus and Antioch: The Unknown Years.* Louisville: Westminster John Knox, 1997.

Holmberg, Bengt. *Paul and Power.* Philadelphia: Fortress, 1980.

Horsley, Richard A. *Galilee: History, Politics, People.* Valley Forge, Penn.: Trinity Press International, 1995.

————. *Sociology and the Jesus Movement.* New York: Continuum, 1994.

Käsemann, Ernst. *Essays on New Testament Themes.* London: SCM, 1964.

————. *New Testament Questions of Today*. London: SCM, 1969.

Kee, Howard Clark. *Christian Origins in Sociological Perspective*. Philadelphia: Westminster, 1980.

Kelly, Joseph F. *The World of the Early Christians*. Collegeville, MN: Liturgical Press, 1997.

Klauck, Hans-Josef. *The Religious Context of Early Christianity: A Guide to Graeco-Roman Religions*. Edinburgh: T. & T. Clark, 2000.

Kloppenborg, John S. and G. S. Wilson, eds. *Voluntary Associations in the Graeco-Roman World*. New York: Routledge, 1996.

Kraemer, Ross S. and M. R. D'Angelo, eds. *Women and Christian Origins*. New York: Oxford University Press, 1999.

Lohfink, Gerhard. *Does God Need the Church? Toward a Theology of the People of God*. Collegeville, MN: Liturgical Press, 1999.

————. *Jesus and Community: The Social Dimension of Christian Faith*. Philadelphia: Fortress, 1984.

MacDonald, Margaret Y. *Early Christian Women and Pagan Opinion: The Power of the Hysterical Woman*. Cambridge, NY: Cambridge University Press, 1996.

————. *The Pauline Churches: A Socio-Historical Study of Institutionalization in the Pauline and Deutero-Pauline Writings*. Cambridge, NY: Cambridge University Press, 1988.

Malherbe, Abraham. *Social Aspects of Early Christianity*. Philadelphia: Fortress, 1983.

————. et al (eds.). *The Early Church in its Context*. Leiden: Brill, 1998.

McDonnell, Kilian and G. T. Montague. *Christian Initiation and Baptism in the Holy Spirit*. Collegeville, MN: Liturgical Press, 1994.

McGowan, Andrew. *Ascetic Eucharists: Food and Drink in Early Christian Ritual Meals*. Oxford: Oxford University Press, 1999.

Meeks, Wayne. *The First Urban Christians: The Social World of the Apostle Paul*. New Haven: Yale University Press, 1983.

————. *The Moral World of the First Christians*. Philadelphia: Westminster, 1986.

————. *The Origins of Christian Morality: The First Two Centuries*. New Haven: Yale University Press, 1993.

Meier, John P. *A Marginal Jew: Rethinking the Historical Jesus*. New York: Doubleday, 1991, 1994, 2001.

Moxnes, Halvor (ed.). *Constructing Early Christian Families*. London, New York: Routledge, 1997.

Nodet, Etienne and Justin Taylor. *The Origins of Christianity*. Collegeville, MN: Liturgical Press, 1998.

Noll, Raymond R. *Christian Ministerial Priesthood: A Search for its Beginnings in the Primary Documents of the Apostolic Fathers*. San Francisco, London: Catholic Scholars Press, 1993.

Osiek, Carolyn, and D. L. Balch. *Families in the New Testament World: Households and House Churches*. Louisville: Westminster John Knox, 1997.

Painter, John. *Just James. The Brother of Jesus in History and Tradition.* Columbia, SC: University of South Carolina Press, 1997.

Pearson, Birger A. *Gnosticism, Judaism and Egyptian Christianity.* Minneapolis: Fortress, 1990.

Richard, Lucien. *Living the Hospitality of God.* New York: Paulist, 2000.

Saldarini, Anthony J. *Matthew's Jewish Christian Community.* Chicago: University of Chicago Press, 1994.

Sanders, Ed P. *Jesus and Judaism.* Philadelphia: Fortress, 1985.

Sanders, Jack T. *Schismatics, Sectarians, Dissidents, Deviants: The First One Hundred Years of Jewish-Christian Relations.* London: SCM Press, 1993.

Schüssler Fiorenza, Elisabeth. *In Memory of Her: A Feminist Theological Reconstruction of Christian Origins.* New York: Crossroad, 1983.

Senior, Donald and Carroll Stuhlmueller. *The Biblical Foundations for Mission.* Maryknoll, NY: Orbis, 1983.

Setzer, Claudia J. *Jewish Responses to Early Christians: History and Polemics.* Minneapolis: Fortress, 1994.

Stark, Rodney. *The Rise of Christianity: A Sociologist Reconsiders History.* Princeton: Princeton University Press, 1996.

Stegemann, Ekkehard and Wolfgang. *The Jesus Movement: A Social History of its First Century.* Minneapolis: Fortres, 1999.

Sullivan, Francis A. *From Apostles to Bishops: The Development of the Episcopacy in the Early Church.* New York: Newman/Paulist, 2001

Theissen, Gerd. *The Religion of the Earliest Churches: Creating a Symbolic World.* Minneapolis, MN: Fortress, 1999.

————. *The Social Setting of Pauline Christianity: Essays on Corinth.* Philadelphia: Fortress, 1982.

————. *Sociology of Early Palestinian Christianity.* Philadelphia: Fortress, 1978.

Vallee, Gerard. *The Shaping of Christianity.* New York: Paulist, 1999.

von Campenhausen, Hans. *Ecclesiastical Authority and Spiritual Power in the Church of the First Three Centuries.* Stanford, CA: Stanford University Press, 1969.

Watson, Francis. *Paul, Judaism, and the Gentiles.* New York: Cambridge University Press, 1986.

Weber, Max. *The Sociology of Religion.* Boston: Beacon Press, 1963.

Wilson, Stephen G. *Related Strangers: Jewish-Christian Relations 70–170.* Minneapolis: Fortress, 1995.

Witherup, Ronald. *Conversion in the New Testament.* Collegeville, MN: Liturgical Press, 1994.

Wright, N. T. *Jesus and the Victory of God.* Minneapolis: Fortress, 1996.

INDEX

abortion, 135
adoptionism, 29
anti-Judaism, 80, 106, 127
antitheses, the, 6, 137
apophthegm, 100
apostates, 123
Apostles, the Twelve, 7, 110, 151–152, 159–160
aposynagogos, 117–118
appearances of Jesus, 14
Ascension, the, 16

baptism
    and Christian life, 35
    and the Body of Christ, 66
    and the Holy Spirit, 33, 44–45, 59
    and the People of God, 74, 75–77, 80
    as initiation into Christ, 43–45
    precedents for, 43–45
    ritual of, 45
Benedictus, the, 38, 39–40, 140
biblical canon, xii, 100
bishops, 93, 95, 136, 149, 160–165
Body of Christ, the 37, 43, 54, 62, 64–68, 87–88
Book of Glory, the 115, 116, 119, 121–122
Book of Signs, the 115, 116, 117, 123

charismatic prophet, the, 21, 23, 61, 159–160
charisms, 61–62, 63, 66, 67, 88, 96, 153–154
Christian assembly, the
    glossolalia in, 53
    problems with, 53, 54–55
    procedures at, 51–52
    role of women in, 53
    timing, 52
Christian life, 31, 34, 67, 112, 156
Church, the
    and ordination, 96
    and the Holy Spirit, 59, 62
    and the kingdom of God, 4, 19–22, 97–98

    as apostolic, 87–88
    as Body of Christ, 64–68
    as "bulwark" for truth, 96
    as community of love, 119–120
    as envisioned in the Pastorals, 94–95
    as God's "holy temple," 87
    as "home for the homeless," 138
    as "household of God," 95
    basis of, 113
    development of, 107
    discipline, 31
    Jesus as foundation stone, 169
    leaders, 31–32, 93–94, 95, 150
    mission of, 72, 73, 88, 89–90, 121
    office in, 159
    order in, 31–32
    Paul's images of, 58–66, 67, 69
    Peter as leader, 168–170
    privileges of, 77–78
    unity in Jesus, 73, 121
church, "catholic" (universal)
    and Paul's legacy, 83–98
    basis of idea, 85
circumcision, 5, 16, 18, 75, 135
commandments, biblical, 6
Commandments, Ten, 18, 52
commandments, two great, 5–6
compassion, 73, 138, 140–141
conventicle, 122–123
conversion, 46
covenant, 71–72, 73
creedal summaries, 70

deaconess, 52
deacons, 93, 95, 136, 149, 160–165
Dead Sea Scrolls, the, 2, 116
Death, 59, 61, 121
deposit of faith, the, 94, 96
Diaspora, the, 17, 18, 74
Disciple, Beloved, 116, 122–123
discipleship, 11, 103–104, 151, 152–153, 156–157, 160
Docetists, 162, 163, 164
"early catholicism," 97–98
elder (presbyter), 150, 160–165
eschatology, 111

Essenes, 2, 21, 44, 52, 150
Eucharist, the
    abuses in, 47
    aligned with Passover, 48
    and Christian life, 45
    and sacrifice, 47, 48
    and the Last Supper, 46
    as Lord's Supper, 49
    as meal, 45–46, 48
    as memorial of Jesus, 47
    as sign of hope, 47
    dimensions of, 48
    memorial theme of, 48–49
    precedents for, 46
Evil One, the, 121

faith, 3, 23, 27, 30, 59, 73, 75, 76–77, 120
fellowship, 66
food and purity laws, 5, 18, 106, 135
forgiveness, 6, 15, 46
form criticism, 27, 100–101

glossolalia, 53
gospel, 100

head/body image (of Church), 86–87
heresy/heretics, 94, 117, 162, 164
Holiness Code, the 138–139
Holy Spirit, the
    and appropriate action, 59–60
    and baptism, 33, 44–45
    and God's victory, 60–61
    and hope, 60
    and prayer, 60
    and "sonship," 59–60
    and the charismatic community,
        61–64, 67
    and the Jesus movement, 15–17, 23
    animates the Church, 107
    as life-force of the Church, 62
    at Pentecost, 90
    "Book of ," 90, 91
    creates the Church, 59
    empowering the Christian mission,
        90
    first fruits of, 61
    Paul's theology of, 58–61
homosexuality, 135
hope, 4, 31–34, 60
hospitality, 138–140

house church, the
    as transitional step, 51
    assemblies, 50
    authority in, 51
    membership of, 49–50
    problematic side of, 50, 52, 54–55
    test for, 50–51
husband/wife image (of Church), 86,
    88–89

Incarnation, the, 31, 33, 115, 127, 147

Jerusalem
    "council," the, 89, 90, 91, 92–93,
        120
    in Luke's Gospel, 111
Jesus
    and Peter, 169
    and the priesthood of Melchizedek,
        165
    as charismatic prophet, 21, 23, 61,
        159–160
    as High Priest, 35, 165, 170
    as mediator, 32
    as Messiah, 84, 102–103
    as new (second) Adam, 84
    as prophet, 110
    as revealer and revelation of God,
        115–116, 156
    as Suffering Servant, 35
    as the "consolation of Israel," 40
    as Wisdom personified, 35–38,
        40–41
    as Word of God, 37–38, 115, 156
    farewell discourse of, 119–121,
        123, 127, 139
    human nature of, 124
    Jewishness of, 73, 80
    mission of, 32
    priesthood of, 165–167
    servant-leadership of, 147–157
    teachings of, 5–8, 146
    the family of, 104
Jesus movement, the
    and disciples, 7–8
    and Paul's letters, 28–31
    and prophetic succession, 16
    and the Beatitudes, 136
    and the Church today, 10–11
    and the death of Jesus, 8–10, 28–31,
        40–41, 103

and the Holy Spirit, 15–17, 23
and the kingdom of God, 4
and the mystery of the cross, 11, 103
and the Pastoral Epistles, 31–34
and the People of God, 1
and the resurrection of the dead,
13–14
and the Twelve Apostles, 160
and women, 142, 161
as reform, 2
charter for, 7
core values of, 5–8, 11, 135–137
development into Church, 10, 13–24
expectation of, 1
external factors, 17–19, 23
goal of teachings, 3
impact in Israel, 8–9
in first-century Palestine, 11
in the twenty-first century, 12, 24,
112–113, 142
internal factors, 19–22, 23
practical situations of, 130
"radical" ethic of, 6, 137
roots of, 1–3, 10
spread of, 8, 170–171
understanding of, 2, 10–11
Jews, negative portrayal of, 118–119
Johannine "school," 122–123
Judaizers, 162, 163, 164
justification, 35, 84

kingdom of God
and the Church, 4, 19–22, 97–98
and the person of Jesus, 4
and the resurrection of the dead,
13–14
as banquet, 46, 111
comes in fullness, 31, 126
Jesus' teachings about, 3–4, 155
presence of, 4, 152
response to, 3
theme in Old Testament, 3

last judgment, the, 3
Law, the, 59, 75, 76–77
leadership
as ministry, 145–146
as service, 145
Jesus' definition of, 146–147
Jesus' teachings about, 146
of Peter, 169–170

patterns of, 149–150
Magnificat, the, 38–40, 140
marriage and divorce, 106, 134
mercy, 73, 138, 140–141
ministry
and charisms, 153–154
and honor, 148–149
and power language, 148
and the Word of God, 156
as response to the Holy Spirit, 148
as service and leadership, 145–146
ideal and goal of, 148
in the Christian tradition, 145–146
in the twenty-first century, 152–153
Petrine, 168–169, 170, 171
mirror reading, 113
monarchical episcopate, 163
monotheism, 18

new heaven, 3
Nunc Dimittis, the, 38, 39–40

ordination, 96
orthodoxy, 94

papacy, the, 168–169, 171
parables, 3–4, 6
Paraclete, 15, 115, 120
passion narratives, 49
Passover, 45–46
Paul
as apostle, 57, 154
as minister of the word, 154–155
images of Church, 58–66, 67, 69
letters of, 57–58
on charisms, 61–64, 66, 67
on Sin, Death, and the Law, 59–61
on the Body of Christ, 64–68
on the Holy Spirit, 58–61
Pentecost, 16, 70, 90, 110
People of God, the,
and baptism, 74, 75
and Gentiles, 78–79
and the covenant, 71–72
and the Exodus, 71
and the Jesus movement, 1
and the Second Vatican Council, 72
as Christ's seed, 76
as the Body of Christ, 87
in the New Testament, 72–81
in the Old Testament, 69–72

    purpose for election, 71–72, 73
    unity in Jesus, 73, 74
prayer, 110
presbyteral model, 161
priest, 165, 167–170

redemption, 31–34, 37
reductionism, 24
repentance, 3, 8, 15, 46
resurrection of the dead, 3, 13–14
Resurrection, the, 13–14, 20, 23, 29–31,
        33, 37, 40–41, 62, 155–156
rewards for righteous, 3
routinization of charisma, 21, 22, 23, 160

Sabbath observance, 5, 18, 106, 135
sacrifice, 41
salvation, 31–34, 35, 69, 70, 73, 78–80, 84,
        110, 155
Second Temple Judaism, 2, 84
Second Vatican Council, the, 72, 99
service
    as leadership, 145
    as response to divine grace, 145
    Jesus' death as, 147
Sin, 59, 61, 121
soteriology, 28, 40, 43
source criticism, 27
suffering, 33, 61
supersessionism, 80
synagogue, 18–19, 49, 51, 150

Temple, destruction of, 105
Torah, 2, 5, 18, 105

women
    in Luke's Gospel, 111
    instruction about, 95

Zealots, 2, 105